iLife® '11
PORTABLE GENIUS

by Guy Hart-Davis

Wiley Publishing, Inc.

iLife® '11 Portable Genius

Published by
Wiley Publishing, Inc.
10475 Crosspoint Blvd.
Indianapolis, IN 46256
www.wiley.com

Copyright © 2011 by Wiley Publishing, Inc., Indianapolis, Indiana

Published simultaneously in Canada

ISBN: 978-0-470-64348-8

Manufactured in the United States of America

10 9 8 7 6 5 4 3 2 1

For general information on our other products and services or to obtain technical support, please contact our Customer Care Department within the U.S. at (877) 762-2974, outside the U.S. at (317) 572-3993 or fax (317) 572-4002.

Wiley also publishes its books in a variety of electronic formats. Some content that appears in print may not be available in electronic books.

Library of Congress Control Number: 2010943061

WILEY

About the Author

Guy Hart-Davis is the author of more than 60 computing books, including *iMac Portable Genius, Second Edition* and *Teach Yourself VISUALLY: iMac*.

Credits

Executive Editor
Jody Lefevere

Project Editor
Chris Wolfgang

Technical Editor
Dwight Spivey

Senior Copy Editor
Kim Heusel

Editorial Director
Robyn Siesky

Editorial Manager
Rosemarie Graham

Vice President and Executive Group Publisher
Richard Swadley

Vice President and Executive Publisher
Barry Pruett

Business Manager
Amy Knies

Senior Marketing Manager
Sandy Smith

Project Coordinator
Kristie Rees

Graphics and Production Specialists
Jennifer Henry
Andrea Hornberger

Quality Control Technician
Melanie Hoffman

Proofreading
Melissa D. Buddendeck

Indexing
Steve Rath

This book is dedicated to Rhonda and Teddy.

Acknowledgments

I'd like to thank the following people for making this book happen:

- Jody Lefevere for getting the second edition approved and asking me to update it.
- Chris Wolfgang for shaping the outline, cutting the chapters down to size, and running the editorial side.
- Dwight Spivey for reviewing the book for technical accuracy and making many helpful suggestions.
- Kim Heusel for copy-editing the book with a light touch.
- Jennifer Henry and Andrea Hornberger for laying out the book in the design.
- Melissa D. Buddendeck for scrutinizing the pages for errors.
- Steve Rath for creating the index.

Contents

How Do I Turn My Content into a Movie? 132

chapter 9

How Can I Make My Song Sound
Great and Then Share It?   258

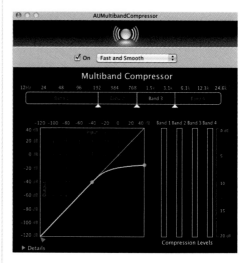

How Do I Build a Web Site with iWeb? 286

chapter 11

How Do I Publish Blogs and Podcasts with iWeb? 326

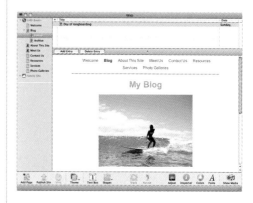

How Do I Design, Build, and Burn DVDs in iDVD?

Introduction

Your Mac is a fantastic tool for enjoying multimedia, and the iLife suite of applications lets you create and share your own multimedia content with the whole wired world.

iLife '11 Portable Genius shows you how to get the most out of the iLife applications. Here's a taste of what you can do with this book:

- **Bring your photos into iPhoto.** Import your digital photos directly from your digital camera or a removable memory card — or from another folder on your Mac or your network. Use Image Capture to scan printed photos so that you can use them on your Mac. If you've upgraded to iPhoto '11 from an earlier version of iPhoto, use Software Update to update iPhoto '11 to the latest version to avoid problems importing your photo library.

- **Organize and improve your photos.** Quickly organize your photos into iPhoto Events and tag them with keywords so that you can instantly find the photos you want. Use iPhoto's powerful features to crop and adjust your photos so that they look exactly as you want them. Keep multiple photo libraries to separate your photos by theme, content, or usage.

- **Share your photos with family, friends, or the whole world.** When your photos look great, use them to create powerful slide shows, share your photos with other people on your network or the Internet, or simply enhance Mac OS X on your Mac.

- **Import your video footage into iMovie.** Bring your video clips into iMovie from your DV camcorder, digital camera, iPhone, or existing files. Swiftly review your clips, mark the footage to use in your projects, and organize related clips into Events. Use the People Finder feature to identify the clips that contain people so that you can easily locate them.

- **Build a movie from your clips.** Grasp iMovie's easy, nondestructive method of handling edits, and learn when to edit in the Event Browser and when to edit on the Storyboard. Build the movie on the Storyboard by arranging the clips and editing them to fit. If you want, add still photos — and enliven them with custom Ken Burns effects.

- **Finish, polish, and share your movie.** Give your movie professional fit and finish by adding titles and transitions and creating a custom sound track complete with music and sound effects. Create a slick, professional-looking trailer to promote your movie. Share the movie with friends by creating a file or a DVD or with the world by posting it to YouTube or other online sites, your MobileMe Gallery, or your Web site.

- **Set up a music studio on your Mac.** Perhaps the best feature of iLife is the way it packs a complete music studio into your Mac. As soon as you've connected your musical keyboard and any physical instruments you're using to your Mac, you're ready to start making music with GarageBand. If you need a kick-start, fire up the Magic GarageBand feature to quickly lay down a backing track that you can play or sing along with. And If you need to improve your playing, study with GarageBand's lessons, and practice with the How Did I Play? feature.

- **Record a song.** To create a song quickly in GarageBand, you can build tracks out of loops, changing them so that they exactly meet your needs. You can then add in your own performances playing either a Software Instrument via your keyboard or a real, physical instrument such as a guitar or drum kit. You can even create your own custom Software Instruments to get exactly the sounds you want.

- **Mix a song and share it.** Even the best performance may need editing, and GarageBand makes it easy to remove mistakes or cut together the best parts of several takes. You can then mix the song, adjusting the balance, panning, and effects on each track so that it fulfils your artistic vision. When the song is finished, you can export it to iTunes; add tags, lyrics, and artwork there; and finally share the song on the Internet.

- **Build your own Web site quickly and easily.** The best place to showcase the photos, movies, and music you create with the iLife applications is by reaching a worldwide audience on the Web. The iWeb application lets you quickly create great-looking Web sites from your content. You can even add Web widgets such as interactive Google Maps and AdSense advertisements.

- **Add blogs and podcasts to your Web site.** If you have rapidly changing information that you need to share, you'll love iWeb's features for adding blogs and podcasts to your Web site. You create the blog entries in iWeb and the podcasts in GarageBand, and can post them to your Web site with minimal effort. You can also add your podcasts to the iTunes Store, which lets you reach a huge audience worldwide.

- **Burn custom DVDs of your movies and photos.** Despite the Internet, DVDs remain a great way of sharing and enjoying movies and photos. iDVD gives you all the features you need to create professional-looking DVDs with customized menu screens and compelling content. And if you need to create a DVD in a hurry, you can use the Magic DVD feature to do the grunt work for you — or use the OneStep DVD feature to burn a movie straight to DVD from your DV camcorder.

How Do I Get My Photos into iPhoto?

You've taken the photos with your digital camera and now you're ready to add them to your iPhoto library so that you can view, improve, and use them. Importing photos from a digital camera takes only moments, but you can also import photos from folders on your Mac (or other computers) or directly from e-mail messages. If you have hard copies of photos (or other documents), you can also add them to your library by using Image Capture. First, take a moment to explore the iPhoto interface and set iPhoto's preferences to suit your needs.

Navigating the iPhoto Interface

iPhoto, iLife's photo-editing and viewing application, packs a ton of power into an easy-to-use interface, so first make sure you know what's what in iPhoto. Figure 1.1 shows the main iPhoto window with the key elements labeled. Most of the action takes place in this window, but you can also expand iPhoto to a full-screen view so that you can see as much as possible of the albums or photos you're working on.

1.1 The main iPhoto window.

Caution If you've upgraded to iPhoto '11, use Software Update to download the latest updates for iPhoto before you run iPhoto for the first time. See the Appendix for details.

Here's what the main elements in the user interface do:

- **Source list.** This pane shows your iPhoto library, recent items, libraries other people are sharing on your network, any connected devices (such as a digital camera), photo albums, MobileMe Gallery, keepsakes (such as books), and slide shows you've created. You can click the gray disclosure triangle to the left of a category to expand or collapse its contents.

- **Viewing area.** This is where you view your photos, either as small thumbnails or taking up the whole area. Drag the Zoom slider to change the size of the thumbnails. From here, you can open a photo for viewing or editing.

- **Toolbar.** This contains buttons for manipulating the photo or photos you've selected.

- **Work pane.** This pane on the right of the iPhoto window shows information about the photo or photos or other items you've selected, as well as tools for working with your selection. For example, when you click the Info button, you see the Information pane shown in the figure. When you click the Edit button, you see tools for editing the current photo.

Setting iPhoto's Preferences so You Can Work Quickly

Before you start importing photos, take a few minutes to choose suitable settings for iPhoto's preferences. Like most applications, iPhoto has several screens of these. Getting settings that suit you enables you to work much more quickly and comfortably.

Choose iPhoto ⇨ Preferences to display the Preferences dialog. Then, work through the following sections, choosing settings in the six categories as you go.

Choosing General preferences

The General preferences (see Figure 1.2) are essential for working quickly and easily in iPhoto, so you'll want to check or change all of them.

If the General preferences are not automatically displayed when you choose iPhoto ⇨ Preferences, click the General button. You can then work through the following sections, choosing settings in the six categories as you go.

On the Sources line, select the Show last check box if you want to show the last 12 months album in the Source list. (An album is one way to group photos in iPhoto.) In the text box, you can change the number of months this album shows. For example, if you take many photos, two or three months may be a better choice than the last 12 months.

If you want to display the number of photos each item contains next to the item in the Source list, select the Show item counts check box. This setting can be helpful if you need to identify large groups of photos, but it can also be distracting.

General

General   Appearance   Sharing   Accounts   Advanced

Sources: ☑ Show last [12] months album
☐ Show item counts

Rotate: ○ ⟲ ⊙ ⟳

Connecting camera opens: [🖼 iPhoto]

Autosplit into Events: [One event per day]

☑ Check for iPhoto updates automatically ⓘ

1.2 The General preferences let you tell iPhoto how to behave.

On the Rotate line, select the clockwise-rotation option or the counterclockwise-rotation option to specify the default direction of rotation. You can reverse the rotation by holding down Option as you click the Rotate button on the panel for editing a photo quickly.

In the Connecting camera opens pop-up menu, choose the application you want Mac OS X to launch when you connect a camera. If you use iPhoto for managing your photos, iPhoto is the best choice here. The alternatives are normally Image Capture and No application.

In the Autosplit into Events pop-up menu, choose how long you want each event to be. Your options are One event per day, One event per week, Two-hour gaps, or Eight-hour gaps.

Note Events are the main means of dividing your photos into different groups. A photo can belong to only one Event, but you can move a photo from one Event to another as needed. iPhoto can automatically create Events for you based on the dates and times of the photos you import. You can also create Events manually if you prefer.

Select the Check for iPhoto updates automatically check box if you want iPhoto to automatically check for software updates when you launch it. Clear this check box if you prefer to use Software Update. The updates contain fixes for problems or other improvements to iPhoto, so it's a good idea to check for them frequently and to install those you find.

Choosing Appearance preferences

In Appearance preferences (see Figure 1.3), choose how you want iPhoto to display and organize your photos.

1.3 In Appearance preferences, you can choose the border style, background color, how to organize the view, and the size of text in the Source list.

Experiment with the Photo Border settings — you can apply an outline, a drop shadow, or both — and the Background slider. iPhoto shows the changes immediately while you work in the Preferences dialog, so you can quickly find settings that suit you.

Select the Show reflections check box if you want to see a small reflection of the Event underneath it. This effect is visually cool, but of no practical use.

Genius

The Photo Border settings and reflections make your Mac's graphics card work harder. If iPhoto runs slowly on your Mac, turn off these options.

Select the Show informational overlays check box if you want iPhoto to display information about the current photos as you scroll down — for example, the month and year. Scrolling information is useful for locating photos within large albums or Events.

To choose the size of the text, click the Source Text pop-up menu, and then select Small or Large.

Choosing Sharing preferences

iPhoto's Sharing preferences (see Figure 1.4) let you share your photos with other iPhoto users on your network and enjoy the photos they're sharing.

```
⊖ ○ ○                          Sharing
 ┌──┐  ┌───┐  ┌───┐  ┌───┐  ┌───┐
 │ 8 │  │▦▦▦│  │ ▦ │  │ ◰ │  │ ⚙ │
 └──┘  └───┘  └───┘  └───┘  └───┘
General  Appearance  Sharing  Accounts  Advanced

        ☑ Look for shared photos
        ☑ Share my photos
           ◉ Share entire library
           ○ Share selected albums:
           ┌──────────────────────────┬─┐
           │ ☐ Last 12 Months         │▲│
           │ ☐ Last Import            │▣│
           │ ☐ Family Photos          │ │
           │ ☐ Work Photos            │ │
           │ ☐ Recent Family Favorites│▼│
           └──────────────────────────┴─┘

        Shared name:  ┌──────────────────────┐
                      │ iMac Photo Albums     │
                      └──────────────────────┘
        ☑ Require password:  ┌───────────┐
                             │ ••••••••  │
                             └───────────┘
        Status: On                           (?)
```

1.4 Choose which of your photos to share and specify if you want to look for photos others are sharing.

To see the photos others are sharing, select the Look for shared photos check box.

To share your own photos, follow these steps:

1. **Select the Share my photos check box.** iPhoto enables all the controls below this check box.

2. **Select the Share entire library option if you want to share all your photos.** To share just some of it, select the Share selected albums option, and then select the check box for each album you want to share.

3. **Type a descriptive name for your shared photos in the Shared name box.**

4. **If you want to password-protect your shared photos, select the Require password check box and type a password.**

Choosing Accounts preferences

In iPhoto's Accounts preferences (see Figure 1.5), you can set up the e-mail accounts and social networking accounts that you will use directly from iPhoto.

Note When you open Accounts preferences, iPhoto automatically loads details for various accounts you have set up on your computer. You'll find instructions for removing an account later in this chapter.

Accounts

General Appearance Sharing Accounts Advanced

Accounts

aconnor@mac...
Email

Account Type: Other

Description: aconnor@macserver.surrealmacs.co

Email Address: aconnor@macserver.surrealmacs.co

Full Name: Anna Connor

Outgoing Mail Server: macserver.surrealmacs.com

Port: 587

User Name: aconnor

Password:

☐ Use Secure Sockets Layer (SSL)

1.5 In Accounts preferences, set up the e-mail and social networking accounts you want to use directly from iPhoto.

When you first open the Accounts preferences pane, it displays the e-mail accounts that you have set up on your Mac. To add another account, such as MobileMe, Facebook, or Flickr, click the add (+) button. iPhoto displays the Add Account pane (see Figure 1.6), and you can then work as described in the following four subsections.

Adding a MobileMe account to iPhoto

To add a MobileMe account to iPhoto, follow these steps:

1. **In the Add Account pane, click the MobileMe button.**

2. **Click Add.** iPhoto displays the Log in to the MobileMe dialog (see Figure 1.7).

3. **Type your username and password.**

4. **Click Log In.** iPhoto validates the information with the MobileMe service and then adds the account to the Accounts list.

Add Account...

Choose which type of account you want to add:

MobileMe

Facebook

Flickr

Email

Cancel   Add

1.6 In the Add Account dialog, click the type of account you want to add to iPhoto, and then click the Add button.

Adding a Facebook account to iPhoto

To add a Facebook account to iPhoto, follow these steps:

1. **In the Add Account pane, click the Facebook button.**

2. **Click Add.** iPhoto displays the Login to Facebook dialog (see Figure 1.8).

3. **Type your e-mail address and password.**

4. **Select the I agree to Facebook's terms check box.** Click the terms link if you want to read through the terms first.

5. **Click Login.** iPhoto validates the information with Facebook and then adds the account to the Accounts list. The main part of the pane displays a message that your Facebook account is enabled.

1.7 To add a MobileMe account to iPhoto you need provide only your username and password.

1.8 When adding a Facebook account to iPhoto you must agree to Facebook's terms.

Adding a Flickr account to iPhoto

To add a Flickr account to iPhoto, follow these steps:

1. **In the Add Account pane, click the Flickr button.**

2. **Click Add.** iPhoto displays the Do you want to set up iPhoto to publish to Flickr? dialog (see Figure 1.9).

3. **Click Set Up.** iPhoto launches or activates your default Web browser (for example, Safari) and displays the Yahoo! login page for Flickr.

1.9 To add a Flickr account to iPhoto, click Set Up in the Do you want to set up iPhoto to publish to Flickr? dialog.

4. **Log in to your Flickr account as usual.** The browser then displays the first Flickr: Authorize iPhoto Uploader page, which checks that you've deliberately made this request from iPhoto (as opposed to malware faking the request).

5. **In the shaded "If you arrived at this page because you specifically asked iPhoto Uploader to connect to your Flickr account, click here" box, click the Next button.** The browser then displays the second Flickr Authorize iPhoto Uploader page, which details the permissions you give to the iPhoto Uploader (such as uploading photos to your Flickr account).

6. **Click the "OK, I'll Authorize It" button.** The browser displays a page telling you that you've authorized iPhoto Uploader.

7. **Close the Flickr tab or window in the browser.** The browser sends iPhoto a signal saying that you've authorized the account. iPhoto closes the Do you want to set up iPhoto to publish to Flickr? dialog, adds the account, and displays a message saying that the Flickr account is enabled.

Adding an e-mail account to iPhoto

To add an e-mail account to iPhoto, follow these steps:

1. **In the Add Account pane, click the e-mail button.**

2. **Click the Add button.** iPhoto displays the Choose Service dialog (see Figure 1.10).

3. **Click the e-mail provider for the account.** For example, if you have a Hotmail account or MSN account, click the Windows Live Hotmail button.

4. **Click the Add button.** iPhoto displays a dialog containing fields for the information required to set up the account. For example, Figure 1.11 shows the Add Hotmail Account dialog.

5. **Click OK.** iPhoto validates the information with the e-mail provider and adds the account to the Accounts list.

Choose Service...

✓ **mobile**me

Windows Live™
Hotmail

YAHOO! MAIL

GM**ail**™

Aol Mail.

Other

(Cancel)　(OK)

1.10 To add an e-mail account to iPhoto, select the e-mail provider in the Choose Service dialog.

11

Removing an account from iPhoto

If the Accounts list includes an account that you don't want to use from iPhoto, you can remove the account from the list. For example, if you have several e-mail accounts set up in Mail by the time you open Accounts preferences, iPhoto grabs all of their details, even if you want to use only some of them.

To remove an account, click it in the Accounts list and then click the Remove (–) button. iPhoto confirms the removal, double-checking about any items that it will remove from your iPhoto library as a result. Figure 1.12 shows the dialog for removing a Flickr account to which you've published albums from iPhoto. Click the Remove button if you want to go ahead.

Choosing Advanced preferences

iPhoto's Advanced preferences (see Figure 1.13) contains widely varied settings — but many you'll find helpful to set.

Add Hotmail Account

Full Name: Chris Smith
Email Address: chrisssmith1@hotmail.com
Password: ••••••••••••••
Description: Hotmail

Cancel   OK

1.11 Type the details of the e-mail account in the dialog that iPhoto displays. The various types of accounts require different pieces of information.

Are you sure you want to remove "Chris Smith's" Flickr account?

One album will be removed from your iPhoto library. It will still be visible on Flickr. Photos downloaded from Flickr that have not been imported will be moved to the iPhoto trash unless you choose to import them.

☐ Import photos to your library before removing this account

Cancel   Remove

1.12 When you remove an account from iPhoto's preferences, iPhoto warns you about any items (such as albums) that it will delete from your library.

In the Importing area, select the Copy items to the iPhoto Library check box if you want iPhoto to make copies of photos you import from folders on your Mac or your network. This is iPhoto's normal behavior, and it's usually helpful because it puts all your photos in one place and makes backup simpler. But if you already have a ton of photos on your Mac and want to use the photos in their current folders, clear this check box to prevent iPhoto from making copies of them. You'll need to make sure you back up the current folders as well as your iPhoto library.

Note

If you clear the Copy items to the iPhoto Library check box, iPhoto adds to your library only a reference to each photo you import — a pointer that tells iPhoto in which folder the photo is located. But if you edit the photo in iPhoto and save the changes, iPhoto creates a copy of the photo so that it can save the changes while leaving the original untouched. This setting doesn't affect files you import from your digital camera.

1.13 In the Advanced preferences, choose whether to copy items to your library, how to edit photos, how to handle RAW photos, and whether to look up Places.

In the Edit Photos pop-up menu, choose how you want to edit your photos. If you want to use iPhoto, which you'll want to do if you don't have another photo-editing application, choose In iPhoto. If you want to use another application, such as Adobe Photoshop CS, choose that application from the list. In the RAW Photos area, choose how to deal with RAW images. If you're unfamiliar with RAW images, see the sidebar, "Understanding What RAW Image Files Are."

- **Use RAW when using an external editor.** Select this check box to use an external graphics editor (such as Photoshop or Aperture) for editing your RAW image files. With this check box selected, iPhoto passes the RAW image file to the external graphics editor, rather than passing the JPEG or TIFF file that iPhoto uses (see the next option).

- **Save edits as 16-bit TIFF files.** When you import or edit a RAW image file, iPhoto normally saves the result as a JPEG file, which has lower quality but takes up less space. Select this check box to make iPhoto save the imported edited file as a 16-bit TIFF file instead, which is higher quality than the JPEG file.

In the Look up Places pop-up menu, choose whether to look up the places in your photos. The choice is simple: Automatically or Never.

Select the Include location information for published photos check box if you want iPhoto to include location information in photos you publish online. Including location information can be useful for both business purposes and personal publishing, but for reasons of privacy you may prefer that others do not know where you took each photo.

Understanding What RAW Image Files Are

RAW image files are minimally processed image files that are also called *digital nega-tives* — the digital equivalent of negatives in film photography. You can set most digital SLR cameras and advanced models of digital compact cameras to produce RAW image files, instead of converted image files in formats such as JPEG or TIFF.

A RAW image file contains every bit of data captured by the camera that took the pic-ture, rather than a converted and compressed form of that data. RAW image files are larger than converted image files and provide higher quality. They're mostly used by professional photographers, but you can use them either within iPhoto or with an external editor such as Apple Aperture (Apple's high-end image-editing application) or Adobe Photoshop.

RAW image files come in various formats. iPhoto supports the same cameras as Aperture, so to see a list of digital cameras that produce RAW image files you can use in iPhoto, see the Aperture list at www.apple.com/aperture/specs/raw.html.

On the e-mail line, select the Automatically Bcc myself check box if you want iPhoto to automati-cally send your e-mail account a BCC copy of each message you send via e-mail. Most e-mail appli-cations and services automatically keep copies of messages you've sent in a folder with a name such as Sent, but if your application or service doesn't, you can select this check box to keep copies.

In the Print Products Store pop-up menu, select the country in which you want to order print prod-ucts, such as books and cards.

Importing Photos

After you choose preferences, you're ready to import photos from your digital camera, memory card, folder, or even an e-mail message.

Importing photos from your digital camera

Here's how to import photos from your digital camera:

1. **If the camera connects directly to your Mac via USB, connect the camera and turn it on if it doesn't turn on automatically.** Otherwise, remove the memory card from the camera and insert it in a memory card reader connected to your Mac.

2. **When Mac OS X notices the camera or memory card containing photos, it launches or activates iPhoto and displays the photos, as shown in Figure 1.14.**

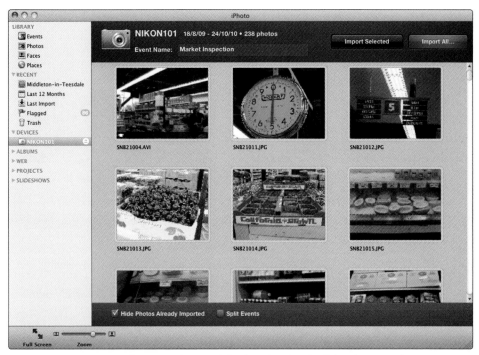

1.14 Mac OS X automatically opens iPhoto and displays thumbnails of the photos on the camera or storage card you've connected.

3. **Type a descriptive name for the event in the Event Name text box.**

4. **If you want iPhoto to split the photos into different events by date and time, select the Split Events check box at the bottom of the screen.** iPhoto uses the event length you set in Events preferences earlier in this chapter — for example, one day or two hours.

5. **If the camera or memory card contains photos you've imported before, select the Hide Photos Already Imported check box to make iPhoto hide these photos so you don't try to import them again.** Hiding the photos you've already imported also lets iPhoto show you the new photos on the camera or memory card more quickly.

Note

If you chose No application or another application than iPhoto in the Connecting camera opens pop-up menu in iPhoto's General preferences (as discussed earlier in this chapter), you must import the photos into iPhoto manually. See the next section in this chapter for details. If you want Mac OS X to activate iPhoto for some cameras but not for others, see the final section in this chapter.

15

Genius If you want to add photos to a specific album, you can simply drag them from the camera or memory card to that album. In the album, iPhoto creates references to the photos so they show up in it. iPhoto also adds the photos to your library, as usual.

6. **Choose which photos you want to import.**

    ○ To import all the photos shown, click Import All.

    ○ To import only some of the photos, select them by dragging across a range, or by clicking the first photo and holding down ⌘ while you click each of the other photos. Then click Import Selected.

7. **iPhoto imports the photos you chose, and then prompts you to delete the photos from the camera or memory card (see Figure 1.15).** To delete the photos, click Delete Photos; to keep them on the camera, click Keep Photos.

Delete Photos on Your Camera?

9 photos were successfully imported into iPhoto.

(Delete Photos)   (**Keep Photos**)

1.15 Choose whether or not you want iPhoto to delete photos from the camera or memory card.

Caution Having iPhoto delete your photos automatically from your digital camera after import can be convenient, but often it's better to keep the photos on the camera until you've checked that iPhoto has imported them successfully. You may also want to keep the photos on the digital camera so that you can import them on another computer.

Dealing with duplicate imported photos

When importing pictures from a camera, it's all too easy to import some of them twice. For example, maybe you forgot to reformat the memory card after putting it back in the camera.

iPhoto helps you avoid duplicate imports by displaying the Duplicate Photo dialog, as shown in Figure 1.16, to warn you when you're about to import a photo you've already added, even if you've changed the version that's already in iPhoto.

Importing Videos from Your Digital Camera

If your digital camera takes video files as well as still photos, you can easily import the videos into iPhoto along with the still photos. iPhoto shows a white camera icon in the lower-left corner of the thumbnail for each video file. Otherwise, the procedure for importing videos is the same as that for still photos.

Select the Apply to all duplicates check box if you want iPhoto to apply your decision to all duplicate photos in the batch you're importing, rather than prompt you to rule on each one. Then, click Import if you want to import the photo anyway, Don't Import to skip importing it, or Cancel if you want to cancel the import.

Ejecting the camera or memory card

After importing all the pictures you want from the camera or the memory card, eject the camera or memory card by clicking the Eject button next to it in the Source list. Alternatively, Control+click or right-click the

1.16 iPhoto makes certain you know you're importing a duplicate photo. In this example, the version that's already in the library has been changed.

camera or memory card in the Source list, and then click Eject. When iPhoto removes the camera or memory card from the Source list, you can safely unplug it.

Caution Never unplug your digital camera or memory card reader without ejecting it. Doing so normally produces a Device Removal error message in Mac OS X, but it can also cause iPhoto or even Mac OS X to stop responding. If iPhoto stops responding, Ctrl-click or right-click its icon on the Dock, and then click Force Quit to close the application.

Importing photos with the Import command

If your photos are in a folder, or on a CD or DVD, rather than on a camera or a memory card, you can bring them into your library by using the Import command:

1. **Choose File ⇨ Import to Library or press ⌘+Shift+I to open the Import Photos dialog.**

2. **Select the photos you want to import.** You can import either an entire folder, or one or more photos from within a folder.

3. **Click Import.**

Importing photos from the Finder or e-mail

Instead of using the Import command, you can also add photos to your library via a Finder window. Simply select a photo — or several, or a folder containing photos — in a Finder window and drag it to the viewing area in iPhoto.

If you receive a photo in the body of an e-mail message, you can also drag the photo from your e-mail application (such as Mail or Entourage) to the viewing area in iPhoto.

If you receive a photo as an attachment in Mail, click and hold down the Save button on the attachment line. Then choose Add to iPhoto from the menu that appears. In other e-mail applications, you may need to save the attached photo to a folder and then drag the photo from a Finder window to the viewing area in iPhoto.

Understanding Which Picture Formats iPhoto Can Handle

You can use the following three photo file formats in iPhoto:

- **JPEG.** A file format developed by the Joint Photographic Experts Group, JPEG is the most widely used format for digital photos. JPEG typically uses lossy compression (compression in which data is discarded) to reduce the file size of the photos, but maintains high-enough quality for general use. Many digital cameras take only JPEGs; others take JPEGs unless you change the file format.

- **TIFF.** The Tagged Image File Format uses either no compression or lossless compression (compression in which no data is discarded) to store images at full quality. Some digital cameras can create TIFF files as well as JPEG files.

- **RAW.** As discussed earlier in this chapter, a RAW file is a digital negative that stores minimally processed data. When you work with RAW files in iPhoto, it saves the results as either a JPEG or TIFF file, depending on what you selected in Advanced preferences.

These three file formats can all contain metadata — information about the photos, such as the date and time they were taken, the camera and exposure used, and other details. You can view this information by choosing Photos ⇨ Show Extended Photo Info or by pressing ⌘+I. iPhoto can read metadata from all three formats, but can write metadata only to the JPEG and TIFF formats.

You can import other types of photos into iPhoto, such as PNG (Portable Network Graphics) files, but iPhoto doesn't fully support them.

Scanning Photos Using Image Capture

To get photos that you have as prints (hard copies) into your iPhoto library, you need to create digital versions of the photos by using a scanner. If your scanner has a film attachment, you can also scan negatives or slides.

Genius Scan at a high bit depth and resolution to get as high-quality a file as possible. You can then create lower-resolution versions from iPhoto if you need them. Watch the little Size readout above the Scan To Folder pop-up menu to see the file size of the scanned image.

Mac OS X includes a powerful scanning application called Image Capture that you can use to control most scanners. However, if your scanner came with its own software, you may prefer to use that application instead because it may offer extra features that tie in with the scanner's capabilities.

Here's how to scan a picture using Image Capture:

1. **Turn on the scanner and place the picture on the scanning surface.** If you want to scan multiple pictures at once, place each of them on the scanning surface with some space between them so that Image Capture can identify each separate picture.

Genius Scanning multiple pictures at the same time can be a great timesaver, but each picture receives the same type of image correction (for example, adjusting the brightness or color temperature). Make sure the pictures you scan at the same time need similar treatment.

2. **Press the Start or Wake-up button on the scanner.** Your Mac notices the scanner and launches Image Capture.

3. **Image Capture makes the scanner run a quick scan of the picture or pictures to provide an overview, which it then displays (see Figure 1.17).** If you're scanning multiple items, make sure the Detect Separate Items check box is selected.

4. **If you want to scan a picture quickly, choose the destination folder in the Scan To pop-up menu.** Click Scan, and skip the rest of these steps. Usually, though, you'll want to choose settings. To do so, click Show Details to display the scanning controls (see Figure 1.18).

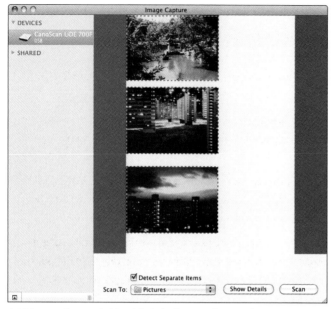

1.17 Image Capture is Mac OS X's built-in application for scanning pictures. Unless you want to scan with default settings, click Show Details to display the scanning controls.

1.18 Image Capture's scanning controls let you choose what kind of scanned pictures to produce, where to store them, and what to name them. You may see different controls depending on your scanner.

5. **In the Kind pop-up menu, choose the scan kind: Color, Black & White, or Text.**

6. **In the second pop-up menu at the top of the right pane, choose how many colors or grays to use:**

   - If you choose Color in the Kind pop-up menu, choose Millions or Billions in the Colors pop-up menu.

   - If you choose Black & White in the Kind pop-up menu, choose 256 Grays or Thousands of Grays in the Grays pop-up menu (which replaces the Colors pop-up menu).

7. **In the Resolution pop-up menu, choose the resolution.** For good results in photographs, choose 300 dots per inch (dpi). Using resolutions higher than this will make the files much larger and also make the scans take longer, so it may not be worthwhile.

8. **When scanning a single picture, use the Size boxes to adjust the width and height of the area you're scanning.** You can choose pixels, inches, or centimeters in the pop-up menu to the right of the boxes. For either a single picture or multiple pictures, you can drag the handles around the selected part or parts of the image.

9. **If you need to rotate the picture or pictures, type the angle in the Rotation Angle text box.** For example, type 90 degrees to rotate the pictures a quarter-turn to the right.

10. **In the Scan To pop-up menu, choose the folder in which you want to store the scanned files.**

11. **Type a name for the scanned files in the Name box.** When you scan multiple pictures, Image Capture adds numbers after this name to distinguish the files — for example, Japan.tiff for the first photo, Japan 1.tiff for the second, and Japan 2.tiff for the third.

12. **Select the format in the Format pop-up menu.** Your choices are JPG, TIFF, PNG, JPEG 2000, and PDF. TIFF is the best choice for high-quality pictures you will use with iPhoto. JPEG 2000 is the best choice for compressed pictures for use with iPhoto. JPG is good for general use on the Web or with older operating systems. PNG is good for high-quality Web use. PDF is good for scanning documents.

13. **If you need to tweak the colors on the image, open the Image Correction pop-up menu and choose Manual instead of Automatic.** You can then use the Brightness, Tint, Hue, and Saturation sliders that Image Capture displays (see Figure 1.19) to produce the colors you want.

14. **Click Scan to scan the picture.** Image Capture saves the files using the folder and filenames you specified.

15. **Scan further images as necessary or quit Image Capture.**

1.19 Choose Manual in the Image Correction pop-up menu if you need to adjust the colors in the picture you're scanning.

Sharing a Scanner or Camera Using Image Capture

Image Capture makes it easy to share a scanner or camera among the Macs on your network. By sharing a scanner, you avoid having to move it from one Mac to another, or buying a scanner for each Mac. You can also share a camera so that any computer on the network can access its contents.

Sharing a scanner using Scanner Sharing

To share a scanner, first set up Scanner Sharing on the Mac to which the scanner is connected:

1. **Choose Apple ⇨ System Preferences to open the System Preferences window.**

2. **Choose View ⇨ Sharing from the menu bar to open the Sharing pane.**

3. **In the Services list on the left, select the Scanner Sharing check box.** Mac OS X turns on Scanner Sharing and displays the Scanner Sharing pane (see Figure 1.20).

1.20 To share a scanner or camera with other Macs and PCs on your network, select the Scanner Sharing check box in Sharing preferences.

4. **In the list of scanners, select the check box for the scanner you want to share.**

5. **Choose System Preferences ⇨ Quit System Preferences or press ⌘+Q to quit System Preferences.**

Sharing a camera using Image Capture

You can also use Image Capture to share a camera on the network. This is great for when you need to give several people access to the same photos directly from the camera, without connecting it to each Mac or PC in turn.

Here's how to set up Image Capture on the Mac to which you connect the camera:

1. **Click the desktop, choose Go ⇨ Applications, and then double-click Image Capture to open Image Capture.**

2. **In the Devices list on the left, click the camera.** Image Capture displays the camera's contents.

3. **In the lower-left corner of the Image Capture window, click the Show Device Settings button (the button with the upward triangle).** Image Capture displays the camera's settings pane in the lower-left corner of the window (see Figure 1.21).

	Name ▲	Date	File Size	Aperture
	SNB20436.JPG	08/22/2009 01:37:18	2.9 MB	f/3.5
	SNB20437.JPG	08/22/2009 01:37:30	2.9 MB	f/3.5
	SNB20438.JPG	08/22/2009 04:10:28	2.9 MB	f/2.8
	SNB20479.JPG	08/25/2009 16:20:02	3 MB	f/4
	SNB20480.JPG	08/25/2009 16:20:02	3.1 MB	f/4
	SNB20481.JPG	08/25/2009 16:20:14	3.2 MB	f/4

DEVICES

Samsung NV5
MassStorage, 6 items

CanoScan LiDE 700F
USB

SHARED

Samsung NV5
Connecting this camera opens:
iPhoto
☑ Share camera
☐ Delete after import

Import   Import All

1 of 6 selected

Show Device Settings button

1.21 Use the Device Settings pane in the lower-left corner of the Image Capture window to share a camera with other Macs and PCs on your network.

4. **Select the Share camera check box.**

5. **Choose Image Capture ⇨ Quit Image Capture if you're ready to quit Image Capture.**

Connecting to a shared scanner or camera

Now that you've shared the scanner or camera, you can connect to it from another Mac like this:

1. **Click the desktop, choose Go ⇨ Applications, and then double-click Image Capture to open Image Capture.**

2. **In the left pane, click the disclosure triangle next to the Shared category to display the shared devices.**

3. **Click the shared scanner or camera you want to use.**

You're now ready to use the scanner or camera across the network, just as if it were connected to your Mac rather than the remote Mac.

Note If you see the message "The scanner is being used by a remote user" when you try to connect to a remote scanner, but you know you're the only remote user, Image Capture is open on the Mac that's sharing the scanner. Quit Image Capture on that Mac, and you'll be able to use the scanner on your Mac.

Telling Your Mac How to Handle Different Cameras

If you use multiple digital cameras, you may want your Mac to treat each one differently. For example, you may want to have iPhoto open when you connect your digital SLR, but not when you connect your iPhone, even though the iPhone has a digital camera.

To tell your Mac how to handle different cameras, you use Image Capture. Follow these steps:

1. **Connect the camera you want to affect.**

2. **Click the desktop, choose Go ⇨ Applications, and then double-click Image Capture to open Image Capture.**

3. **In the Devices list on the left, click the camera.** Image Capture displays the camera's contents.

4. **In the lower-left corner of the Image Capture window, click the Show Device Settings button (the button with the upward triangle).** Image Capture displays the camera's settings pane in the lower-left corner of the window.

5. **Open the Connecting this camera opens pop-up menu, and then click the item you want:**

   - **No Application.** Select this item if you don't want Mac OS X to launch an application when you connect this camera.

   - **iPhoto.** Select this item to launch iPhoto. On most Macs, this is the default setting.

   - **Image Capture.** Select this item to launch Image Capture.

   - **Preview.** Select this item to launch Preview. You can then import photos by choosing File ⇨ Import from *Camera*, where *Camera* is the name by which Mac OS X knows the camera.

   - **AutoImporter.** Select this item to import photos automatically using Image Capture's AutoImporter feature. If you use this, you need to choose settings for AutoImporter. Open a Finder window, go to the /System/Library/Image Capture/ Support/Application/ folder, and then double-click the AutoImporter item to launch the AutoImporter application. Choose AutoImporter ⇨ Preferences from the menu bar to display the AutoImporter Preferences window (see Figure 1.22), and then choose the destination folder for imports, whether to create a subfolder, and whether to delete items from the camera after import. Choose AutoImporter ⇨ Quit AutoImporter when you've made your choices.

AutoImporter Preferences

Import folder: Pictures

☑ For each import create a subfolder named:

(camera name) (sequence #) (date)

CAMERA sequence # 10/28/2010   (date)
                                       (camera name)
                                       (user name)
                                       (sequence #)

☐ Delete items from camera after successful import

1.22 If you decide to use Image Capture's AutoImporter feature to import photos automatically, set the destination folder in AutoImporter Preferences.

⊙ **Other.** Click this item to display a dialog in which you can choose a different application to open when you connect the camera.

6. **Choose Image Capture ⇨ Quit Image Capture if you're ready to quit Image Capture.**

How Do I Organize and Edit My Photos?

After importing your photos into your iPhoto library, you're ready to start making the most of them. The first thing to do is organize the photos effectively using iPhoto's Events, Faces, and Places tools, and to create albums so that you can quickly find the photos you want. Next, you can use iPhoto's powerful tools effectively to give your photos full power and impact. You may also want to separate your photos into two or more libraries for ease of use.

Organizing Your Photos

To get the most out of your library, you need to organize your photos effectively into Events and albums. iPhoto also lets you organize photos by people's faces using its face-recognition technology, and by location using its Places feature.

To sort through your photos easily, you need to flag photos of interest and add keywords, descriptions, and ratings to as many photos as possible.

Working with Events

iPhoto gives you four main ways of organizing your photos: by Event (which iPhoto capitalizes like that), by Faces, by Places, and by album.

Understanding what an Event is

An *Event* is a way of organizing related photos together. Each time you import a set of photos from a digital camera or from a folder, iPhoto organizes them into Events by time and date. You can set iPhoto to create different Events for intervals of two hours, eight hours, one day, or an entire week by choosing the appropriate setting in the Autosplit into Events pop-up menu in General preferences. For more on setting Event intervals, see Chapter 1.

Note To organize your photos, you can easily rename an Event or move photos from one Event to another.

To display your library's Events in Events view, click the Events item in the Library category of the Source list. iPhoto displays the events, as shown in Figure 2.1.

In Events view, you see each Event represented by a single photo — the *key photo,* which you can choose (I cover how to do this later in the chapter). But you can position the mouse pointer over an Event to scroll through each of the Event's photos. This is a great way of browsing quickly to the photo you want.

Genius Events and albums can seem confusing at first. The big difference between the two is that a photo can appear in only one Event at a time, whereas you can add a photo to as many albums as you want.

2.1 You can quickly browse your photos in Events view. Drag the Zoom slider if you want to make the Event pictures larger or smaller.

Viewing an Event's photos

To display the photos in an Event, double-click the Event. iPhoto displays the photos the Event contains, as shown in Figure 2.2. You can change the size by dragging the Zoom slider at the bottom of the iPhoto window.

From here, you can double-click a photo to make iPhoto zoom in to the full area of the preview pane and display the other photos as miniatures in a bar across the bottom of the window. You can also hold the mouse pointer over a photo, click the disclosure triangle that appears, and then use the resulting pop-up panel (see Figure 2.3) to quickly manipulate the photo. For example, click the Rotate button to rotate the photo, click Edit in iPhoto to open the photo for editing, or click the number of stars (from one star to five stars) for the rating you want to give the photo.

Note

At any point, you can click the Full Screen button in the lower-left corner of the iPhoto window to switch to full screen view, which you can see on the opening page of this chapter. iPhoto remains in full screen view until either you click the Full Screen button again to exit or you activate another application.

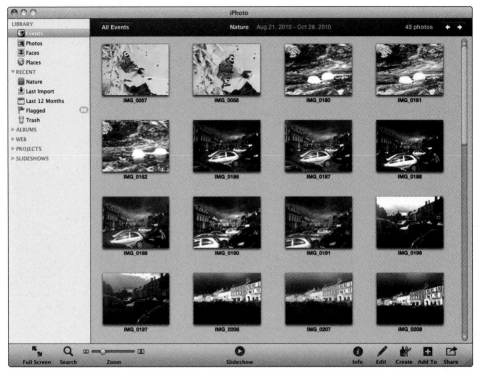

2.2 Viewing the photos within an Event.

Click the All Events button (shown in Figure 2.2) on the bar at the top of the window when you want to go back to viewing all Events. Alternatively, click the Previous Event button (the button with the left-pointing arrow) in the upper-right corner of the window to display the photos in the previous Event, or the Next Event button (the button with the right-pointing arrow) to display those in the next Event.

Renaming an Event

iPhoto names each Event by dates, but often you'll want to give an Event a more descriptive name. You can rename an Event in any of these ways:

- **While browsing All Events.** Click the Event's name below its preview, type the name in the edit box that appears, and then press Return.

- **While browsing the Event.** Click the Event's name at the top of the window, type the new name, and then press Return.

- **Any time.** With the Event selected or opened, click the Info button to display the Information pane, select the name field, type the new name, and then press Return.

Setting the key photo for an Event

The photo that appears at the top of an Event's stack in the Events view is called the key photo. When iPhoto creates an Event for you (or when you create one yourself), iPhoto makes the first photo in the Event the key photo.

Sometimes this first photo summarizes the Event perfectly, but often you'll want to pick a key photo yourself. You can do so in two ways:

- **While browsing All Events.** Position the mouse pointer over the Event, and then move the mouse until iPhoto displays the photo you want. Control+click or right-click, and then click Make Key Photo.

2.3 To quickly manipulate a photo, hold the mouse pointer over it, click the disclosure triangle that appears, and then choose the command from the pop-up panel.

- **While browsing the Event.** Control+click or right-click the photo and then click Make Key Photo. You can also hold the mouse pointer over the photo, click the disclosure triangle that appears, and then click Make Key Photo on the pop-up menu, or you can click the photo and then choose Events ⇨ Make Key Photo.

Moving photos from one Event to another

Often, you'll need to move photos from one Event to another. You can do that easily like this:

1. **In the Source list, click Events to display all the Events.**

2. **Click one Event, and then ⌘+click the other Event.**

3. **Double-click either of the selected Events.** iPhoto displays the photos from both Events.

4. **Drag one or more photos from one Event to the name bar at the top of the other Event (see Figure 2.4).**

2.4 To move a photo from one Event to another, open both Events, and then drag the photo to the name bar of the destination Event.

Merging two Events

If you find that iPhoto's automatic splitting has separated photos that you want to keep in the same Event, you can easily merge the two Events. Here's what to do:

1. **In the Source list, click Events to display all the Events.**

2. **Drag the Event whose name you want to lose onto the Event whose name you want to keep.** iPhoto displays the Do you want to merge these Events? dialog, as shown in Figure 2.5).

3. **Select the Don't Ask Again check box if you want to merge more quickly in the future, and then click Merge.** iPhoto merges the photos into the first of the Events.

Genius

If the Events are so widely separated in the Events list that dragging one Event to another is difficult even if you zoom out, click one Event and then ⌘+click the other Event. Control+click or right-click one of the selected Events, and then click Merge Events on the context menu. In the Do you want to merge these Events? dialog, click Merge. iPhoto merges the photos into the first Event, which you can then rename if necessary.

Do you want to merge these Events?

All photos in the Event you are dragging will be moved into the Event "Scenery."

☐ Don't Ask Again

(Cancel)　(**Merge**)

2.5 Click Merge in the Do you want to merge these Events? dialog to merge two Events. Select the Don't Ask Again check box if you want to suppress this confirmation in the future.

Splitting an Event

There may be times when you want to split an Event into two or three. Follow these steps:

1. **In the Source list, click Events to display all the Events.**

2. **Double-click the Event you want to split.**

3. **Select the photos from which you want to create the new Event.** For example, drag through the photos; or click the first photo you want, and then ⌘+click each of the others.

4. **Click the Split button or choose Events ⇨ Split Event.** If the original Event contains photos before and after the ones you selected, iPhoto creates a new Event containing the photos and names it Untitled Event. If the original Event contains photos —both before and after the ones you selected — iPhoto creates two new Events, one containing the photos you selected and another containing the photos after them.

5. **Rename the new Event or Events.** Click the name, type the new name, and then press Return.

6. **Control+click or right-click the photo you want to use as the key photo, and then click Make Key Photo on the context menu.**

Organizing photos with the Faces feature

Faces uses face-recognition technology to automatically identify the people in your photos. Here's how it works:

● **You teach iPhoto the name for a face.** You pick a face that's important to you and assign the name. The face must be human — Faces doesn't match animal faces, no matter how cute.

● **iPhoto scans your other photos for other instances of the same face.** iPhoto does this in the background as you do other things.

● **You check the photos iPhoto has found and confirm those that are right.**

Caution Faces is a terrific feature, but it's not all that accurate. While it can work apparent wonders, such as correctly picking one face out of a whole group, it also tends to give false positives — it's biased to finding matching faces in your photo library. Be prepared to check every suggested match or you'll get some surprises.

Once you identify the faces, you can quickly pull together albums, slide shows, or keepsakes featuring your favorite faces.

Teach iPhoto the name that matches a face

You can teach iPhoto the name for a face like this:

1. **Open the photo you want to use.** For best results, choose a picture that shows the person's face close up, looking straight at the camera, and unobscured. The higher the resolution, the better. If you use a group photo, iPhoto picks out all the faces looking toward the camera; click the face for which you want to provide the name.

2. **Click the Info button to display the Info pane.**

3. **If the Faces pane in the Info pane is collapsed, click its bar or disclosure triangle to display it.**

4. **If the Faces pane has a "1 unnamed" button, move the mouse pointer over the photo to display the white square where Faces has detected a face.** If the Faces pane doesn't have a "1 unnamed" button, click the Add a Face button to make Faces detect the face and place a white square around it. iPhoto picks out the face and puts a white square around the area from above the eyebrows to below the mouth, including the eyes and nose but not the ears, as shown in Figure 2.6.

5. **If the square is in the wrong place, correct it.** Drag the square to the face, and then resize it if necessary. Drag a corner handle to resize it around the center. Option+click and drag a corner handle to keep the opposite corner stationary as you drag.

6. **Click the click to name label below the frame and start typing the name.** As you type, iPhoto displays matching entries from your Address Book. If one of them is correct, click it; otherwise, finish typing the name and then press Return. iPhoto adds the name and displays a right-arrow button next to it. Click the arrow to see other photos in which iPhoto thinks this face appears.

2.6 You may need to help the Faces feature identify the face in the photo by placing the white square. You can then type in the name.

Confirm the faces iPhoto has found

Now check the photos iPhoto has found and confirm which are right. Follow these steps:

1. **Click the right-arrow button next to the name you just added.** iPhoto selects the Faces item in the Source list and opens the Face for the name. Figure 2.7 shows an example for a different photo.

2. **Click Confirm Additional Faces to display the photos that appear to contain the face (see Figure 2.8).** The Confirm Additional Faces button is unavailable if Faces hasn't identified any other photos with this face.

Genius

To confirm photos quickly, drag around them. iPhoto displays a green bar with the person's name across the bottom of each photo. If you realize you've chosen a photo you shouldn't have, click the green bar to change it to a red bar.

3. **Confirm or reject each photo:**

- Click a photo to confirm it. iPhoto adds a green bar with the person's name across the bottom of the photo.

- Option+click a photo to reject it. iPhoto adds a red bar with "Not" and the person's name across the bottom of the photo.

- Click again to change a green bar to a red bar or a red bar to a green bar.

4. **When you finish confirming and rejecting photos, click Done.**

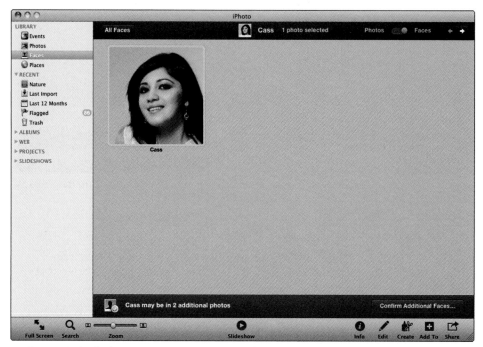

2.7 From an individual's Face page in Faces, click Confirm Additional Faces to see any other photos Faces has found that seem to match this face.

Managing Faces

After you add one or more faces, you can manage them from the Faces corkboard (see Figure 2.9). To display the corkboard, click the Faces item in the Source pane.

From the corkboard, you can take the following actions:

- **Skim through the pictures.** Move the mouse pointer over one of the people and then around the picture to skim through all the pictures.

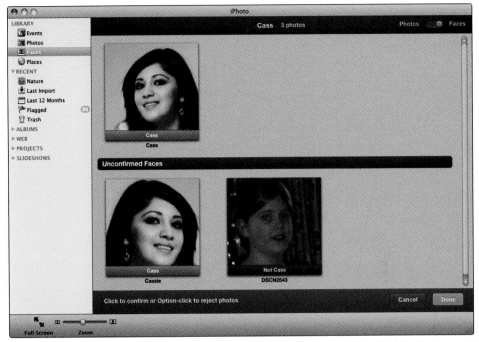

2.8 In the Unconfirmed Faces area, click a photo to confirm that iPhoto has identified the face correctly. Option+click a photo to reject the match.

- **Open a collection.** Double-click a collection to open it. You can then browse and work with the photos as usual. Click the All Faces button at the top of the window when you want to return to the corkboard. Alternatively, click the Previous button or the Next button to display another collection.

- **Add information about the person.** Move the mouse pointer over the person's picture, and then click the Info button on the toolbar. iPhoto displays the Info pane for the person, in which you can change the name you assigned, add a full name, add an e-mail address, or click the unconfirmed matches button to review any suspected matches you haven't yet confirmed. Click Done when you finish.

Genius

To delete a face, click Faces in the Source list, and then click the face you want to delete. Press ⌘+Delete, and then click Delete Face in the Are you sure you want to delete this person from Faces? dialog. The photos remain in your photo library.

2.9 From the Faces corkboard, you can display a collection of faces.

Organizing photos by Places

iPhoto's Places feature gives you another way to sort and organize your photos — by using the location in which the photos were taken.

If your camera has a built-in GPS (as the iPhone's camera and various other modern cameras do), the GPS information is recorded right in the photo. The photo is then ready for you to use in Places. If your camera doesn't have a GPS, or if your pictures are older, you can add a location to them manually.

Adding a location manually

Here's how to add a location to a photo manually:

1. **Display the Info pane.** Click the photo and then click Info on the toolbar.

2. **If the Assign a Place pane at the bottom is collapsed, click its bar or disclosure triangle to display it (see Figure 2.10).**

Genius

If you know your camera has a GPS (and you've turned the feature on) but Places seems not to have noticed that the photos contain GPS information, open the Advanced preferences (choose iPhoto ⇨ Preferences, and click Advanced) and choose Automatically in the Look up Places pop-up menu.

2.10 Click Assign a Place in the lower part of the Info pane for a photo to display the Places map.

3. Use the controls in the Assign a Place pane to find the location you want to assign to the photo. For example:

- Click in the search box, type the city name or ZIP code, and then press Return to display a map of the place, as shown in Figure 2.11.

- On the bar at the bottom of the pane, choose the view you want: Terrain, Satellite, or Hybrid.

- Click + to zoom in or – to zoom out.

- Click the pushpin on the map and drag it where you want it.

- Click Center (the circular button on the bar at the bottom of the pane) to center the map on the pushpin.

- Type the name of the place in the text box at the top of the pane.

2.11 Use the Assign a Place area in a photo's Info pane to manually assign a place to a photo. You can switch among Terrain, Satellite, and Hybrid views to find the exact spot.

41

Once you add a place like this you can apply it quickly to another photo by selecting the photo, displaying the Info pane, and then typing the name in the text box in the Assign a Place pane.

Viewing photos by place

After you or your camera assign location data to some of your photos in iPhoto, you can click Places in the Source pane to browse by place.

At first, Places displays a map showing marker pins in the locations your photos were taken. Double-click the map to zoom in on an area (see Figure 2.12); keep double-clicking to zoom in closer. You can also drag the map to display the area you want, or drag the Map Size slider to zoom in or out. For larger movements, choose a different country, state, city, or place in the bar in the upper-left corner of the Places pane.

To view the photos taken at a place, move the mouse pointer over a marker pin to display its name, and then click the arrow button to its right. From the photos for that place, click the Map button in the upper-left corner when you want to return to the map.

2.12 Click Places in the Source list and then zoom in on the pins that mark where your photos were taken.

Managing your places

To get an overview of the places your photos use, choose Window ⇨ Manage My Places. iPhoto displays the Manage My Places dialog, as shown in Figure 2.13, in which you can take the following actions:

- **Move a place.** Click the place in the My Places list, and then drag the pushpin on the map to where you want the place to be. Click + to zoom in or – to zoom out.

- **Resize a place.** Click the place in the My Places list, click its pushpin on the map, and then drag the sizing handle to enlarge or reduce the circle around the place.

- **Rename a place.** Click the place in the My Places list and then click the place's name to display an edit box around it. Type the new name and press Return.

- **Delete a place.** Click the place in the My Places list, and click the Remove (–) button that appears next to it. iPhoto displays a confirmation message to make sure you know that deleting the place will remove it from the photos to which it's assigned. Click Delete to proceed.

When you finish working in the Manage My Places dialog, click Done to close it.

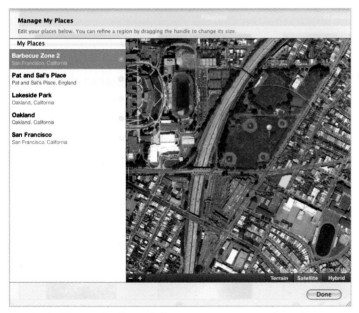

2.13 In the Manage My Places dialog, you can move or resize a place, rename it, or delete it.

Organizing photos into albums

Organizing your photos into suitable Events (as described earlier in this chapter) gives you the basic structure of your iPhoto library. But you'll most likely want to create photo albums that draw photos from different Events. An album gives you an easy way of browsing related pictures in iPhoto. You can also use an album as the basis for a slide show, calendar, book, or card.

iPhoto lets you create both standard photo albums (which don't change unless you change them) and Smart Albums — albums in which iPhoto selects photos based on criteria you specify.

Creating a standard album

Here's how to create a standard album:

1. **If you're looking at photos you want to put in the new album, select them first.** If not, you can add the photos after creating the album.

2. **Click the Create button on the toolbar to display the Create pop-up menu.** Then click Album, as shown in Figure 2.14. You can also choose File⇨New Album or press ⌘+N.

   iPhoto creates a new album, names it untitled album, and puts any selected photos into it (see Figure 2.15).

3. **In the Albums category in the Source list, type the name you want to give the album over the default name (for example, untitled album).**

4. **Add photos to the new album by dragging them from one of the collections in the Source list.** For example, you can click Events and add photos from there, or click Faces and add photos from a person's collection.

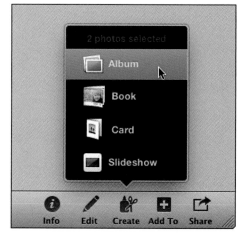

2.14 To create a new album, choose Create⇨ Album from the toolbar, or File⇨New Album from the menu bar.

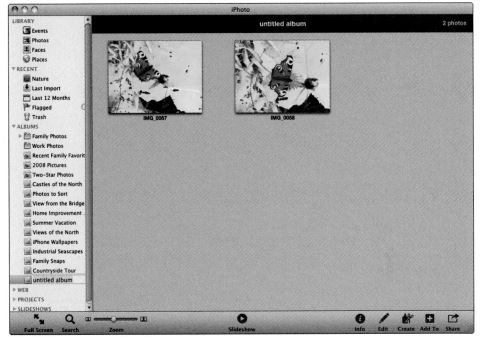

2.15 Type the name for the new album over the untitled album default name in the Source list.

Creating a Smart Album

If you want iPhoto to pick photos for you based on criteria you specify, create a Smart Album. This example shows you how to create a Smart Album that contains recent family photos.

1. **Option+click the Create button on the toolbar.** Then, click Smart Album to display the dialog shown in Figure 2.16. Alternatively, choose File ⇨ New ⇨ Smart Album or press ⌘+Option+N.

2.16 Beginning to create a new Smart Album.

2. **In the Smart Album name box, type the name you want to give the Smart Album over the default name (untitled album).**

3. **Use the line of controls under Match the following condition to set up the first condition for the Smart Album.** Here's what you would do to create the example Smart Album (see Figure 2.17):

- In the first pop-up menu, choose Date.

- In the second pop-up menu, choose is in the last.

- Type 6 in the text box.

- In the third pop-up menu, choose months.

Smart Album name:	Recent Family Favorites					
Match the following condition:						
Date	is in the last	6	months		⊖ ⊕	
				Cancel	OK	

2.17 Creating the first condition for a Smart Album.

4. **Add one or more further conditions as needed.** To add another condition, click + at the end of the current row. For the example Smart Album, you would create two more conditions, which are shown completed in Figure 2.18:

- Keyword is Family.

- My Rating is in the range **** to ***** (four to five stars).

Smart Album name:	Recent Family Favorites				
Match	all	of the following conditions:			
Date	is in the last	6	months	⊖ ⊕	
Keyword	is	Family		⊖ ⊕	
My Rating	is in the range	★★★★☆ to ★★★★★		⊖ ⊕	
			Cancel	OK	

2.18 The Smart Album with all three conditions completed.

5. **Click OK to close the dialog.** iPhoto adds the new Smart Album to the Albums category in the Source list.

Deleting an album

When you tire of an album, you can delete it. Deleting an album removes only the album's links to the photos it contains; the photos themselves remain in your library.

To delete an album, Control+click or right-click it in the Source list. Choose Delete Album and click Delete in the confirmation message that appears.

Renaming and duplicating albums

If you need to rename an album, just double-click its name in the Source list. Type the new name in the edit box that iPhoto displays and then press Return.

To duplicate an album so that you can create another album from it, Control+click or right-click the album, and then click Duplicate. iPhoto gives the duplicate album the same name with a number added — for example, the duplicate of an album named Christmas is named Christmas 2. You can than rename the duplicate as described above.

Arranging your albums in order

iPhoto adds each new album you create to the bottom of the Source list. You can then move the album to a different position in the list as needed by dragging it up the list, or by dragging other albums down.

To sort the albums alphabetically, Control+click or right-click any album, and then click Sort Albums. iPhoto keeps the list of Smart Albums before the list of regular albums.

Arranging your albums into folders

If you create scads of albums, the Source list can become too full and awkward to navigate. To get your albums under control, you can create folders and put the albums in them.

Folders are easy to use:

- **Create a folder.** Choose File ➪ New ➪ Folder or press ⌘+Option+Shift+N. iPhoto creates a new folder named untitled folder in the Albums category and displays an edit box so that you can change the name. Type the new name and press Return to apply it.

- **Create a folder within a folder.** Create a new folder and drag it to the folder in which you want to keep it.

- **Put an album in a folder.** Drag the album to the folder.

- **Rename a folder.** Double-click the folder's name, type the new name in the edit box, and press Return.

- **Delete a folder and its contents.** Control+click or right-click the folder, and click Delete Folder. Then, click Delete in the confirmation message that appears.

Adding keywords, titles, descriptions, and ratings

Each photo you bring into your library includes the filename assigned to it by the camera. It also includes all of the metadata from the camera — for example, the date and time the photo was taken, the camera used, the shutter speed and aperture used for the exposure, the GPS coordinates, and so on.

To help you identify your photos more easily, iPhoto lets you add a title, a rating, a description, and keywords to your photos. You can also add people's names and photo locations, as described earlier in this chapter.

It's easiest to start with the information that's embedded within the photo.

Viewing the information for a photo

To view the information available for a photo, select it, and click the Info button on the toolbar or press ⌘+I. iPhoto displays the photo's information in the Info pane, as shown in Figure 2.19.

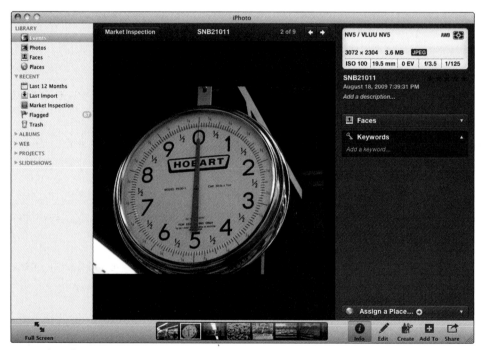

2.19 In the Info pane, you can change a photo's name, add a description or a star rating, as well as assign Faces, keywords, and Places.

The box at the top of the Info pane contains the technical details of the photo:

- **Camera name.** This is the text at the top left (NV5/VLUU NV5 in the example shown).
- **Automatic White Balance.** The icon in the top-right corner of Figure 2.19 appears if the photo uses Automatic White Balance.
- **Resolution.** In the example, 3072 × 2304 pixels.
- **File size.** In the example, 3.6MB.
- **File format.** In the example, JPEG.
- **ISO rating.** In the example, ISO 100.
- **Focal length.** In the example, 19.5mm.
- **Exposure bias.** In the example, 0 EV.
- **Aperture.** In the example, f/3.5.
- **Shutter speed.** In the example, 1/125.

While the Info pane is open, you can click another photo in the iPhoto window to view its details. You can also move to another photo using the arrow keys on the keyboard.

When you finish examining the information, click the Info button on the toolbar, or press ⌘+I again to close the Info pane.

Adding titles, descriptions, and ratings to your photos

To make your photos easy to find, you can give each one a title and a description. Click the photo, click the Info button, and then type the text you want in the Info pane.

To apply a rating of one to five stars to a photo, click the appropriate number of stars in the Info pane.

Changing the date and time of a photo

Ideally, each photo gets the correct date and time stamp when the camera takes it. But it's all too easy to let battery failure reset the camera's clock to its default date, and then take a stack of photos before noticing the date is wrong.

Luckily, you can change the date for one or more selected photos in iPhoto. To do so, choose Photos ➪ Adjust Date and Time, and the Adjust date and time of selected photos dialog that appears (see Figure 2.20). Select the Modify original files check box if you want to apply the date change to the original files, rather than to iPhoto's copies.

Adjust date and time of selected photos

The original date and time of your photo is shown below. Adjust it to the correct time.

Original: 8/18/2009 7:40:12 PM

Adjusted: 1/11/2011 7:40:12 AM

☑ Modify original files

The original photo will be adjusted by 510 days, 12 hours, 0 minutes, and 0 seconds

Cancel   Adjust

2.20 iPhoto lets you adjust the date and time of one or more photos.

You can also change the date or time by using the Batch Change feature, described next.

Making batch changes to photos

If you find you need to change the date, time, or description on two or more photos at once, use the Batch Change feature like this:

1. **Select the photos you want to affect.**

2. **Choose Photos ➪ Batch Change, or press ⌘+Shift+B to open the Batch Change dialog.**

3. **In the Set menu, choose the item you want to change: Date, Title or Description.** Figure 2.21 shows the Batch Change sheet for changing the date. If you choose Title or Description, you see different controls.

   * **Date.** Select the date and time to apply. Choose whether to add one or more seconds, minutes, hours, or days between each pair of photos.

Set Date   to

Date: 2/ 8/2011 9:56:35 AM

☑ Add 1   Minute   between each photo
☑ Modify original files

Cancel   OK

2.21 The Batch Change dialog enables you to change the date, time, or description on multiple photos at once.

Select the Modify original files check box if you want to apply the date change to the original files, rather than to iPhoto's copies.

- **Title.** Choose Empty to remove the current title. Choose Text to apply the text you type, and select the Append a number to each photo check box if you want to add a number (giving you titles such as Vacation - 1, Vacation - 2, and so on). Choose Event Name to apply the Event's name, or Filename to apply the file's name. Choose Date/Time to apply the date, time, or both in the format you choose.

- **Description.** Type the text you want to use. Select the Append to existing Description check box if you want to add the new description to the existing description, rather than replace it.

4. **Click OK to close the Batch Change dialog.** iPhoto applies the changes to the photos.

Creating your Quick Group list of keywords

Keywords are a great way of identifying photos because you can apply them in moments.

Your first move should be to set up a Quick Group list of keywords. Follow these steps:

1. **Choose Window ⇨ Manage My Keywords to display the Keywords window.**

2. **If the Keywords area contains keywords or symbols (such as the check box) you want to use frequently, drag them to the Quick Group area (see Figure 2.22).**

3. **To add keywords of your own to the list, click Edit Keywords.** iPhoto displays the Manage My Keywords dialog.

4. **Click the Add (+) button, type a keyword (see Figure 2.23), and then press Return.**

5. **iPhoto automatically suggests a shortcut letter for the keyword.** If the keyword's first letter hasn't yet been used for a shortcut, iPhoto suggests that letter. If the letter is already in use, iPhoto suggests the keyword's next letter if that letter is free.

2.22 Drag existing keywords to your Quick Group list.

2.23 You can add your own keywords and set up shortcuts in the Manage My Keywords dialog.

6. **To change a shortcut letter, click the keyword, and then click in the Shortcut column.** Type the letter you want. If it's already in use, iPhoto warns you, and lets you decide whether or not to use it.

Note

To remove an existing keyword, click it, and then click the Remove (–) button. iPhoto warns you if you've applied the keyword to any photos, and confirms that you want to remove it. To rename an existing keyword, click it, click Rename, type the new name, and press Return.

7. **Click OK when you finish editing keywords.** iPhoto returns you to the Keywords window.

8. **Drag your new keywords to the Quick Group area as needed, and then close the Keywords window.**

Adding keywords to your photos

To add keywords to your photos, follow these steps:

1. **Select the photo to which you want to assign keywords.**

2. **If the keyword has a shortcut, type that letter.** If not, click the Info button to display the Info pane, expand the Keywords pane in it, and click the Add a keyword placeholder. Start typing the keyword. iPhoto automatically completes the keyword as soon as it recognizes it uniquely, or offers you a choice of keywords starting with the letters you've typed.

3. **To remove a keyword, click it in the Keywords pane in the Info pane, and then press Delete.**

Searching for photos via dates, keywords, or ratings

To find your photos, you can search using dates, keywords, ratings, filenames, or descriptions. Here's how to search:

1. **In the Source list, choose the item through which you want to search.** For example, click Photos in the Source list to search all your photos, or click a particular album to search only that album.

2. **Click the Search button on the toolbar to display the Search box.** You can also choose Edit ➪ Find or press ⌘+F.

3. **If you want to search by only Date, Keyword, or Rating, click the Search pop-up menu and choose the item you want.** Otherwise, choose All in the Search pop-up menu (it may already be selected).

4. **Enter your search criteria:**

   - **All.** Type the text for which you're searching.

   - **Keywords.** In the panel that appears, click each keyword you want to use (see Figure 2.24).

   - **Date.** In the panel that appears, choose the year and month.

   - **Rating.** Click the number of stars in the Search box itself.

2.24 You can quickly search by one or more keywords using the Search box.

5. **Work with the photos the search returns, or click the X at the right side of the Search field to clear it.**

Editing and Improving Your Photos

No matter how good you are at taking photos, at some point you'll most likely need to edit some of them, either to bring out their best features or reduce any deficiencies. iPhoto packs a powerful set of editing tools that handles everything from rotating and cropping a picture, to comprehensively changing its color balance.

Opening a photo for editing

For most editing tasks, you must first open the photo for editing. iPhoto lets you edit photos either in the main iPhoto window or full screen. You can also open a photo for editing in an external graphics application, such as Adobe Photoshop, if you have one installed on your Mac.

To open a photo for editing, click it, then click Edit on the toolbar. This opens the photo for editing in the way you set in the Edit Photos pop-up menu in iPhoto's General preferences (see Chapter 1 for details).

Two Ways to Avoid Photo Disasters

iPhoto lets you undo edits you've made to a photo or revert to the original version. Even so, it's a good idea to duplicate a photo before editing it. Having an extra copy of the photo gives you the freedom to make more extensive edits — and then trash the photo if you ruin it. You may also want to edit the same photo in different ways.

To duplicate a photo, click it and choose Photos ⇨ Duplicate or press ⌘+D.

If you do manage to delete a valuable photo, you should be able to recover it from backup if you're using Mac OS X's Time Machine feature. From iPhoto, choose File ⇨ Browse Backups to launch Time Machine.

If you chose In iPhoto in the Edit Photos pop-up menu, iPhoto resizes the photo to take up the main part of the application window, and displays the Edit pane (see Figure 2.25). The Edit pane contains three tabs—Quick Fixes, Effects, and Adjust—which you'll meet shortly. If you've selected another application (for example, In Adobe Photoshop CS), iPhoto tells that application to open the photo.

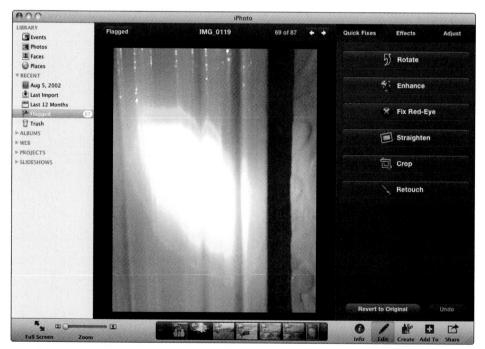

2.25 The Edit pane contains three tabs: Quick Fixes, Effects, and Adjust.

When editing a photo, you can press either the right- or down-arrow key to move to the next photo, or the left- or up-arrow key to move to the previous photo.

You can override your default way of editing by Control+clicking or right-clicking a photo, and then clicking Edit in iPhoto or Edit in External Editor, as appropriate.

When you finish editing a photo, you can click Edit on the toolbar to close the Edit pane, or click the Next button (the button with the right arrow) or the Previous button (the button with the left arrow) to start editing another photo.

Zooming in on a photo

When you open a photo for editing, iPhoto displays it at the largest size at which the whole photo will fit in the iPhoto window, or the whole screen (depending on which view you're using). You can zoom in further if needed by dragging the Zoom slider on the toolbar.

Genius Press 1 to zoom to 100 percent, 2 to zoom to 200 percent, and 0 (zero) to fit the picture in the window or screen. Press Option+1 to zoom to 100 percent on the center of the photo, or Option+2 to zoom to 200 percent on the center of the photo.

When you zoom in far enough that the whole photo doesn't fit in the available area, iPhoto displays the Navigation pane (see Figure 2.26). Then you can drag the rectangle to move the photo.

Rotating and straightening a photo

If you've turned your camera vertically to take a photo, you'll need to rotate the photo after importing it into iPhoto.

You can rotate a photo without opening it for editing. To do so, Control+click or right-click the photo, and then click the Rotate button on the pop-up panel. Option+click the Rotate button to rotate the photo in the opposite direction.

2.26 After zooming in until only part of a photo fits in the available space, drag the rectangle in the Navigation pane to move around the photo.

Note

Press ⌘+R to rotate a photo in the direction set in General preferences. Press ⌘+Option+R to rotate the photo in the opposite direction.

When you open a photo for editing, you can rotate it by clicking Rotate on the Quick Fixes tab in the Edit pane. Option+click Rotate to rotate the photo in the opposite direction.

After you fix the rotation, you can apply any straightening needed. To straighten a photo, click Straighten on the Quick Fixes tab of the Edit pane, and then drag the Angle slider to the left or right (see Figure 2.27). Use the gridlines that iPhoto displays to align horizontal or vertical features in the photo. Click Done when you finish the straightening.

2.27 Drag the Angle slider in the Straighten area to straighten a photo.

Cropping a photo

To make your photos look their best, you often need to crop them. iPhoto lets you crop either to a specific size or size ratio — for example, so that a photo is the right size for your desktop, a book page, or a frame — or to whatever custom dimensions the photo's subject needs.

Here's how to crop a photo:

1. **Open the photo for editing.**

2. **Click Crop on the Quick Fixes tab of the Edit pane.** iPhoto displays the cropping tools, as shown in Figure 2.28.

2.28 iPhoto lets you quickly crop a photo to exclude parts you don't want, and emphasize those you do.

3. **If you want to constrain the crop area to a particular size, open the Constrain pop-up menu and choose that size.** For example, to constrain the crop area to the size of your Mac's desktop, choose the size whose name is followed by (Display), for example, 1680 × 1050 (Display).

4. **Set the size of the crop area.** Drag one of the corner handles to change the cropping area in two dimensions, or drag an edge of the cropping area to change it in only one dimension (if you're not using a constraint). To temporarily override the constraint without turning it off, Shift+drag a corner handle or an edge.

5. **Reposition the crop area as needed by clicking inside it, and dragging it where you want it.**

6. **Click Done to apply the cropping to the photo.**

7. **If you've finished editing the photo, click Edit on the toolbar to close the Edit pane.**
Otherwise, leave the photo open for further editing.

Adjusting the colors in a photo

To quickly pump up the colors in a photo, click Enhance on the Quick Fixes tab of the Edit pane. This is well worth trying as a quick fix for any photo that looks anemic. If you don't like the effect, simply press ⌘+Z or choose Edit ➪ Undo Enhance Photo. You can click Enhance more than once if you want to intensify the effect.

For more subtle changes, click the Adjust tab in the Edit pane to display the Adjust controls (see Figure 2.29), and then use the controls to change the color balance. Table 2.1 explains what the tools in the Adjust window do.

2.29 The Adjust tab of the Edit pane provides powerful tools for changing the color balance of a photo.

Genius

The tools in the Adjust window affect the entire photo — you can't select part of the photo to work on. If you need to apply different adjustments to different parts of a photo, use an application such as Apple Aperture or Adobe Photoshop.

Table 2.1   Tools in the Adjust Tab of the Edit Pane

Tool	Effect
Levels histogram	The histogram shows how the colors in your picture are distributed between pure black (at the left end, 0 percent) and pure white (at the right end, 100 percent). The red, green, and blue show the individual Red, Green, and Blue color channels in the image.
Black slider	Adds black tones to the photo (drag the slider to the right).
White slider	Adds white tones to the photo (drag the slider to the left).
Levels slider	Adjusts the gray balance (drag to the left or right).
Exposure slider	Adjusts the brightness of the photo.
Contrast slider	Adjusts the contrast of the photo.
Saturation slider	Changes the intensity of the color.
Avoid saturating skin tones check box	Lets you tell iPhoto not to saturate skin tones in the photos. Selecting this check box helps your subjects avoid getting rosacea.
Definition slider	Increases the clarity in the photo, letting you make details easier to see.
Highlights slider	Recovers contrast in highlights that have become too bright.
Shadows slider	Recovers contrast in shadows that have become too dark.
De-noise slider	Reduces the graininess of the photo, giving it a smoother look.
Temperature slider	Changes the color temperature. The left end of the slider gives a "cool" blue effect, and the right end gives a "warm" golden effect.
Tint slider	Changes the amount of green and red tones in the photo. Drag to the left to add red and reduce green; drag to the right to reduce red and add green.
White Balance	Lets you correct the photo's white balance by clicking a neutral white area dropper in the photo.
Revert to Original button	Resets all the sliders to how they were when you started editing.
Undo	Undoes the last change you made.

Applying effects to photos

To make a photo look different, you can apply any of 15 effects to it like this:

1. **Open the photo for editing.**

2. **Click the Effects tab in the Edit pane to display the Effects controls (see Figure 2.30).**

3. **Click the effect you want and adjust it as needed:**

   ⦿ The Lighten, Darken, Contrast, Warmer, Cooler, and Saturate buttons are an easy way to make adjustments that you can also make using the Adjust tab. Lighten has the opposite effect of Darken, and Warmer has the opposite effect of Cooler.

   ⦿ The B&W and Sepia effects can only be On or Off.

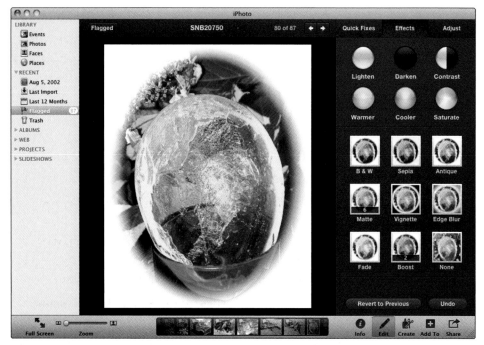

2.30 Use the controls on the Effects tab of the Edit pane to give a photo a different look.

- The Antique, Fade, Boost, Matte, Vignette, and Edge Blur effects have various settings. Click the effect to apply level 1, and then click the right arrow to increase the effect, or the left arrow to reduce it.

- Click the None effect to restore the original look.

4. **When you're satisfied with the result, click Edit to stop editing the photo.**

Retouching a photo

If a photo has a blemish or embarrassing detail you want to remove, use the Retouch tool like this:

1. **Open the photo for editing.**

2. **Click Retouch on the Quick Fixes tab of the Edit pane to display the Retouch control.** The mouse pointer becomes a circle that you use for retouching.

3. **Drag the Size slider to adjust the size of the circle.**

4. **Click on the blemish, or drag over it.** iPhoto covers it using the surrounding color or colors.

5. **When you finish retouching, click Done to close the Retouch tool.**

Removing red-eye from a photo

iPhoto is great for removing red-eye — the red pupils you get when the light from your camera's flash goes through your subject's eye, and reflects off the blood-rich retina just in time for the camera to capture it. Here's how to fix red-eye:

1. **Open the photo for editing.**

2. **Zoom in on the eyes.**

3. **Click Fix Red-Eye on the Quick Fixes tab of the Edit pane to display the Red-Eye control (see Figure 2.31).**

4. **If the Auto-fix red-eye check box is not selected, select it.** iPhoto tries to remove the red-eye automatically. Usually, it succeeds.

5. **If iPhoto can't remove the red-eye automatically, drag the Size slider to adjust the size of the mouse pointer's circle to match the red-eye spot.** Then position the mouse pointer over one of the red spots and click. Repeat for any other feral eyes.

6. **When you have fixed the red-eye problems, click Done to close the Fix-Red Eye tool.**

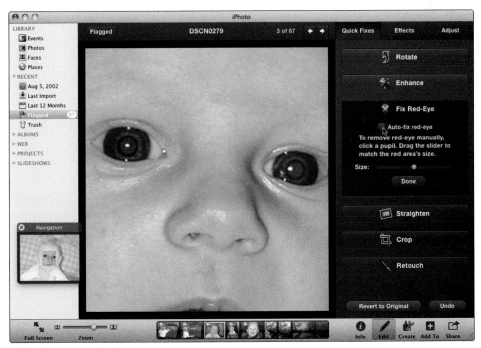

2.31 iPhoto's Red Eye tool can quickly restore normality to a wild youth.

Keeping Backups of Your Photos

iPhoto does its best to keep your photos safe, but it's a good idea to back them up regularly.

For most Macs, the best way to back up photos and other data is to use Mac OS X's Time Machine feature. To set up Time Machine, choose Apple ⇨ System Preferences, and then click the Time Machine icon in the System area. In the Time Machine preferences pane, move the master switch from the Off position to the On position, and follow Time Machine's prompts to select the external hard drive you want to use.

After you back up your photos using Time Machine, you can choose File ⇨ Browse Backups in iPhoto to locate the backup from which you want to restore lost or damaged photos.

You may also want to back up your most valuable photos to an online storage site such as MobileMe, or burn them to CDs or DVDs.

Reverting to the original photo

If you mess up your edits, don't worry — you can revert to the original photo by clicking Revert to Original in the Edit pane. If iPhoto warns you that you're about to lose all the changes you've made, click OK.

Keeping Multiple iPhoto Libraries

Normally, iPhoto puts all your photos into a single library, which it loads every time you open the application. But if you take so many photos that your library is slow to load, or if some of your photos are suitable for some audiences but not for others, you may prefer to separate your photos into different libraries. iPhoto lets you do this too with minimal effort.

Creating a new iPhoto library

First, create a new library. To create one, follow these steps:

1. **Quit iPhoto if it's running.** Press ⌘+Q or choose iPhoto ⇨ Quit iPhoto.

2. **Hold down Option and click the iPhoto icon on the Dock to display the What photo library do you want iPhoto to use? dialog (see Figure 2.32).** Keep holding down Option until the dialog appears — a quick Option+click doesn't usually do the trick.

2.32 The What photo library do you want iPhoto to use? dialog lets you create a new iPhoto library, or select one of your existing libraries.

3. **Click Create New to display a dialog for creating a new library.**

4. **Type a descriptive name for the library (for example, Family Photos) in place of iPhoto's suggestion (iPhoto Library_2, and so on).** Choose the folder in which to store the library, and then click Save.

Note

iPhoto suggests saving each library in the Pictures folder in your user account (~/Pictures). If you have plenty of hard drive space, and will share the photos via iPhoto's sharing features, this folder is a good choice. But if you want to put the new library in another folder (for example, so that you can share the photos with other people through a network), click the disclosure triangle to the right of the Save As box to expand the dialog, and then navigate to that folder

5. **iPhoto opens using the library you just created, so it is empty.** You can now add photos to the library as discussed in Chapter 1. For example, drag photo files from a Finder window, or choose File ⇨ Import to Library.

After you add photos to the library, you can use the library as normal. For example, you can edit the photos, organize them into Events, use Faces and Places, or create slide shows from them.

Selecting the library you want to load

To switch from one library to another, you use the What photo library do you want iPhoto to use? dialog you saw a moment ago. To do this

1. **Quit iPhoto if it's running.** Press ⌘+Q or choose iPhoto ➭ Quit iPhoto.

2. **Hold down Option and click the iPhoto icon on the Dock to display the What photo library do you want iPhoto to use? dialog.** Keep holding down Option until the dialog appears.

3. **Select the library you want, and then click Choose.** If the library doesn't appear in the dialog, click Other Library, locate the library manually, and then click Open.

Caution The What photo library do you want iPhoto to use? dialog may show backups of your iPhoto libraries — for example, those on external hard drives. If you see multiple entries for the same library, make sure you open the right one. Click the library in the list, and then look at the folder path shown below the list.

When you want to switch to another library, quit iPhoto, and then hold down Option as you restart it. If you open iPhoto without holding down Option, iPhoto opens the last library you used.

Them with Others?

After importing and editing your photos, you're ready to share them with others. iPhoto makes it easy to create compelling slide shows, either in just moments by using standard settings or taking your time to customize each photo's settings. You can easily share your photos on your local network with other iPhoto users; on Web sites such as MobileMe, Facebook, and Flickr; or in the applications you use. You can create books, cards, and calendars; you can also use your photos in several ways within the Mac OS X user interface, as desktop backgrounds, account icons, or the background of a folder in Finder.

Creating Powerful Slide Shows

iPhoto lets you create attractive slide shows in moments, complete with music and transition effects if you like. You can either create a slide show quickly, using the same setting for each photo, or spend the time to create a customized slide show that plays exactly the way you want it to.

Running a quick slide show

Here's how to run a quick slide show without saving it:

1. **In iPhoto, select the photos you'll use in the slide show.** If you want to quickly review your most recent photos, click Last Import in the Source list.

2. **Click the Slideshow button on the toolbar.** iPhoto displays the first photo full screen and opens the Slideshow dialog with the Themes tab at the front, as shown on the opening page of this chapter.

3. **Click the Classic box or the Ken Burns box.** The Ken Burns Effect — zooming and panning over the photos — adds visual interest, but you'll want to turn it off when you're just checking out your latest photos.

4. **Click the Music tab to bring it to the front of the dialog (see Figure 3.1).**

5. **Select the Play music during slideshow check box if you want music with the slide show.** If you prefer peace, deselect the check box and skip the next step.

3.1 You can accompany your slide show with music from GarageBand or iTunes, or stick with the theme music that iPhoto offers.

6. **Choose the song you want to play from the Theme Music folder, your GarageBand compositions, or your iTunes library.** You can search by using the Search box and preview music by clicking Play.

7. **Click the Settings tab to bring it to the front of the dialog (see Figure 3.2).**

Genius

If you want to create a playlist just for this slide show, select the Custom Playlist for Slideshow check box. iPhoto displays an extra box at the bottom of the Music tab. Drag songs into this box, and then drag them into the order in which you want them to play.

8. **In the Play each slide for a minimum of box, choose how many seconds to dwell on each slide.** If you prefer to use music to control the length of the slide show, you can select the Fit slideshow to music option instead.

9. **If you want to use transitions between slides, follow these steps:**

   ○ Select the Transition check box.

   ○ In the Transition pop-up menu, choose the transition. None is a good choice when you're simply reviewing your photos and don't need extra pizzazz. For consistent changes,

3.2 Choosing settings for a slide show.

   choose a transition such as Dissolve, Flip, or Twirl. If you feel more adventurous, choose Random to have iPhoto pick a different transition for each change.

   ○ Look to see whether the four direction buttons are available (the arrows are white) or not available (the arrows are gray). If two or more are available, click the direction you want to use for the transition.

   ○ Drag the Speed slider to set the speed of the transition.

10. **Choose other options to suit your preferences:**

    ○ If you want to include captions, select the Show Caption check box. In the pop-up menu, choose the text: Titles, Descriptions, Titles and Descriptions, Places, or Dates.

    ○ Select the Show title slide check box if you want to have a title slide at the beginning of the show.

    ○ Choose whether to shuffle the slides, repeat the slide show at the end, and scale the photos to fill the screen.

    ○ Select the Use settings as default check box if you want to make these settings the default for future slide shows.

11. **Click Play.** iPhoto closes the Slideshow dialog and starts the slide show full screen.

Use the slide show controls and navigation miniatures (see Figure 3.3) toward the bottom of the screen to navigate the slide show or to adjust the slide show settings. You can summon these controls at any point by moving the mouse pointer. To end the slide show, click the X button on the control bar or press Esc.

Creating and saving a slide show

If you want to create a slide show and save it for future use, follow these steps:

1. **Click the album on which you want to base the slide show, or select the photos you want to use.**

2. **Click the Create button on the toolbar, and then click Slideshow on the pop-up panel.** iPhoto creates a new slide show, adds it to the Slideshows category in the Source list, and displays the Slideshow toolbar (see Figure 3.4).

3.3 Move the mouse to display the slide show controls and navigation miniatures.

3. **Type the name for the slide show over the default name that iPhoto suggests.** iPhoto automatically selects the default name for you, so you can type the new name over it. Press Return to apply the name.

4. **Choose the theme for the slide show.** Click the Themes button; choose Classic, Ken Burns, or another theme in the Choose a Slideshow Theme dialog; and then click Choose. The Choose a Slideshow Theme dialog is like the Themes tab of the Slideshow dialog (shown on the opening page of this chapter).

5. **Choose the music — or lack of it — for the slide show:**

   - Click the Music button to display the Music Settings dialog, which closely resembles the Music tab of the Slideshow dialog (shown earlier in this chapter).

   - If you want music, select the Play music during slideshow check box, and then select the song. To build a custom playlist for the slide show, select the Custom Playlist for Slideshow check box, drag songs into the box that the Music Settings dialog displays, and then drag the songs into the order in which you want them to play.

   - Click Choose to close the dialog.

6. **Choose default settings for the whole slide show:**

   - Click the Settings button to display the Slideshow Settings window (see Figure 3.5). Make sure the All Slides tab is at the front.

3.4 Creating a slide show with custom settings.

   - Choose how long to display each slide for, or select the Fit slideshow to music option if you want the slide show to play for the same length of time as the music you chose.

71

- To use transitions, select the Transition check box. Choose the transition in the pop-up menu, and pick a direction if the direction buttons are available. Drag the Speed slider to set the default speed. Watch the Preview box to see how the transition looks.

- Choose whether to show captions (and if so, select the text) and a title slide.

- Choose whether to repeat the slide show and scale the photos to fill the screen.

- In the Aspect Ratio pop-up menu, choose This Screen if you want to display the slide show on your Mac's screen. Otherwise, choose the HDTV (16:9) format for HDTV or widescreen displays, the iPad/TV (4:3) format for an iPad or a TV, or the iPhone (3:2) format for the iPhone and iPod touch.

- Leave the Slideshow Settings window open for the moment.

3.5 Choosing default settings for a slide show on the All Slides tab of the Slideshow Settings window.

7. **In the filmstrip at the top of the iPhoto window, drag the pictures into the order in which you want them to play.** Put the first slide on the left. If your slide show contains more photos than will fit in the filmstrip, you'll need to drag to the left to reach the starting position.

8. **Click the first picture, click the This Slide tab in the Slideshow Settings dialog (see Figure 3.6), and then choose settings for the slide:**

   - **Effect.** To apply an effect, click Black & White, Sepia, or Antique.

   - **Duration.** Select the Play this slide for check box, and then set the number of seconds. This setting overrides the setting you applied to the slide show as a whole.

Transition. Choose the transition from this slide to the next. Select the Transition check box to use a transition, and choose it in the Transition pop-up menu.

To change the direction (for a transition that supports different directions), click the appropriate direction button; to change the speed, drag the Speed slider until the preview in the Preview box changes at the speed you want. Again, you're overriding the setting applied to the slide show as a whole.

Ken Burns Effect. Select the Ken Burns check box if you want to use the panning and zooming effect. If necessary, zoom in by dragging the Size slider in the main iPhoto window, and then drag the picture to where you want its starting position. Move the Start/End switch to the End position, and then zoom and drag to set the end position.

3.6 The This Slide tab of the Slideshow Settings dialog lets you apply an effect to the slide, control how long it appears for, add a transition, and apply the Ken Burns effect.

In the main iPhoto window, click the Preview button to preview the effect. Make any changes needed in the Slideshow Settings dialog, and then preview it again until it's right.

Note

iPhoto automatically saves the changes you make to your slide show, so you don't need to save them manually.

9. **Repeat Step 8 for each of the other slides in the slide show.**

10. **Click Play when you're ready to view your slide show.**

11. **To create a version of the slide show you can use on an iPad, iPhone or iPod, Apple TV, computer, or a MobileMe gallery, click the Export button on the toolbar, and then follow the export process.**

Sharing Your Photos with Others

To get the most enjoyment out of your photos, you'll likely want to share them with other people. iPhoto lets you share photos in several ways: directly with other iPhoto users on your local network, via your Gallery on Apple's MobileMe service, on Facebook or Flickr, through your Web site or your applications, or even via video chat. You can also go old-school and order hard-copy prints of your photos, photo books, cards, or calendars.

Sharing your photos with other iPhoto users

iPhoto makes it easy to share your photos with other Macs on your local network. After you set up sharing, as described in Chapter 1, your iPhoto library (or the albums you've chosen to share) appears under the shared name you chose in the Shares category in the Source list in iPhoto running on other Macs on the network.

iPhoto doesn't give you any indication when someone connects to your shared library or albums. The only way to find out is by quitting iPhoto, which warns you (see Figure 3.7) that you're about to disconnect all sharing users (it doesn't tell you how many). Click Disconnect Sharing Users if you want to quit iPhoto anyway.

Are you sure you want to quit iPhoto and disconnect all sharing users?

One or more users are connected to your shared photo library.

(Disconnect Sharing Users)   (Cancel)

3.7 When you go to quit iPhoto, the application warns you if other users are connected to your shared photos.

Viewing and copying other people's shared photos

If you selected the Look for shared photos check box in iPhoto's Sharing preferences, iPhoto shows other people's shared photo libraries in the Shared category in your Source list. To view the contents of a library, follow these steps:

1. **Click the library you want to view.**

2. **If iPhoto displays the Photo Library Password dialog prompting you for the password, type the password.**

3. **Click OK.**

4. **After you connect to someone else's library, you can browse through it much as you can your Mac's own library.**

5. **Click the library's gray disclosure triangle to display the list of shared albums, and then click the album you want to display.**

Because the photos are on someone else's Mac, you can't change them. But you can copy photos to your library by dragging them from the shared library to your Photos library or an album in the Source list. You can also drag an album from the shared library to your library.

When you finish using the shared library, click the Eject button to the right of the shared library's name in the Source list to disconnect from the shared library. You can also disconnect by quitting iPhoto.

Exporting your photos to your MobileMe Gallery

If you have a MobileMe subscription, you can share your photos with a wider audience by publishing an album to your MobileMe Gallery. You can make an album public so that anybody can access it, limit access to only the people you choose, or keep it to yourself.

Follow these steps to export an album to your MobileMe Gallery:

1. **Get the album ready for publishing.** Edit the photos so that they look just the way you want them, and add any names and descriptions needed.

2. **Click the album in the Source list to display its photos.**

Note

If you've already set up accounts in iPhoto's Accounts preferences, the Share pop-up panel may show your account names (for example, Chris Smith) rather than the service names (for example, MobileMe). The symbol to the left of each account name indicates the type of account: a white cloud on a blue background for MobileMe, a blue dot and pink dot for Flickr, a lowercase f on a blue background for Facebook, and a stamp for e-mail.

3. **Click the Share button on the toolbar to display the Share pop-up panel (see Figure 3.8), and then click MobileMe Gallery.**

4. **If iPhoto displays the Log in to MobileMe dialog, type your username and password, and then click Log In.**

5. **In the MobileMe Galleries pop-up panel that iPhoto displays, click the New Album button.** iPhoto displays the dialog for publishing to your MobileMe Gallery, as shown in Figure 3.9.

6. **In the Album Name text box, change the album name if necessary.**

7. **In the Album Viewable by pop-up menu, choose who may view the album:**

3.8 Click MobileMe Gallery on the Share pop-up panel to start exporting an album to your MobileMe Gallery.

Would you like to publish "Sharp Shots" to your MobileMe Gallery?

This will create an album in Chris Smith's MobileMe Gallery. The album can be viewed with Safari or any modern web browser. The title of this album will be visible to everyone viewing your Gallery.

Album Name: `Sharp Shots`

Album Viewable by: `Everyone ▲▼`

Allow: ☑ Downloading of photos or entire album
☐ Uploading of photos via web browser
☑ Adding of photos via email

Show: ☑ Photo titles
☐ Email address for uploading photos

(Show Advanced)　　　　　　(Cancel)　(Publish)

3.9 Publishing an album to your MobileMe Gallery.

- **Everyone.** Anyone on the Web can view the album.

- **Only me.** You keep the album to yourself — good for personal or work photos.

- **Public.** Anyone who knows your MobileMe public password can view the album.

- **Edit Names and Passwords.** To add the name of a person or group and assign a password, click this item, and work in the dialog that appears. Click OK when you finish.

8. **Choose options in the Allow area:**

    - Select the Downloading of photos or entire album check box if you want visitors to be able to download high-quality versions of the photos. Click the Show Advanced button (changes to the Hide Advanced button) to display the hidden section at the bottom of the dialog and choose the quality you want in the Download quality pop-up menu. Choose Optimized if you want to provide high-quality images with reasonably small file sizes. Choose Actual Size when you need to provide the full-quality photos. These will take longer to upload to your Gallery (and longer for visitors to download).

Caution

Clearing the Downloading of photos or entire album check box doesn't prevent visitors from downloading the photos in your album: Users can still right-click a photo in their Web browsers and save it to a file on their computers. The difference is that they get only the photo displayed on their screen, not the higher-resolution version that your MobileMe Gallery enables you to provide.

    - Select the Uploading of photos via web browser check box if you want visitors to be able to add photos to the album using a Web browser.

    - Select the Adding of photos via email check box if you want to be able to add photos by e-mail from any computer or from an iPhone or iPod touch.

9. **Choose options in the Show area:**

    - Select the Photo titles check box if you want to include titles in the Gallery. Usually, having the titles is helpful.

    - If you chose to allow uploading via e-mail and want to let visitors to the Gallery see the address, select the Email address for uploading photos check box. A visitor can then click the Send to Album icon in the Gallery to display the address.

10. **If you want to hide the album on your Gallery page, click the Show Advanced button, and then select the Hide album on my Gallery page check box.**

Hiding an album so that it doesn't appear on your MobileMe Gallery page is good for when you need to share different albums with different people. Instead of needing to password-protect a gallery to keep out people you don't want to see it, you can simply prevent the album from appearing and give the album's URL to the people who need to be able to access it.

11. **Click Publish.** iPhoto publishes the album to your MobileMe Gallery and displays an icon to the right of the album's name in the Source list. After making changes online or in iPhoto you can synchronize the album by clicking this icon.

Adding photos to a Gallery from an iPhone, iPad, or iPod touch

If you have an iPhone, iPad, or iPod touch, you can add photos to a MobileMe Gallery directly from the device. This is great both for when you take a photo on the iPhone that you need to share immediately and for when you want to share one of the other photos you're carrying on the device.

Here's how to add a photo to a MobileMe Gallery from the iPhone, iPad, or iPod touch:

1. **On the iPhone, iPad, or iPod touch, open the photo.** For example, open the Camera Roll on the iPhone and touch the picture.

2. **Touch the leftmost button on the toolbar (the button with the curving arrow).**

3. **Touch the Send to MobileMe button on the panel that appears.** The device displays the Publish Photo dialog box (see Figure 3.10).

4. **In the first box, type the name you want to give the photo.**

5. **In the Description box, optionally type a description for the photo.**

6. **In the list of albums, touch the album you want to place the photo in.**

Cancel	Publish Photo	Publish

mobileme

Latest product craze

Description (Optional)

The World's Greatest Cliffs ✓

Wood and Rocks

Station Scenes

The World's Greatest Cliffs

Industrial Decay

Pictures for Mom

Latest Photos

3.10 In the Publish Photo dialog, type the photo's name and (optionally) a description, choose the MobileMe album to put it in, and then touch the Publish button.

7. **Touch the Publish button.** The device publishes the photo to your MobileMe Gallery.

8. **The device displays a dialog saying that the photo was published.** Touch the View on MobileMe button to check that the photo appears as you want it to, touch the Tell a Friend button to start a boilerplate e-mail message to one or more friends telling them where to find the photo, or click the Close button to close the dialog without taking either action.

Adding photos to a Gallery from your Web browser

If you selected the Uploading of photos via web browser check box when exporting an album to your Gallery, any visitor can upload photos to the album by clicking the Upload button and using the form that appears.

Even if you deselected this check box, you can add photos and edit your albums from a browser by logging into MobileMe, clicking the Switch Apps button on the toolbar, clicking the Gallery icon on the switching bar, and then working with the Gallery tools.

Sharing your photos on Facebook

If you have an account on the Facebook social networking site, you can use the iPhoto Uploader to upload photos directly from iPhoto. This is a great way to publish your photos quickly.

To publish photos to Facebook, follow these steps:

1. **Select the photo or photos you want to upload.** When publishing to an album, you can use multiple photos. When publishing a profile picture or to your Wall, you can use only a single picture.

2. **Click the Share button on the toolbar, and then click Facebook on the pop-up panel.** This item may be called *Facebook* or it may have the name of your Facebook account. iPhoto displays the Facebook Albums pane, as shown in Figure 3.11.

Note

If you haven't yet set up iPhoto to use your Facebook account, iPhoto displays the Login to Facebook dialog. Type your e-mail address and password, select the I agree to Facebook's terms check box, and click Login. iPhoto validates your login information and then displays the Facebook Albums pane.

3.11 In the Facebook Albums pane, choose whether to publish the photo to your profile picture, a new album, your Wall, or an existing album.

3. **Choose where to put the photos:**

   ● Click the New Album button if you want to create a new album. iPhoto displays the confirmation dialog shown in Figure 3.12. Type the album name, choose who may view the photos — Everyone, Friends of Friends, or Only Friends — and then click Publish.

Do you want to publish "Quick Tour" to Facebook?

This creates an album in Chris Smith's Facebook account.

Album Name: Quick Tour

Photos Viewable by: Everyone

I certify that I have the right to distribute these photos and that they do not violate Facebook's terms.

Cancel   Publish

3.12 Confirm that you want to publish your photos to Facebook, and decide who's allowed to see them.

- Click Wall if you want to put the photos on your Facebook Wall. iPhoto displays the dialog shown in Figure 3.13. Type your comment for the photo in the Comment box, and then click Publish.

Do you want to publish this photo to your Facebook Wall?

This photo will show up on Chris Smith's Facebook account. Enter a comment for the photo below.

Comment: Classic skies courtesy of Nature!

Cancel   Publish

3.13 Click Publish to publish the photo to your Wall in Facebook.

- Click the Profile Picture item if you want to use the photo as your Facebook profile photo. iPhoto displays the confirmation dialog shown in Figure 3.14. Click Set to use the picture.

Do you want to set this photo as your Facebook profile picture?

Cancel   Set

3.14 Click Set to use the photo as your profile picture in Facebook.

- Click an existing album to place the photo or photos in that album. iPhoto doesn't display a dialog — it just goes ahead and publishes the photo or photos to the album.

4. **Click Publish.** iPhoto publishes the photo or photos to the Facebook area you chose.

Sharing your photos on Flickr

If you have an account on the Flickr photo-sharing site, you can publish photos directly to Flickr. Follow these steps:

1. **Select the photo or photos you want to publish.**

2. **Click the Share button on the toolbar, and then click Flickr on the pop-up panel.**
   This item may be called *Flickr* or it may have the name of your Flickr account. iPhoto displays the Flickr Sets pane (see Figure 3.15).

3.15 In the Flickr Sets pane, choose whether to publish the photo to a new set, to your photostream, or to an existing set.

Note If you haven't yet set up iPhoto to use your Flickr account, iPhoto displays the Do you want to set up iPhoto to publish to Flickr? dialog. Click the Set Up button to launch your Web browser and display the Flickr site. Follow through the process of giving the iPhoto Uploader permission to access your Flickr account, as discussed in Chapter 1. When you complete the process, choose Share ⇨ Flickr from the toolbar again; this time, iPhoto displays the Flickr Sets pane.

3. **Choose where to put the photos:**

- Click the New Set button if you want to create a new photo set. iPhoto displays the dialog shown in Figure 3.16.

- Click the Photostream button if you want to publish the photos to your photostream. iPhoto displays a confirmation dialog that has the Photos Viewable by pop-up menu and the Photo size pop-up menu but not the Set Name text box.

- Click an existing set if you want to add the photos to that set. iPhoto displays a confirmation dialog that has the Photos Viewable by pop-up menu and the Photo size pop-up menu but not the Set Name text box.

Do you want to publish "Sharp Shots" to Flickr?

This creates a "set" of photos in Chris P. Smith's Flickr Photostream.

Set Name: Sharp Shots

Photos Viewable by: Only You

Photo size: Web (fit within 1024 × 1024)

Cancel   Publish

3.16 Confirm that you want to publish your photos to Flickr, choose who may view them, and select the size.

4. **For a new photo set, type the name in the Set Name text box.**

5. **In the Photos Viewable by pop-up menu, choose who may view the photos: Only You, Your Friends, Your Family, Your Friends and Family, or Anyone.**

6. **In the Photo size pop-up menu, choose the size at which to publish the photos: Web (for viewing on-screen), Half Size, or Actual Size.** The Half Size and Actual Size options are available only for Flickr Pro accounts.

7. **Click Publish.** iPhoto publishes the photos on Flickr and adds the album to the Flickr category in the Source list.

Exporting your photos to a local Web site

If you have your own Web site, you can quickly create Web pages containing photos from your iPhoto library. iPhoto creates an index page containing a thumbnail version of each picture, and a detail page containing the full photo.

To export photos to Web pages, follow these steps:

1. **Select the photos you want to export.**

2. **Choose File ⇨ Export to open the Export dialog, and then click the Web Page button to display the Web Page tab (see Figure 3.17).**

83

3.17 Use the Web Page tab of the Export dialog to create Web pages containing your photos.

3. **In the Page area, choose the details for the index page:**

- **Title.** Type the title you want to give the page. This appears at the top of the page and in the browser's title bar.

- **Columns and Rows.** Choose how many rows and columns to create. Watch the read-out that shows the number of pages.

- **Template.** Choose Plain for unadorned photos. Choose Framed to include a frame around each photo.

- **Background and Text Color.** Pick the colors you want for the page background and the text.

4. **In the Thumbnail area, set the size and text for the thumbnails on the index page.** Set the maximum height and width, and choose whether to include the photos' titles and descriptions.

5. **In the Image area, set the size and text for the photos on their individual pages.**
Set the maximum height and width, and choose whether to include the photos' titles, descriptions, metadata, and location. Titles are usually helpful; descriptions are sometimes helpful; metadata is usually overkill; and locations can be fascinating, an invasion of your privacy, or both.

6. **Click Export, choose the folder in which to store the pages, and then click OK.**
iPhoto suggests storing the pages in the Sites folder in your Home folder, but you may prefer to use a folder on a shared drive.

To view the pages you've created, open a Finder window to your Sites folder or the folder you chose, open the site's subfolder, and then double-click the index.html file. Mac OS X opens the index page in your Web browser.

Exporting your photos for use in other applications

If you need to use your photos in other applications, you can export them from iPhoto like this:

1. **Select the photo or photos you want to export.**

2. **Choose File ⇨ Export to open the Export dialog, and then click the File Export tab (see Figure 3.18) if it's not displayed.**

3.18 The File Export tab of the Export dialog lets you choose the format, size, and naming convention for the photo files you export.

3. **In the Kind pop-up menu, choose the format to use for the exported files:**

   - **Original.** The format in which you imported the files (typically JPEG or RAW if you imported the files from a camera).

   - **Current.** The format in which iPhoto is storing the photo (JPEG unless you've set iPhoto to store RAW files in TIFF format to preserve quality).

   - **JPEG.** The best choice for general use, although you lose quality. Choose the quality in the JPEG Quality pop-up menu: Low, Medium, High, or Maximum.

   - **TIFF.** A good choice for use in publishing.

   - **PNG.** The high-quality choice for general computer or Web use.

4. **Select the Titles and keywords check box and the Location information check box if you want to include these details in the files.** These options aren't available for PNG files.

5. **In the Size pop-up menu, choose the size: Small, Medium, Large, Full Size, or Custom.** For Custom, an extra section of the dialog appears that lets you choose the maximum dimension and the orientation.

6. **In the File Name pop-up menu, choose how to name the files: Use title, Use file-name, Sequential, or Album name with number.** If you choose Sequential, type the text in the Prefix for sequential box. For example, type House to get files named House 01, House 02, and so on.

7. **Click Export, choose the folder in which to save the photos, and then click OK.** iPhoto exports the files and then closes the Export Photos dialog.

Sharing your photos via video chat

When you need to discuss your photos with someone across the Internet, you have several options, such as sending photos via e-mail, posting them on a sharing site, or creating an album on your MobileMe Gallery. But here's another great option: Share the photos via iChat Theater with another Mac user, so you can both view the photos at the same time and talk them over.

To use iChat Theater to share photos, follow these steps:

1. **Launch iChat from the Dock or from the Applications folder.**

2. **Choose File ⇨ Share iPhoto With iChat Theater to open the iPhoto dialog.**

3. **Choose the album or Event you want to share, and then click Share.** iChat displays a dialog telling you that iChat Theater is ready to begin and prompting you to invite a buddy to a video chat.

4. **Click your buddy in the main iChat window, and then click the Start a Video Chat button on the toolbar at the bottom of the window.** iChat establishes the connection and starts displaying the photos.

Getting high-quality prints of your photos

iPhoto has a built-in connection to Apple Photo Services that makes it easy to order prints online and pay via your Apple account. Select the photos, and then choose File ⇨ Order Prints to open the Order Prints dialog, which makes the ordering process simple.

Caution When you order large prints, double-check that the Order Prints dialog isn't showing a yellow exclamation icon next to the size. This means that this photo's resolution is too low for getting good results at the size you've chosen.

Given that the resolution of digital cameras keeps increasing, resolution is usually a problem these days only if you crop your photos heavily.

When you need to get prints made more quickly than Apple Photo Services can deliver, use the File ⇨ Export command to export the photos to a memory card that you can take to your local photographic specialist.

Creating books, cards, and calendars

iPhoto also makes it easy to create books, cards, and calendars from your photos. To do so, follow these steps:

1. **Select the photos you want to use.**

2. **Click the Create button on the toolbar to display the Create pop-up panel, and then click Book, Card, or Calendar, as appropriate.** iPhoto displays the control screen for that type of item. Figure 3.19 shows the control screen for creating a book.

3. **Choose options for the book, card, or calendar.** For example, for a book, click the Hardcover button, Softcover button, or Wire-bound button at the top of the screen to choose the binding. Then click the book layout (the arc of books), the size (XL or L, in the lower-left corner), and the paper color (in the lower-right corner).

4. **Click Create.** iPhoto displays a screen on which you can start the process of paying for the item.

3.19 iPhoto lets you use your photos to create picture books, cards, or calendars.

Using Your Photos within Mac OS X

To get the greatest enjoyment from your photos, you'll probably want to use them as widely as possible within Mac OS X. For a quick and easy use of a photo, you can put a single photo on your desktop; for a more entertaining background, you can use a sequence of photos. Better yet, you can create custom screen savers, make a personal icon for your user account, and display a photo as the background in a Finder window for that custom touch.

Put a photo on your desktop

To put a photo on your desktop, click the photo, and then choose Share ⇨ Set Desktop from the menu bar. Your desktop displays the photo immediately; you don't need to make any choices.

Put a sequence of photos on your desktop

Instead of having a single, unchanging photo on your desktop, you may prefer to display a sequence of photos. You can do this easily, too:

1. **In iPhoto, select the photos you want to use.** You have several options:

   - Select the photos by clicking the first and then ⌘+clicking each of the others.

   - Select an existing album. Alternatively, create a new album.

   - Flag the photos you want. This is a handy way of picking desktop photos from more than one Event or album without adding the photos to an album.

2. **Choose Share ⇨ Set Desktop from the menu bar.** iPhoto applies the first photo to the desktop and sets the others to change periodically. (The interval depends on the last settings you've used for multiple pictures in Desktop & Screen Saver preferences. I'll show you how to change this next.)

To adjust how your sequence of pictures runs as a background, follow these steps:

1. **Control+click or right-click the desktop and click Change Desktop Background to display the Desktop & Screen Saver pane in System Preferences with the Desktop tab at the front (see Figure 3.20).**

3.20 Use the Desktop tab in Desktop & Screen Saver preferences to control how a sequence of photos on your desktop runs.

2. **If you're using flagged photos, expand the iPhoto Albums list and then click Flagged.** If you're using photos you selected, expand the Folders item and then click iPhoto Selection. Your photos appear in the box on the right.

89

3. **In the pop-up menu, choose how to display the photos:**

   - **Fill Screen.** Fills the screen with the picture, hiding any parts that are too large to fit.

   - **Fit to Screen.** Displays the photo at the largest size where the whole photo fits on the screen. You can choose a background color for the uncovered parts of the screen by clicking the color swatch and working in the Colors window that appears.

   - **Stretch to Fill Screen.** Changes one of the photo's dimensions as needed to make the photo fit the screen exactly. Stretching a photo often makes it look wrong.

   - **Center.** Displays the photo centered in the screen. You can choose a background color for the uncovered parts of the screen by clicking the color swatch and working in the Colors window that appears.

   - **Tile.** Uses multiple instances of the photo to cover the screen. This setting is good for small photos or patterns.

4. **Select the Change picture check box and choose the frequency of change in the pop-up menu.** You can choose intervals from every 5 seconds to every day, or have the photo change when you log in or when you wake your Mac from sleep.

5. **Select the Random order check box if you want to go through the photos in random order rather than in sequence.**

6. **Select the Translucent menu bar check box if you want the desktop background to show through the menu bar.**

7. **Press ⌘+Q or choose System Preferences ⇨ Quit System Preferences to quit System Preferences.**

Now the photos will change automatically in the background as you work or play on your Mac.

Making screen savers from your photos

A great way to enjoy your photos full screen on your Mac is to make a screen saver from them. Here's what to do:

1. **In iPhoto, create an album or Smart Album containing the photos you want to use.** If you already have a suitable album, you're all set. Alternatively, you can use an existing category (for example, Last Import or Flagged) or even your whole library if you want.

2. **Control+click or right-click the desktop and choose Change Desktop Background to display the Desktop & Screen Saver preferences pane.**

3. **Click the Screen Saver tab to display its contents.**

4. **In the Screen Savers box on the left, expand the Pictures section if it's collapsed.** Then click the album or item that contains the photos. The Preview box displays the first of the photos (see Figure 3.21), showing the effect of the screen saver with its current settings.

Desktop & Screen Saver

Show All

Desktop | Screen Saver

Screen Savers

- Forest
- Nature Patterns
- Paper Shadow
- iPhoto
- Flagged
- Last 12 Months
- Quick Tour
- Apr 1, 2010
- Apr 2, 2010
- Apr 5, 2010
- Aug 18, 2009

Preview

+ −

☐ Use random screen saver
☐ Show with clock

Display Style

Options...   Test

Start screen saver:

3   5   15   30   1hr   2hr   Never

Hot Corners...

3.21 You can easily create custom screen savers that use the photos in your iPhoto library.

5. **Choose the display style for the screen saver by clicking one of the three Display Style buttons:**

   - **Slideshow.** The screen saver shows each photo for a few seconds. You can choose whether to use cross-fading transitions and panning across the photos (the Ken Burns Effect).

   - **Collage.** The screen saver spins in each photo in turn, adding it to those already there to make a collage. You can display the titles and comments on the photos if you want.

   - **Mosaic.** The screen saver slowly zooms out to form a mosaic that shows all the photos in miniature. It repeats the photos as necessary to fill the whole screen.

Note

The Mosaic screen saver is visually entertaining, but you don't get much of a view of the photos. The Collage screen saver, on the other hand, is good for getting an overview of the photos in the album or collection — and seeing their titles and comments if you choose.

6. **Click Options and choose options in the dialog that appears.** Apart from an option for presenting the slides in random order, the options are different for the Slideshow (see Figure 3.22), Collage, and Mosaic screen savers:

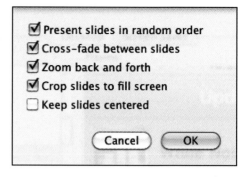

- **Slideshow.** Choose whether to cross-fade between slides, zoom back and forth, crop the slides to fit the screen, and keep the slides centered.

- **Collage.** Choose between a Classic-style (unadorned) slide show or one annotated with the filenames and dates.

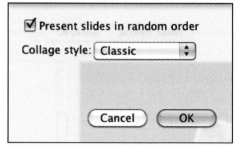

- **Mosaic.** Choose the number of rows to include in the mosaic and the speed at which to generate it.

7. **Click Test to test the screen saver.** Move the mouse to end the test. Change your settings as needed, and test again until satisfied.

8. **Drag the Start screen saver slider to tell Mac OS X how soon to start the screen saver when you leave your Mac inactive.**

9. **Select the Show with clock check box if you want to include a clock on the display.**

10. **Select the Main screen only check box if your Mac has multiple screens but you want to use only the main one.** This check box appears only if your Mac has two or more screens.

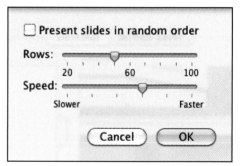

3.22 For a Slideshow screen saver, you can use cross-fades, zooming, and cropping. For a Collage screen saver, you can choose the style and whether to use random order. For a Mosaic screen saver, you can choose the number of rows, set the speed, and decide whether to use random order.

11. **Press ⌘+Q or choose System Preferences ➪ Quit System Preferences to quit System Preferences.**

Creating an account icon from a photo

Another fun use of a photo is to create a custom icon for your user account in Mac OS X. This is a great way of personalizing the Mac OS X login screen, either with portraits of the users — flattering or distorted, whichever you like — or simply with photos you and the other users like.

Genius

If you've changed your user account icon before, you can quickly return to a picture you've used before by opening the Recent Pictures pop-up menu at the top of the Edit Picture dialog and choosing the picture you want from the panel.

Here's how to create a custom icon for your user account:

1. **Click the System Preferences icon on the Dock or choose Apple menu ⇨ System Preferences to open the System Preferences window.**

2. **Click Accounts (in the System section) to open the Accounts preferences.**

3. **Click your existing account picture (to the left of the Change Password button), and then click Edit Picture on the pop-up panel that appears (see Figure 3.23).**

3.23 Click Edit Picture on the pop-up panel to start creating a custom icon for your user account.

4. **In the Edit Picture dialog that appears (see Figure 3.24), add a picture in one of these three ways:**

- Click the Take photo snapshot button to take a picture using your Mac's iSight or another webcam you've plugged in. If no camera is available, the Edit Picture dialog displays a prompt to plug in a camera instead of the Take photo snapshot button.

- Click Choose, select the picture in the Open dialog that appears, and then click the dialog's Open button to close the dialog box and apply the picture.

- Drag a photo from iPhoto or from Photo Booth. Open iPhoto or Photo Booth, position the application so that you can see the System Properties window as well, and then drag the photo you want to the Edit Picture dialog.

3.24 The Edit Picture dialog lets you take a video snapshot of yourself or choose a photo either from a folder or directly from iPhoto or Photo Booth.

5. **If you want to use only part of the picture, click and drag the Size slider to zoom in.**

6. **After zooming, or if the photo is bigger than the icon area, you can click in the preview and drag to change the part of the photo that appears.**

7. **Click Set to close the Edit Picture dialog and apply your new icon to the Accounts window.**

8. **Press ⌘+Q or choose System Preferences ➪ Quit System Preferences to quit System Preferences.**

Displaying a photo as the background in a Finder window

Icon view in the Finder is a great way of getting an overview of your files — and you can make it even better by adding one of your own photos as the background in the Finder window.

You can set a different photo as the background in any folder. This is a handy way of making your key Finder windows easier to recognize, especially when they're displayed in miniature on the Dock. For example, if you give the Documents folder a background photo with a predominantly blue color, and the Macintosh HD folder a background with a predominantly green color, you'll be able to distinguish the miniature icons even at a glance.

Note Folder background pictures appear only in Icon view, not in List view, Columns view, or Cover Flow view.

Here's how to set a photo as the background for a folder:

1. **Click the Finder icon on the Dock to open a Finder window.** Navigate to the folder in which you want to display the photo.

2. **Make sure the folder is displayed using Icon view.** If it's not, choose View ⇨ As Icons or click the Icons button on the toolbar (the leftmost of the four View buttons).

3. **Choose View ⇨ Show View Options to open the View Options window.**

4. **Select the Always open in icon view check box to make the folder use Icon view every time you open it (so that you can see the background picture).**

5. **Select the Picture option in the Background area, and then click the picture place-holder (it appears at first with the text Drag image here) to open the Select a Picture dialog.**

6. **Select the picture you want to use.**

   ● To go straight to your iPhoto library, expand the Media category in the sidebar, and then click Photos. You can then choose a photo much as you would in iPhoto itself — for example, from an Event, an album, or your Last Import.

   ● To choose a picture from a folder, simply navigate to the folder.

7. **Click Select to close the Select a Picture dialog.** The Finder window displays the photo as its background.

8. **Close the View Options dialog by clicking the red button (the Close button) on the window or choosing View ⇨ Hide View Options.**

How Do I Import Video into iMovie?

Movie not only packs a huge amount of power but it also includes lots of great features that enable you to create, edit, and share movies quickly and easily. If you've wanted to get started with iMovie but felt daunted by its complexity, start at the beginning of this chapter. If you're ready to go ahead and start importing your video from your DV camcorder or another source, jump in at the middle of the chapter. And if you've already imported video and want to review and sort it, go directly to the end of the chapter.

troductory screen that highlights the application's new features. From here, you can click the deo Tutorials button to see walkthroughs of iMovie's main features, or simply click OK to close e introductory screen and get right to iMovie itself.

Note

When you open iMovie for the first time, it automatically creates a new movie project called My First Project for you and displays that project. The iMovie window should look like Figure 4.1.

Open camera import   Project Library
window button   button   Project frames   Project Storyboard   Toolbar   Viewer

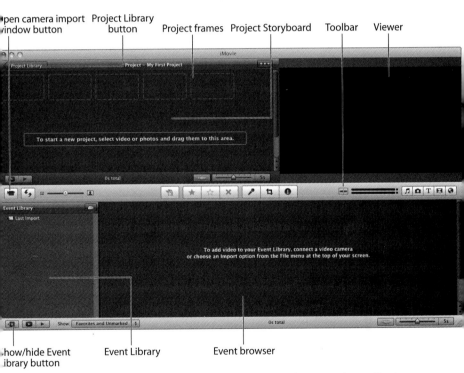

Show/hide Event   Event Library   Event browser
Library button

4.1 The main parts of the iMovie window as it appears when you first open the application.

Here are the main parts of the iMovie interface that you see in Figure 4.1, with brief details on what they do:

- **Project Storyboard.** This area is where you put your movie projects together. iMovie displays the current project on the Project Storyboard as a series of filmstrips, sequences of frames from the clips you're using. To leave the Project Storyboard and go to the Project Library (which you meet in a moment), click the Project Library button.

- **Toolbar.** This strip across the middle of the iMovie window contains most of the controls you use for manipulating content and for displaying other parts of the iMovie interface, such as the Music & Sound Effects Browser or the Title Browser.

- **Event Library.** This pane lets you browse the Events that contain all the movie footage you import into iMovie. If you don't need to keep the Event Library open, click the Show/ Hide Event Library button to hide it and give yourself more space for the Event browser.

Genius

Events in iMovie work in a similar way to Events in iPhoto (see Chapter 1). An Event is a tool for organizing your movie footage into categories that suit you. iMovie creates Events for you automatically when you import video, but you can also rearrange iMovie's Events and create your own Events as needed.

- **Event browser.** This pane displays the clips of movie footage contained in the Event you select in the Event Library. You use the Event browser to pick the footage you want to add to the Project Storyboard.

Note

When you restart iMovie, it automatically opens the last movie project you worked with. You can switch quickly to another movie project by clicking it in the Project Library.

The one main component of the iMovie interface that you don't see when you first launch iMovie is the Project Library, which shares space with the Project Storyboard. From the Project Storyboard, click the Project Library button in the upper-left corner to move back from the project to the Project Library (shown in Figure 4.2 with just the default project created).

The Project Library pane lists all your movie projects, along with a few frames from each project to help you identify them so you can easily move from one project to another. When you're ready to work on a project, either double-click it or click it and then click Edit Project. iMovie displays the Project Storyboard in place of the Project Library pane.

Open camera import
window button

New project button

4.2 The Project Library gives you quick access to all your iMovie projects.

Choosing Preferences to Make iMovie Work Your Way

Before you start importing video and building a movie project, take a couple of minutes to make sure iMovie's preferences are set to suit you. Choose iMovie ➪ Preferences to open the Preferences window (see Figure 4.3), and then choose settings, as described next. When you finish choosing preferences, click the Close button (the red button) to close the Preferences window.

Choosing general preferences

The General tab of the iMovie Preferences window displays the following assorted preferences:

- **Show Advanced Tools.** If you select this check box (which is cleared by default), iMovie displays several additional tools. You meet these tools later in this chapter and in Chapters 5 and 6.

⦿ **Display time as HH:MM:SS:Frames.** Select this check box if you want iMovie to display clip lengths using professional-style timecodes in hours, minutes, seconds, and frames (such as 01:45:22:10 – 1 hour, 45 minutes, 22 seconds, and 10 frames) instead of seconds (such as 22.3 s – 22.3 seconds).

4.3 Use the iMovie Preferences window to set up iMovie to suit your movie-editing style.

⦿ **Show "Play" reminder in viewer.** Deselect this check box if you want to suppress the Press the space bar or double-click to Play message that appears when you move the mouse pointer over a filmstrip in the viewer window. This check box is available only when the Show Advanced Tools check box is cleared.

⦿ **Exit full-screen mode after playback is finished.** iMovie comes with this check box selected, so when it finishes playing back a movie in full-screen mode, it displays the iMovie window again. Normally, this behavior is handy, but if you want iMovie to stay in full-screen mode until you switch it back manually, deselect this check box.

⦿ **Full-screen playback.** In this pop-up menu, choose the size at which you want iMovie to play back movies when you use full-screen view. Normally, iMovie uses the Entire Screen setting, which stretches or squeezes the movie as needed to fill the screen. If you find your Mac struggles to play back video smoothly at full screen, try Entire Screen – Reduced Resolution instead. Otherwise, choose Actual Size if you want to see the movie at its "real" size or Half Size for a smaller view.

- **Check for iMovie updates automatically.** Select this check box if you want iMovie to automatically check for updates when your Mac is online. Usually, installing the latest updates is a good idea because they may fix bugs in iMovie. If you deselect this check box, Mac OS X checks for iMovie updates when checking for other updates at the interval you've set in Software Update preferences.

Choosing browser preferences

The Browser tab of the iMovie Preferences window (see Figure 4.4) lets you tell iMovie what to do when you click a filmstrip in the Event browser:

- **Show date ranges in Event Library.** Select this check box if you want iMovie to display the beginning and end date of each Event in the Event Library. Showing the date ranges is helpful when you're working by date as well as by content, but it can make the Event Library appear cluttered.

4.4 Take a minute to set the Browser preferences because they make a big difference in how you work in the Event browser.

- **Use large font in Project Library and Event Library.** Select this check box if you want the Project Library and Event Library to use a larger font that's easier to read.

- **Always show active clip badges.** Select this check box if you want iMovie to display badges (tiny icons) on the active clip indicating which edits and effects you've applied to it. For example, if you've cropped a clip, iMovie displays a clip icon in its upper-left corner when the clip is active.

- **Always show clip durations.** Select this check box if you want iMovie to display the duration of every clip. Showing the durations can be helpful when you select footage and build your projects, but it makes the iMovie interface that much busier.

- **Use project crop setting for clips in Event Browser.** Select this check box if you want the Event browser to show clips using the cropping that you've applied to the project as a whole.

- **Automatically stabilize clips that have been analyzed.** Select this check box if you want iMovie to automatically apply stabilization to clips you analyze for stabilization. If you need to stabilize many clips, try selecting this check box to see if it saves you time overall. Otherwise, it's usually best to apply stabilization only to clips you've decided to use.

- **Apply rolling shutter correction for clips that have been analyzed.** Select this check box if you want iMovie to automatically minimize problems with clips shot on a camera that uses a rolling shutter (such as the iPhone or many digital cameras). Because a rolling shutter records each frame in a pass from top to bottom rather than all at once, a moving subject can appear blurred in the frame. This feature tries to correct such blur.

- **Show Fine Tuning controls.** If you select this check box, when you point to a clip that you've already shortened, iMovie displays a button that you can use to change the clip's length. You'll learn how to do this in Chapter 5. If you deselect this check box, you can display the Fine Tuning buttons by pressing ⌘+Option while pointing to a clip.

- **Double-click to.** Choose the action you want to occur when you double-click an event: Edit or Play.

- **Clicking in Event Browser deselects all.** Select this option button if you find it easier to select by clicking and dragging than by merely clicking.

- **Clicking in Event Browser selects entire clip.** Select this option button to make a click select an entire clip rather than just the first part of it.

- **Clicking in Event Browser selects.** Select this option button, and then click and drag the slider to choose how many seconds you want to select at the beginning of a clip you click in the Event browser. The default setting is 4.0 seconds. Select the Add automatic transition duration check box if you want iMovie to include the length of any transitions you've decided to apply automatically.

103

Choosing video settings

The Video tab of the iMovie Preferences window (see Figure 4.5) contains only a single control, the Import HD video as pop-up menu. In this pop-up menu, choose the size at which to import high-definition video:

- **Full – Original Size.** Select this item to import the high-definition video at its full size. Doing this gives you the highest quality in your projects, but it takes up a lot of hard drive space.

- **Large – 960×540.** Select this item to import high-definition video at a smaller size. This size takes up around a quarter as much space as full-quality HD video.

Genius

Unless you have a professional-quality HD camcorder or you must keep your high-definition video full quality, choosing Large in the Import 1080i video as pop-up menu is usually a good idea. Consumer HD camcorders typically record less data than the 1920×1080 format technically requires, which means the image is not full quality — so if you reduce the image to 960×540, the drop in actual image quality is so small few people notice it.

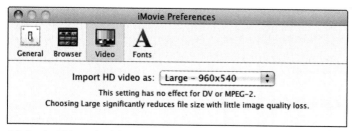

4.5 On the Video tab of the iMovie Preferences window, choose whether to import high-definition video at full size or at the reduced "Large" size.

Choosing fonts settings

The Fonts tab of the iMovie Preferences window (see Figure 4.6) displays the list of fonts that comprise iMovie's Choose Font panel, which is a subset of your Mac's complete list of system fonts. For each of the nine listed fonts, you can choose a typeface and a color.

iMovie Preferences		
General Browser Video **A** Fonts		
Helvetica Neue	÷	
Futura Medium	÷	
Impact	÷	
Coolvetica	÷	
Sign Painter House Script	÷	
Chalkboard	÷	
American Typewriter	÷	
Big Caslon Medium	÷	
Baskerville	÷	

4.6 On the Fonts tab of the iMovie Preferences window, choose the fonts and colors you want to be able to apply quickly in your projects.

Genius

The Choose Font panel is the quick way of applying fonts, so use the Fonts tab of the iMovie Preferences window to line up the fonts and colors you'll want to use most often. You can apply other fonts as needed using the Font window, but it takes a little longer.

Starting a Movie Project

If you've just opened iMovie, and iMovie has created a project called My First Project for you, you're ready to start. First, though, you may want to rename the movie project and check that its properties are set the way you need them.

If you've already added material to My First Project, you may prefer to create a new project. To do so, follow these steps:

1. **Click the New Project button in the lower-right corner of the Project Library, or choose File ⇨ New Project from the menu bar, or press ⌘+N.** iMovie displays the dialog shown in Figure 4.7.

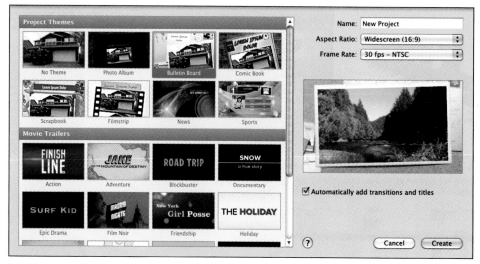

4.7 When you create a new project, you give it a name, choose its aspect ratio and frame rate, and apply a theme if you want to use one.

2. **In the Name box, type the name you want to give the project.** You can change this at any point, so go ahead and assign a working title if you haven't chosen a killer name yet.

3. **In the Aspect Ratio pop-up menu, choose the aspect ratio you want — the proportion of the frame's width to its height.** These are your choices:

   - **Widescreen (16:9).** Choose this aspect ratio (16 units wide by 9 units high) for playing back on a high-definition TV or a widescreen monitor. If you play the project back on a standard TV or monitor, the video appears letter-boxed, with black bands above and below it.

   - **Standard (4:3).** Choose this aspect ratio (4 units wide by 3 units high) for playing back on a standard-shaped TV or monitor.

Note

You can change a project's aspect ratio later if necessary by working on its Properties dialog, as described shortly.

4. **In the Project Themes box, click the predefined iMovie theme you want to use (or click No Theme if you don't want to use a theme).** Each theme comes with a predefined set of scene transitions, as well as titles and other effects, so you can create a movie simply by snapping your content into place.

5. **In the Frame Rate pop-up menu, choose the frame rate and format for the movie.** These are your choices:

- **30 fps – NTSC.** Choose this item to create a movie using the NTSC (National Television Standards Committee) format. This is the format used in North America, South America, and Japan. It runs at 30 frames per second (fps).

- **25 fps – PAL.** Choose this item to create a movie in the PAL (Phase Alternating Line) format. This is the format used in Europe, Australia, China, Africa, and the Middle East. It runs at 25 frames per second.

- **24 fps – Cinema.** Choose this item to create a movie using the 24 fps frame rate used in cinemas.

Genius

Unless you've bought your DV camcorder or TV in another country, or you're creating a movie for playback in a cinema, you'll normally want to choose your local standard in the Frame Rate pop-up menu. For example, if you're in the United States, you'll probably want to choose the 30 fps – NTSC format.

6. **Tell iMovie whether you want it to add scene transitions automatically.** How you do this depends on whether you selected a theme in Step 4:

- **If you selected No Theme.** In this case, select the Automatically add check box and then use the pop-up menu to click the type of transition you want iMovie to apply throughout your project. You learn about the various transitions in Chapter 6, but the best transition for automatic use is Cross Dissolve.

- **If you selected a theme.** In this case, iMovie selects the Automatically add transitions and titles check box for you. Deselect this check box if you don't want the automatic transitions and titles. To get the most benefit from using a theme, leave the Automatically add transitions and titles check box selected.

7. **Click Create.** iMovie creates the movie project for you, adds it to the Project Library, and opens it in the Storyboard so that you can start working on it. If you want to adjust project properties (as discussed in a moment), click the Project Library button to return to the Project Library.

Genius

Notice that unlike most applications, iMovie doesn't let you choose the folder in which to store your project. Instead, iMovie automatically stores the project in the ~/ Movies/iMovie Projects folder (where the tilde [~] represents your home folder). iMovie also automatically saves the changes you make to your projects, so you don't need to save them yourself.

Renaming a movie project

My First Project isn't the greatest of names, so you may want to change it to something more suitable. To do so, double-click the existing name in the Project Library to display an edit box, type the new name, and then press Return to apply the change.

Setting properties for a movie project

Before you start working on a project, make sure its properties are set the way you need them. Follow these steps:

1. **Control+click or right-click the project in the Project Library and choose Project Properties.** iMovie displays the Project Properties dialog (see Figure 4.8).

2. **In the Aspect Ratio pop-up menu, choose the aspect ratio you want: Standard (4:3) or Widescreen (16:9).**

3. **In the Frame Rate pop-up menu, choose the frame rate and format to use: 30 fps – NTSC, 25 fps – PAL, or 24 fps – Cinema.** Frame rates are covered earlier in this chapter.

4.8 It's usually a good idea to set properties in the Project Properties dialog before working on a project.

4. **Click and drag the Transition Duration slider to set the default length for transitions in this project.** You can set from 0.5 seconds up to 4 seconds.

5. **Click and drag the Theme Transition Duration slider to set the length of the theme transitions.** You can set from 0.5 seconds up to 4 seconds. This slider is disabled if you've set the project to use no theme.

6. **If you've set the project not to apply transitions automatically, select the appropriate option under the Theme Transition Duration slider.** If you have set the project to apply transitions automatically, these option buttons are not available.

   - **Applies to all transitions.** Select this option button if you want iMovie to use these settings for all transitions — those you've placed so far (if any) and those you add from now on.

   - **Applies when added to project.** Select this option button to apply automatic transitions only to clips you add from now on.

7. **Click and drag the Title Fade Duration slider to tell iMovie how long to fade the titles in and out.** You can set from 0 seconds to 2 seconds.

8. **Choose settings for still photos you add to the project:**

   - **Photo Duration.** Click and drag the slider to tell iMovie how long to play a photo for by default (from 1 second to 10 seconds).

   - **Applies To.** Select the Applies to all photos option button if you want to apply this duration to all photos you've already placed as well as to any you place from now on. Select the Applies when added to project option button if you want to apply the duration only to photos you place from now on.

   - **Initial Photo Placement.** In this pop-up menu, choose the standard placement for photos: Fit in Frame, Crop, or Ken Burns. You're just setting your default placement here; you can always change the placement for a photo after you place it.

Genius

The Fit in Frame placement makes iMovie add letterboxing to photos and videos that are the wrong aspect ratio for the project. The Crop placement makes iMovie enlarge the photo or video so that it occupies the full aspect ratio, cropping off parts of the dimension that was already fitting. For example, if a photo's aspect ratio makes it too wide and short for the frame, Crop increases the photo's height to match the frame, and then crops the extra parts of the width.

9. **In the Initial Video Placement pop-up menu, choose the initial video placement: Fit in Frame, or Crop.** See the nearby Genius note for an explanation of these options.

10. **Click OK to close the Project Properties dialog.** iMovie applies your preferences to the project.

Genius

If you create stacks of movie projects, the Project Library can get crowded. To ease the congestion, you can use folders within the Project Library to organize your movie projects. To create a folder, Control+click or right-click in the Project Library window, choose New Folder, type the name, and then press Return. You can then drag a movie project to a folder.

Importing Video

You can bring your video content into iMovie in several ways:

- **Import video directly from your digital video camera.** The process is different for a DV camcorder that uses tape than for one that doesn't.

- **Copy video from your digital video camera, digital camera, or iPhone to your iPhoto Library, and then access the files from iMovie.**

- **Import existing video files you have on your Mac.** You can also import video from iMovie HD projects, an older version of iMovie (this chapter doesn't cover importing video from iMovie HD).

- **Record live video directly into iMovie using an iSight or a DV camcorder.**

Importing video from a DV tape camcorder

To import video from a DV camcorder that records onto tape, follow these steps:

1. **Connect the DV camcorder to your Mac.** Most DV camcorders connect via a FireWire cable, usually with a four-pin (small) plug at the camcorder end and a regular nine-pin FireWire 800 plug at the Mac's end.

Caution

Connecting a DV camcorder via FireWire can disconnect an external FireWire drive you're using. This shouldn't happen — but it does. So before you connect your DV camcorder for the first time, close any files that you've opened from any external FireWire drive you're using just in case the DV camcorder knocks the drive off your Mac's FireWire chain.

2. **Switch the DV camcorder to Play mode or VCR mode.** When iMovie recognizes the DV camcorder, it automatically displays the Import From window, as shown in Figure 4.9. If you don't see the window, click the Open Camera Import Window button (you can also choose File ⇨ Import from Camera or press ⌘+I).

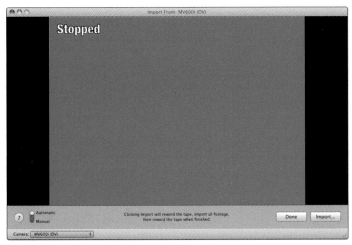

4.9 iMovie displays the Import From window when it recognizes a DV camcorder connected and switched on. This is a tape camcorder.

Once iMovie recognizes the camcorder, you can either import all the video on the tape (as discussed next) or just parts of it (as discussed after that).

Importing all the video on the tape automatically

If you want to import all the video on the tape, follow these steps:

1. **Make sure the mode switch in the lower-left corner of the Import From window is set to Automatic.**

2. **Click Import.** iMovie displays the dialog shown in Figure 4.10.

3. **In the Save to pop-up menu, choose the hard drive on which you want to save the video.** Your Mac's internal hard drive is usually the best bet unless you've attached an external hard drive to give yourself extra space for working with video.

4. **Tell iMovie which Event to make the video part of:**

   - **Add to existing Event.** Select this option button to add the video to an existing event, and then choose the Event in the pop-up menu.

● **Create new Event.** Select this option button to create a new Event. Type the name for the new Event in the text box; iMovie suggests New Event and the date, but you'll find that more descriptive names are more helpful. Select the Split days into new Events check box if you want iMovie to create a separate Event for each day on the imported video.

Save to: [Macintosh HD (312.4GB free / 24 hours ... ◆]

◉ Add to existing Event: [Scenery ◆]

○ Create new Event: [New Event 02-15-2011]

☐ Split days into new Events

☐ After import analyze for: [Stabilization ◆]

Selecting this option will analyze all clips for stabilization, but will result in longer import times.

(Cancel) (Import)

4.10 Choose which hard drive or storage device to save the video on; whether to create a new Event or add it to an existing Event; and whether to analyze the imported video for stabilization, people, or both.

5. **If you want iMovie to apply stabilization to your clips or find people in them after importing the video, select the After import analyze for check box, and then make the appropriate choice in the pop-up menu:**

● **Stabilization.** Analyzing the video for stabilization adjusts your clips to compensate for the telltale signs of shakiness that are the hallmark of handheld video footage.

Caution

Analyzing the imported video for stabilization, people, or both can make the import process take much longer than a straightforward import. Unless you're sure the video is all high quality, you may do better to analyze only selected clips for stabilization or people (or both) after importing the video and grading it for quality.

● **People.** Select this item to have iMovie try to pick out faces in the clips.

● **Stabilization and People.** Select this item to have iMovie both analyze the video for stabilization and try to identify faces.

6. **Click OK.** iMovie rewinds the tape to the beginning, and then imports the video, displaying it in the Import From window as it does so (see Figure 4.11).

4.11 Letting iMovie import all the video from a tape automatically

7. **When iMovie displays the Camera Import Complete dialog, as shown in Figure 4.12, click OK.** You can now turn off your DV camcorder and start working with the imported video.

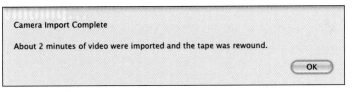

4.12 iMovie tells you when it finishes importing the video.

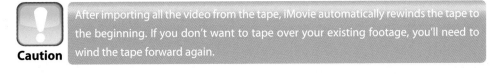

Caution After importing all the video from the tape, iMovie automatically rewinds the tape to the beginning. If you don't want to tape over your existing footage, you'll need to wind the tape forward again.

Importing video from your DV camcorder manually

If you want to grab only some of the video from your DV camcorder, follow these steps:

1. **Move the mode switch in the lower-left corner of the Import From window to the Manual position.** iMovie displays the transport controls for the DV camcorder (shown in Figure 4.13 with an import running).

4.13 Move the mode switch to Manual to access iMovie's transport controls for your DV camcorder.

2. **Use the transport controls to reach the part of the tape you want to import.** For example, fast-forward to approximately the right part of the tape, play the video until where you want to start importing, and then stop it.

3. **Click Import.** iMovie displays the dialog for choosing where and how to save the video.

4. **In the Save to pop-up menu, choose the hard drive on which you want to save the video.**

5. **Choose whether to make the video part of an existing Event or to create a new Event for it, as discussed earlier in this chapter.**

6. **If you want iMovie to analyze your clips for stabilization, people, or both (as described in the previous section), select the After import analyze for check box.** In the pop-up menu, choose People, Stabilization, or Stabilization and People, as needed.

7. **Click OK.** iMovie starts importing the video from the point you chose.

8. **Click the Stop button when iMovie reaches the end of the video you want to import.** iMovie processes the clip you imported and then displays the blue screen of the Import From window again.

9. **If you want to import more video from the DV camcorder, follow Steps 2 through 8 to select and import it.** When you finish, click Done to close the Import From window.

Importing video from a DV tapeless camcorder

If your camcorder stores the video on a hard drive, memory card, or DVD, import the video files like this:

1. **Connect the camcorder to your Mac.** Most tapeless camcorders connect via USB rather than FireWire.

Caution Don't use the low-power USB port on a desktop Mac's keyboard — it normally doesn't work. If possible, connect the tapeless camcorder to a USB jack on your Mac rather than on a USB hub connected to your Mac. Plugging the camcorder in directly helps avoid connection problems and gives you the best transfer speeds.

2. **Switch the camcorder on and put it into Playback mode.** Some camcorders call this mode PC mode or VCR mode.

3. **Your Mac should open or activate iMovie automatically when it notices the camcorder in Playback mode.** If not, try quitting iMovie (if it's running) and then reopening it manually.

4. **iMovie automatically transfers or generates thumbnail previews for the clips on the camcorder, and then displays the thumbnails in a panel at the bottom of the Import From window.** Figure 4.14 shows an example.

4.14 When you connect a tapeless camcorder, iMovie shows you thumbnails of the clips it contains.

115

5. **Choose which clips you want to import:**

   - **If you want to import all the clips, simply click Import All, and go to the next step.** Otherwise, click and drag the switch in the lower-left corner of the Import From window from Automatic to Manual. iMovie adds a check box to each clip, as shown in Figure 4.15.

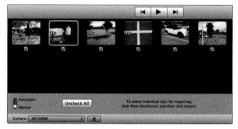

4.15 Move the switch to Manual to reveal check boxes for selecting the clips you want to import.

   - **To play a clip, click its thumbnail, and then click the Play button.** You can then click the Previous button or the Next button to play another clip.

   - **Select the check box for each clip you want to import.** If you want to import most of the clips, click Check All, and then deselect the check boxes for those clips you don't want.

   - **Click Import Selected.**

6. **In the Save to pop-up menu, choose the hard drive on which you want to save the video.**

7. **Choose whether to make the video part of an existing Event or to create a new Event for it, as discussed earlier in this chapter.**

8. **If you want iMovie to analyze your clips for stabilization, people, or both (as described in the previous section), select the After import analyze for check box.** In the pop-up menu, choose People, Stabilization, or Stabilization and People, as needed.

9. **Click OK.** iMovie starts importing the video, displaying a progress indicator so you can see how it's doing. iMovie displays an Import Complete dialog to let you know when it has finished.

10. **Click OK to close the Import Complete dialog.**

11. **Click Done to close the Import From window.**

Importing video from a digital camera

If your digital camera takes video clips, you may want to use these in iMovie. Depending on your digital camera, you can import the clips into iMovie in one of these ways:

- **Import the clips into iPhoto.** If iPhoto recognizes your digital camera, but iMovie does not, import the clips into iPhoto. You can then use the iPhoto Videos Event in iMovie's Events browser to browse the clips. This is how you import video clips from an iPhone.

- **Click and drag the clips from the Finder.** Connect your digital camera to your Mac via the camera's USB cable, and Mac OS X mounts the camera's storage as a drive in the Finder. Open the drive, locate the video clips you want, and then click and drag them to the Event in which you want to place them in the Event Library.

Genius

If Mac OS X doesn't recognize your digital camera, remove the storage medium from the camera and insert it in a card reader built into or connected to your Mac. For example, remove a CompactFlash card or an SD card from your camera and insert it in a card reader. Once Mac OS X mounts the volume and displays it in the Finder, you can click and drag the video clips from the Finder to an Event in the Event Library in iMovie.

Importing existing video files

If you already have video files on your Mac that iMovie doesn't know about, you can import them into iMovie by using either the Finder or the Import Movies command.

The simplest way to import existing video files is by clicking and dragging them from the Finder to the Event Library in the iMovie window. Drop the files on the Event to which you want to add them. If the video files are high definition, iMovie imports them at the resolution you set on the Movies tab in iMovie Preferences.

If you want to put the video files you're importing in a new Event or control the resolution at which iMovie imports high-definition video, use the Import Movies command instead. Follow these steps:

1. **In iMovie, choose File ⇨ Import ⇨ Movies.** iMovie displays the dialog shown in Figure 4.16.

2. **Navigate to the video files and select them as usual.**

3. **In the Save to pop-up menu, choose the hard drive on which you want to store the imported video.**

117

4.16 This importing dialog lets you choose whether to create a new Event and whether to copy or move the files you're importing.

4. **Choose whether to add the files to an existing Event or whether to create a new Event.** If you create a new Event, type its name in the text box.

5. **If you're importing high-definition video, select the Optimize video check box if you want to optimize the video for the size you choose in the pop-up menu.** As when importing from a camera, your choices are Large – 960×540 and Full – Original Size.

6. **Select the Copy files option button or the Move files option button.** Copying the files lets you change the files in iMovie without worrying about the originals, but it takes twice as much hard drive space. If the files are large, you may want to move them rather than copy them.

7. **Click Import.** iMovie imports the files and then generates thumbnails for them, keeping you informed of its progress (see Figure 4.17).

4.17 iMovie generates thumbnails for the video files you import.

118

Recording live video from an iSight or a camcorder

Another option is to record video directly from an iSight video camera or a DV camcorder connected to your Mac. The iSight can be either built into your Mac or connected via FireWire.

To record live video, follow these steps:

1. **If you're using an external iSight or another external DV camera, connect it to your Mac via FireWire.** For a camera other than an iSight, turn its control knob to the Record position or Camera position (depending on the model).

2. **Open the Import From window by clicking the Open Camera Import Window button, choosing File ⇨ Import from Camera, or pressing ⌘+I.** If you're using an external camera other than an iSight, the Import From window may open automatically when you switch the camera to the Record position or Camera position. The illustration on the opening page of the chapter shows iMovie ready to record from an iSight.

3. **If you have two or more cameras connected, choose the camera you want from the Camera pop-up menu.**

4. **If the Video Size pop-up menu appears, choose the resolution you want.** Some DV camcorders and iSight cameras can provide different resolutions (for example, 640×480 or 1024×576), while others can manage only a single resolution.

5. **Aim the iSight or camera and any external microphone you're using.**

6. **Position your subject (for example, yourself) in the frame.**

7. **Click Capture when you're ready to start recording.** iMovie displays the dialog shown in Figure 4.18.

8. **In the Save to pop-up menu, choose the hard drive on which you want to store the imported video.** Your Mac's internal hard drive is usually the best choice.

9. **Choose whether to add the files to an existing Event or whether to create a new Event whose name you type in the text box.** Select the Split days into new Events check box if you want iMovie to create a new Event for each day you film. Unless the clock is ticking toward midnight or you're planning a marathon filming session, you don't normally need to worry about this check box when recording live.

10. **If you want iMovie to analyze your clips for stabilization, people, or both (as described in the previous section), select the After import analyze for check box.** In the pop-up menu, choose People, Stabilization, or Stabilization and People, as needed.

| Save to: | Macintosh HD (310.7GB free / 71 hours ... | ⬍ |

○ Add to existing Event: Monuments Footage ⬍

◉ Create new Event: Talking Headshots\

☐ Split days into new Events

☐ After import analyze for: People ⬍

Selecting this option will detect people in all clips, but will result in longer import times.

Cancel Capture

4.18 Choose where to store the footage, which Event to make it part of, and whether to analyze it for people or stabilization after import.

11. **Click Capture.** iMovie starts recording through the camera.

12. **Click the Stop button when you want to stop capturing video.**

13. **Click Done when you're ready to close the Import From window.** iMovie adds your new footage to the Event you chose.

Reviewing and Sorting Your Video Clips

After you import your video clips as described earlier in this chapter, review them to see what footage you have and what parts of it you want to keep. iMovie lets you quickly identify known people in your clips, mark clips you want to keep as favorites, and mark clips that don't make the grade as rejects. To make your clips easy to sort and search, you can add keywords to them, and you can organize them into different Events so that you can easily find the footage you need.

Navigating through your Events

As you've seen in this chapter, when you import video clips, iMovie assigns them to Events. To work with Events, you use the Event Library in the lower-left corner of the iMovie window. Figure 4.19 shows the Event Library with various events added.

Swap events and projects | Thumbnail Size slider | Group events by disk | Keyword filtering | Show/hide audio waveforms

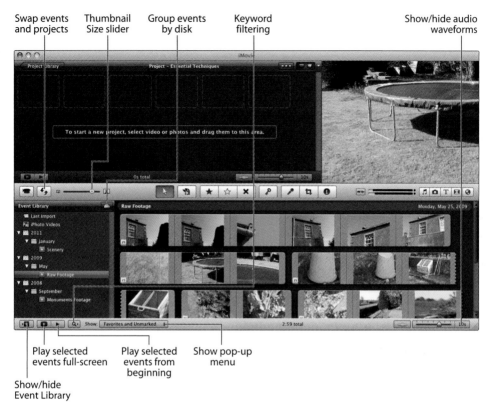

Play selected events full-screen | Play selected events from beginning | Show pop-up menu

Show/hide Event Library

4.19 The Event Library with various events.

The Event Library organizes your Events like this:

- **Last Import.** This Event contains the last batch of clips you imported from your video camera. If you've just imported some video, this is the place to start.

- **iPhoto Videos.** This Event contains the videos you've imported into iPhoto from your digital camera.

- **Year folders (2011, 2010, and so on).** Each folder contains the Events for footage shot in that year. For example, if you dredge up a tape from 2008 and import it, iMovie puts it in the 2008 folder rather than the folder for the current year. (iMovie picks up the date from the timecode on the video.)

Changing the Event Library's sort order

Normally, the Event Library sorts the Events and folders in reverse date order, so the most recent items appear at the top of the list, where they're handiest. If you want to switch to conventional date order, choose View⇨Most Recent Events at Top to remove the check mark by this command.

Viewing Events by month or day

If you want to see the Events listed by month in the Event Library, choose View⇨Group Events by Month. iMovie adds a separate category for each month that has footage. Choose the same command again if you want to hide the months again.

Viewing Events and folders by drives

If you want to see the Events and folders listed by the drives on which they're stored (see Figure 4.20), click the Group Events by Disk button in the upper-right corner of the Event Library (this button is labeled in Figure 4.19). Alternatively, choose View⇨Group Events By Disk to place a check mark by this item.

To return to the reverse date order, just click the Group Events by Disk button again. Alternatively, choose View⇨Group Events by Disk again to remove the check mark.

4.20 Viewing Events by disk lets you tell easily which drive an Event's clips are stored on.

Viewing the clips in an Event

To view the clips in an Event, click the Event in the Event Library. iMovie displays the clips in the Event browser (see Figure 4.21) as filmstrips, sequences of frames that show you the contents of the clips.

To change the size of the video thumbnails, drag the Thumbnail Size slider to the left or the right. (Figure 4.19 shows where this slider is.)

To change the number of frames iMovie displays for a filmstrip, drag the Filmstrip length slider to the left or right. If you drag the slider all the way to the left, iMovie displays a single frame for each clip.

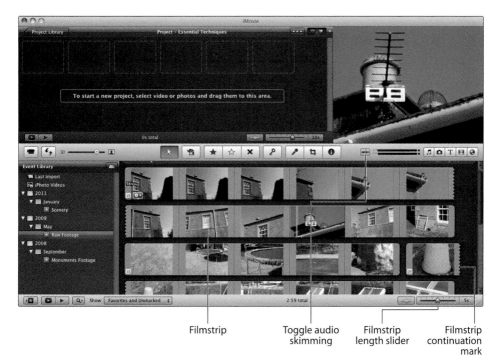

Filmstrip   Toggle audio   Filmstrip   Filmstrip
skimming   length slider   continuation
mark

4.21 Viewing an Event's clips as filmstrips in the Event browser.

You can play clips in any of these ways:

● **In the viewer.** Control+click or right-click the clip and then click Play Clip on the context menu.

● **Full screen.** Control+click or right-click it and choose Play Full Screen.

- **Play all clips in the selected Event (or Events) in the viewer.** Click the Play selected Events from beginning button.

- **Play all clips in the selected Event (or Events) full screen.** Click the Play selected Events full screen button. This way you can get the full impact of the clips.

Skimming through a clip

To move through a clip at your own pace, position the mouse pointer over the filmstrip in the Event browser so that iMovie displays a red line representing the playhead (see Figure 4.22), and then move the mouse to the left or right to move through the frames. iMovie

4.22 Drag the Playhead (the red line) to skim through a clip.

shows the current frame both in the Event browser and in the viewer so you can get a good view of what's happening. iMovie calls this technique skimming.

When you skim through a clip, iMovie plays the audio. If you don't want to hear the audio, click the Toggle Audio Skimming button on the toolbar to turn off audio skimming. (Figure 4.21 shows where the Toggle Audio Skimming button is.) Click the button again when you want to turn it on again.

Genius

After placing the playhead in a clip, you can press the Left Arrow key or the Right Arrow key to move through the clip one frame at a time.

Switching the Event and Project areas

When you review your clips, you may want to switch the Event area and the Project area around so that the Event Library and Event browser appear at the top of the iMovie window alongside the viewer. Switching the Event area and the Project area is also useful when you work on the Storyboard and you want more space.

To switch the two areas, click the Swap Events and Projects button. iMovie swaps them over with a swirly animation. Figure 4.23 shows iMovie with the Event Library and Event browser at the top of the window. Click the button again when you want to switch the areas back.

4.23 You can swap the Event area and the Project area to make browsing your clips easier or to give yourself a larger Storyboard area to work in.

Selecting the footage to keep

To save space on your Mac's hard drive, you'll usually want to trim down your clips by selecting only the footage you want to use. Use these techniques to select the footage:

- **To select a standard-length chunk of video, click the clip.** iMovie displays a yellow outline around it starting from the point you clicked. By default, iMovie selects 4 seconds.

Note To change the number of seconds of video that iMovie selects when you click a clip, choose iMovie ⇨ Preferences, click the Browser tab, and then click and drag the Clicking in Events Browser selects slider to the number of seconds you want.

- **To select as much video as you want, click and drag through a clip.** iMovie displays a yellow outline around the part you selected (see Figure 4.24).

4.24 Click and drag to select as much of a clip as you want.

- **To change the length of the selection, drag the handle at either side to the left or right.** Alternatively, Shift+click another point in the clip to make the nearest handle snap to where you click.

- **To move the selection without changing its length, drag its top or bottom border to the left or right.**

- **To select an entire filmstrip, Option+click it.** Alternatively, Control+click or right-click and choose Select Entire Clip.

- **To select multiple filmstrips, click the first one, and then ⌘+click each of the others.** The first click gets you however many seconds iMovie is set to select, but as soon as you ⌘+click the second clip, iMovie selects the whole of the first clip as well.

Identifying clips that contain people

When your video clips include shots of people, you can use iMovie's People Finder feature to locate the clips that contain people — or, strictly speaking, people's faces.

Genius

Unlike iPhoto's Faces feature, People Finder doesn't recognize the faces of individuals and allow you to assign names to them. It just finds people in your clips by identifying their faces so that you can easily locate the clips that feature people.

To use People Finder, click the Event you want to analyze, and then choose File⇨Analyze Video⇨People. iMovie displays the Detecting People dialog (see Figure 4.25) as it scans the clips for people. This process may take several minutes, depending on how much footage there is and how powerful your Mac is.

> **Detecting People**
>
> ━━━━━━━━━━━━━━━ (Cancel)
>
> Time remaining: less than a minute

4.25 iMovie may take several minutes to detect all the people's faces in an Event.

Note

You can also have iMovie run People Finder when you import clips, as discussed earlier in this chapter. And if you want to analyze the video for stabilization needs at the same time as searching for people, choose File⇨Analyze Video⇨Stabilization and People. As you'd imagine, performing both forms of analysis at the same time takes longer, but it can save you time overall if you need to run both operations.

When iMovie finishes analyzing the clips for people, it displays a purple bar across the clips that contain faces and adds the People button to the bar across the bottom of the window, as shown in Figure 4.26.

People button

4.26 iMovie shows a purple bar across the clips and footage that contain people and displays the People button.

Now you can click the People button to filter down the clips displayed to only those that contain people. This is a great way of finding the footage that contains people quickly without having to skim through many clips.

But it gets better. Click the Show/hide Keyword Filtering pane button to display the Filter by Keyword pane, and you can turn on filters to find exactly what you need. For example, try this:

1. **Click the green side of the People button at the top to turn on filtering by people.**
    This may be on already.

2. **Click the red side of the One Person button to tell iMovie not to display footage containing one person.**

3. **Click the green side of the Two People button to tell iMovie to display footage containing two or more people.**

4. **Click the green side of the Closeup button to tell iMovie to display closeups.**

5. **Click the green side of the Medium button to include medium-distance shots.**

6. **Click the red side of the Wide button to strip out wide shots of people.**

Figure 4.27 shows the type of result you'll see: clips that contain two or more people in closeup or medium shots.

127

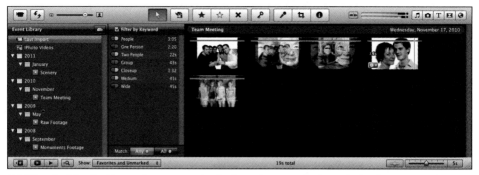

4.27 Use the Filter by Keyword pane to make the Event browser display only the footage containing the number of people and types of shot you want.

Marking your video clips as favorites or rejects

After you select the footage you want, you can quickly mark it as a favorite. Similarly, you select footage you don't want to keep and mark it as a reject:

- **Mark as a favorite.** Click the Mark Selected Video as Favorite button on the toolbar (see Figure 4.28) or press F. iMovie puts a green bar across the top of the selected part of the clip.

- **Mark as rejected.** Click the Reject Selected Video button or press R. iMovie puts a red bar across the top of the selected part of the clip.

- **Remove the marking.** Click the Unmark Selected Video button or press U. iMovie removes the green bar or red bar.

Unmark selected video

Mark selected video as favorite

Reject selected video

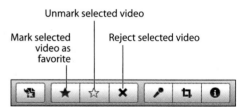

4.28 Use these toolbar buttons to quickly mark favorites and rejects.

After marking favorites and rejects, you can narrow down the clips displayed by opening the Show menu and choosing Favorites Only, Favorites and Unmarked, or Rejected Only, as appropriate. When you want to see all the clips again, open the Show pop-up menu once more and choose All Clips from it.

Adding keywords to video clips

To make your video clips easier to sort and to find, you can add keywords to them. Follow these steps:

1. Choose iMovie ⇨ Preferences, click the General tab, select the Show Advanced Tools check box, and then click the Close button (the red button on the title bar) to

close the Preferences window. iMovie displays the Advanced tools.

2. **Click the View Keywords for Selection button — the button with the key icon — that appears in the middle of the toolbar.** iMovie displays the Keywords window with the Inspector tab at the front (see Figure 4.29).

3. **Change the list of keywords to suit your needs:**

   - **To change an existing keyword, double-click it on either tab.** Type the replacement word, and then press Return.

   - **To add a keyword, type it in the box in the lower-left corner of the Auto-Apply tab, and then click Add.**

   - **To rearrange the list of keywords, drag them up and down the list.** iMovie automatically assigns the numbers 1 to 9 to the first nine keywords so that you can apply them quickly.

4. **To apply keywords to a selected clip, click the Inspector tab, and then select the check box for each keyword you want to apply.** You can also press the 1 through 9 keys to apply the keywords currently assigned those numbers.

5. **To apply the same keywords quickly to several clips, use Auto Apply like this:**

   - **Click the Auto-Apply tab.**

   - **Select the check box for each keyword you want to apply.**

   - **Drag across each section in the filmstrip that you want to give the keywords.** To apply the keywords to a whole filmstrip, Option+click it.

6. **When you finish working with keywords, close the Keywords window.** Either click the Close button (the X button) in the upper-left corner of the Keywords window, or simply click the Keywords button in the middle of the toolbar.

Filtering your clips by keywords

After you apply keywords to your clips, you can use the keywords to filter the clips so that you see only the clips that have the keywords you choose. Here's how to do this:

4.29 Use the Keywords window to tag clips with keywords that make them easier to identify.

1. **Click the Keyword Filtering button to display the Keyword Filter panel (see Figure 4.30).** The panel appears between the Event Library (if it's displayed) and the Event browser.

4.30 Use the Keyword Filter panel to display only the clips that match the keywords you select.

2. **Click the green part of the button for each keyword by which you want to filter.**

3. **In the Match line at the bottom of the pane, click the Any button if you want to see clips that have any of the keywords you've selected.** Click the All button if you want only clips that have all the keywords.

4. **When you finish using the Keyword Filter panel, click the Keyword Filtering button to close the panel again.**

Organizing clips into Events

To make your clips more manageable, you often need to move a clip from one Event to another. You may also need to split, merge, or rename Events — or even delete Events and their contents.

Moving a clip from one Event to another

To move a clip from one Event to another, follow these steps:

1. **Control+click or right-click the clip and choose Select Entire Clip.** iMovie puts a yellow hoop around the clip.

2. **Click and drag the clip to the Event in which you want to place it.** iMovie displays the Move Clip to Event dialog, as shown in Figure 4.31.

3. **Click OK.** iMovie moves the clip to the Event you chose.

4.31 Click OK in the Move Clip to Event dialog box to move a clip to a different Event.

Splitting an Event into two Events

Here's how to split an Event into two events:

1. **Click the Event in the Event Library to display its clips.**

2. **Control+click or right-click the clip before which you want to split the Event, and then choose Split Event Before Clip.** iMovie creates a new Event containing the clip you clicked and those clips that follow it.

3. **Double-click the default name for the new clip, type a new name, and then press Return.**

Merging two Events into one

If you find that iMovie has split clips that belong together into separate Events, you can easily merge the Events. Follow these steps:

1. **Click the Event whose name you want to lose and drag it on top of the Event whose name you want to keep.** iMovie displays the renaming dialog shown in Figure 4.32.

Name for merged Event: Raw Footage

The combined clip dates will determine the new position in the Events Library.

Cancel   OK

4.32 You can merge two Events into a single Event to pool their clips.

2. **If necessary, type a new name for the merged Event.** If you simply want to use the name of the second Event you used, you're all set.

3. **Click OK.** iMovie merges the Events and puts the merged Event in the appropriate place in the Events list.

131

As most directors will be quick to tell you, shooting the film is only the first part of the long process of creating a movie. Once you shoot your footage, import it into iMovie, and choose favorite clips as described in Chapter 4, you're ready to edit your clips and put your movie together on the Storyboard. You can also add still photos to your movies and create a custom Ken Burns Effect to bring them to life. First, though, you need to know how iMovie applies edits to your clips because you can edit clips either in the Event browser or on the Storyboard — and the effects are different.

How Editing Affects Your Clips

For most editing maneuvers, iMovie gives you the choice of editing a clip either in the Event browser or after you place it on the Storyboard. This may seem puzzling at first, but it makes good sense when you get used to it.

As you saw in Chapter 4, the Event Library is where you store all the footage you may want to use in your projects. All the clips you import from your DV camcorder, digital camera, or other sources go into the Event Library, and you can use the clips for any project. You narrow down the amount of footage available by creating favorites, by rejecting clips and footage you don't want to keep, and by organizing the clips into Events.

Changes you make to a clip in the Event browser apply to any project in which you use that clip. By contrast, changes you make to a clip after you place it on the Storyboard for a project apply only to that project.

This means you'll want to make general changes to clips in the Event browser and more specific changes to clips after placing them on the Storyboard. Here's a quick example using cropping:

- **Event browser.** If a clip has a cropping problem such as a bystander's head and shoulders appearing in the corner of the frame at a sporting event, you'll probably want to crop it in the Event browser. This obstruction will be a problem in any project you add the clip to.

- **Storyboard.** If you need to create a special effect by emphasizing the subject of the clip, crop the clip after placing it on the Storyboard. This way, you can use the clip as normal in other projects.

Either way, the edits you make to your clips in iMovie are still nondestructive — they don't actually change the video footage you've shot, just the way in which it appears. This means that you can undo any of your edits or redo the edits differently as needed, even when you make changes in the Event browser rather than in the Storyboard.

Arranging the Clips on the Storyboard

After choosing the footage you like, you can start creating your movie by arranging clips on the Storyboard, the area that appears when you hide the Project Library in the iMovie window.

If you're like me, you'll find the easiest way to start putting your movie together is by adding clips to the Storyboard in the order in which you want them to appear in the movie. Doing this lets you lay out the story of the movie in a natural and logical way.

Other times, though, you may need to add a clip to a different part of the Storyboard. This takes only a moment longer.

Adding a clip to the end of the Storyboard

iMovie gives you two easy ways to add a selected clip to the end of the Storyboard:

- **Keyboard.** Press E.

- **Mouse.** Click the Add selected video to Project button on the toolbar (see Figure 5.1).

5.1 Click the Add selected video to Project button or press E to add the selected clip to the Storyboard.

When you add a clip to the Storyboard, iMovie places an orange bar across the bottom of the clip in the Event browser (see Figure 5.2) to indicate that you've used the clip in the current project. (If you click another project in the Project Library, iMovie changes the bars to show the clips used in that project, so you can always see exactly what you've used in your current project.)

5.2 The orange bar on a clip in the Event browser indicates you've already used this clip in the current project.

Adding a clip elsewhere in the Storyboard

When you need to add a clip to another part of the Storyboard than the end, click the clip and drag it to where you want it.

You can drop the clip either between two clips that are already on the Storyboard or inside a clip. When you drop a clip inside another clip, move the mouse pointer over the destination clip to skim through the footage to the point at which you want the clip you're dragging to appear (see Figure 5.3), and then drop the clip there.

5.3 You can also click and drag a clip to the point in the Storyboard where you want it to appear.

When you drop a clip on another clip, iMovie displays the pop-up menu shown in Figure 5.4. Click Insert to insert the clip at the position of the playhead.

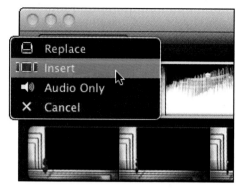

5.4 Click Insert on the pop-up menu to insert the clip where you've placed the Playhead.

Adding multiple clips to the Storyboard

If you want, you can add two or more clips to the Storyboard at the same time like this:

1. **Select the first clip you want to add, and then Shift-click each of the other clips.**

2. **Press E or click the Add selected video to Project button on the toolbar.** iMovie displays the Editing Tip dialog (see Figure 5.5) suggesting that your movie will be optimal if you use only your best video segments. Little does it know that you've selected them already.

3. **Click Continue.** iMovie adds the clips to the end of the Storyboard.

5.5 iMovie objects to your adding two or more clips to the Storyboard at once. Click Continue to proceed.

Adding clips quickly with the Edit tool

Adding clips to the Storyboard using the techniques discussed so far in this chapter is quick enough for most people. But if you want to be able to add footage even faster, try the Edit tool.

First, you need to display iMovie's advanced tools because iMovie hides the Edit tool until you do this. Choose iMovie ⇨ Preferences, click the General tab, select the Show Advanced Tools check box, and then click the Close button (the red button) at the left end of the window's title bar.

Now, you can click the Edit Tool button on the toolbar (see Figure 5.6) to turn on quick-add mode.

5.6 Click the Edit Tool button to turn on quick-add mode when you need to build a movie project quickly.

When you turn on quick-add mode, the mouse pointer appears as an arrow with a little sheet bearing a star. With this pointer, skim across a clip to where you want to start selecting, and then click and drag. As you drag, iMovie turns the selected footage light orange (see Figure 5.7). When you release the mouse button, iMovie adds the selected footage to the end of the Storyboard.

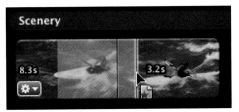

5.7 After clicking the Edit Tool button, click and drag across clips in the Event browser to select the footage you want.

Keep selecting footage using this technique. When you finish, click the Edit Tool button again to turn off the Edit Tool and restore normality.

Genius

If you find yourself dragging across the wrong part of a clip when using quick-add mode, press Esc to cancel the selection without adding it to the end of the Storyboard, and then release the mouse button.

Playing back video on the Storyboard

To see how your movie looks with the clips you've added so far, you can play back the footage you've placed on the Storyboard. Without effects, transitions, titles, and added sound, the movie may seem pretty bald, but you'll be able to see how it's developing.

Playing back everything on the Storyboard

To play back in the viewer everything you've put on the Storyboard from the beginning, choose View ⇨ Play from Beginning or press the \ (backslash) key. Press \ again to stop playback.

To play everything full screen, click the Play Project full screen button. Alternatively, Control+click or right-click in the Storyboard and choose Play Full Screen.

When playing full screen, you can move the mouse to display the navigation bar (see Figure 5.8). Here's how it works:

- **Play/Pause.** Click the Play/Pause button at the left end of the navigation bar. You can also press the spacebar.

- **Skim through clips.** Pause playback and then move the mouse pointer through the clips on the navigation bar.

- **Change location.** Double-click another clip in the navigation bar to start playback there. Or else click another clip in the navigation bar to move there and pause playback.

- **Exit full screen.** Click the X button in the bottom-left corner of the navigation bar or press Esc.

5.8 Use the navigation bar to move around a project you're playing full screen.

Playing back from a particular point

To start playback in the viewer, click at the point at which you want playback to start, and then click the Play button (or choose View⇨Play). You can also skim through the footage to the point where you want to start, and then press the spacebar to start playback. Click anywhere in the iMovie window or press the spacebar to stop playback.

To start playback full screen, skim to the point at which you want to start, and then press ⌘+G.

Genius

If you find your movie looks weird when playing full screen, it may be because it's stretched out of its aspect ratio. Choose iMovie⇨Preferences, click the General tab, and use the Full Screen playback size pop-up menu to choose Actual Size or Half Size instead of Entire Screen. Try playing back again, and full screen playback will have black borders rather than actually filling your screen, but the project will appear at its correct aspect ratio.

Playing back just a short section

If you want to play back just part of what you've placed on the Storyboard, click and drag to select it, and then press the / (forward slash) key. Press / again if you want to stop playback before the end of your selection.

Genius

To play just a couple of seconds of video, point to the area of interest, and then press the [key (to play 1 second) or the] key (to play 3 seconds) around where you point.

Moving a clip to a different point

Here's how to move a clip to a different point on the Storyboard:

1. **Select the clip or the part of it you want to move.** You can move either an entire clip or just a selected part of one.

2. **Click the clip or selection and drag it to where you want to place it.** iMovie displays a vertical green line between the existing clips to indicate where the clip or selection will land.

If you want to place the clip you're moving inside another clip, Option+drag it instead of plain dragging. iMovie displays a playhead on the clip over which you drag the clip you're moving, so that you can skim through the footage to the right place. Drop the clip at the appropriate place, and then click Insert in the pop-up menu that iMovie displays (see Figure 5.9).

5.9 When you move a clip on the Storyboard to a position inside another clip, click Insert on the pop-up menu that appears.

Editing Your Clips

To get your clips looking just right, you'll almost certainly need to edit them, if only to trim them to exactly the length you need. iMovie provides easy-to-use editing tools that enable you to make good video look great and even salvage video that has problems with cropping, exposure, or color balance.

First, it's a good idea to set up iMovie to give you a better view of what you're doing.

Preparing to edit a clip

Normally, when you edit a clip, you'll want to see as much of it as possible. Use these five suggestions to improve your view:

- **Zoom the iMovie window as large as possible.** Unless you need to see other applications at the same time, give all your screen space to iMovie. Click the green Zoom button in the upper-left corner or choose Window ⇨ Zoom.

- **Increase the size of the viewer by choosing Window ⇨ Viewer ⇨ Large or pressing ⌘+0.** Alternatively, you can play your clips full screen.

Genius You can quickly change the size of the viewer window by pressing ⌘+8 (Small size), ⌘+9 (Medium size), or ⌘+0 (Large size) instead of fiddling about by choosing Window ⇨ Viewer.

- **Show only the clips you're interested in.** When you're working in the Event Library, select the Event that contains the clips you want to work with. Then open the Show pop-up menu and choose Favorites Only or Favorites and Unmarked to make the Event browser hide clips you've rejected.

- **Make the thumbnails larger.** Click and drag the Thumbnail Size slider to the right to pump up the size of the thumbnails and make their contents easier to see.

- **Adjust the number of frames per filmstrip.** Either in the Event browser or in the Storyboard, click and drag the Filmstrip Length slider to increase or decrease the number of frames each filmstrip displays.

Genius How many frames you need to have displayed in a filmstrip depends on how long the clip is and how much its contents change. For example, a long clip of a little-changing scene usually needs fewer frames displayed than a shorter take in which the camera pans or the subjects move. You may well need to change this setting as you move from clip to clip.

Adjusting the length of a clip

One of the most important edits you'll need to make is adjusting the length of a clip. You can do this by trimming off a selected part of the clip or cutting the clip down to only the part you selected, adjusting the clip's playing length using the Trim Clip pane, or making precise adjustments using the Fine Tuning buttons.

Trimming off the beginning or end of a clip

When you need to trim off the beginning or end of a clip, follow these steps:

1. **On the Storyboard, click the clip to display a yellow selection rectangle around it.**

2. **Click and drag the left selection handle to the point at which you want to start deleting.** If you want to start deleting from the beginning of the clip, you don't need to move the selection handle.

3. **Click and drag the right selection handle to the point where you want to stop deleting.** If you want to stop deleting at the very end of the clip, you don't need to move the selection handle. Figure 5.10 shows an example of dragging the right selection handle.

Action button

5.10 Click and drag the yellow selection handle to select the part of the clip you want to delete. The white figures show the clip's length in seconds and tenths of seconds. The cog button is the action button, which you'll meet shortly.

4. **Press Delete, choose Edit ⇨ Delete Selection, or Control+click or right-click and click Delete Selection.**

If you want to remove the selection and paste it into another part of the movie, Control+click or right-click and choose Cut instead of deleting the selection. Move the mouse pointer to where you want to paste the selection, Control+click or right-click, and then choose Paste.

You can also cut and paste a selection by using the menu commands (Edit ⇨ Cut and Edit ⇨ Paste) or the standard keyboard shortcuts (⌘+X for cut and ⌘+V for paste).

Note

Trimming a clip to only the part you want

The second way to approach the process of trimming a clip is to select the part you want and then dispose of the rest. Here's how to do that:

1. **On the Storyboard, click the clip to display a yellow selection rectangle around it.**

2. **Click and drag the left selection handle to the beginning of the part you want to keep.**

3. **Click and drag the right selection handle to the end of the part you want to keep.**

4. **Control+click or right-click in the selection and choose Trim to Selection.** iMovie gets rid of the parts you didn't select, leaving those you selected.

Genius

You can also trim a clip to the current selection by pressing ⌘+B or choosing Clip ➪ Trim to Selection.

Trimming a clip to the playhead's position

When you need to trim a clip quickly, try using the Trim to Playhead command. This command trims all the frames in the clip that lie to the right of the playhead's current position.

To use the Trim to Playhead command, skim through the clip on the Storyboard until you reach the last frame you want to keep. Then Control+click or right-click at that point, and click Trim to Playhead on the context menu.

Adjusting a clip with the Clip Trimmer

When you need to dig deeper into a clip than you can on the Storyboard, open the clip in the Clip Trimmer.

Here's how to use the Clip Trimmer:

1. **Open the Clip Trimmer (see Figure 5.11) by moving the mouse pointer over a clip, clicking the Action button that appears (pointed out in Figure 5.10), and then clicking Clip Trimmer.** You can also choose Window ➪ Clip Trimmer, or press ⌘+R.

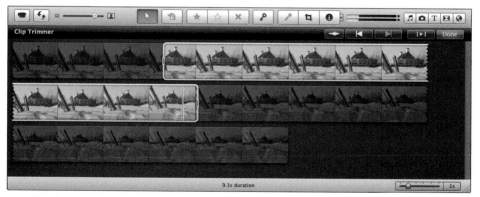

5.11 The Clip Trimmer appears in place of the Event browser and gives you a full-length view of the clip you're editing. The selection rectangle shows the part of the clip you're using.

2. **Change the part of the clip you're using.** For example

  - Click and drag one of the selection handles to increase or reduce the amount of footage selected.

  - Click and drag the bottom edge or top edge of the selection rectangle to move it along the clip without changing its length.

  - Point at the end of the clip you want to move, and then press Option+left arrow or Option+right arrow to move it one frame at a time.

3. **When you select the part of the clip you want, click Done to close the Clip Trimmer and return to the Storyboard.**

Making a short adjustment with the Fine Tuning buttons

When you need to adjust the length of a clip by less than a second, use the Fine Tuning buttons. The Fine Tuning controls are turned off by default in iMovie, so you must turn them on before you can use them. To do so, choose iMovie ⇨ Preferences, click the Browser tab, and then select the Show Fine Tuning controls check box.

To use the Fine Tuning controls, follow these steps:

1. **Move the mouse pointer over the clip so that the Fine Tuning control buttons appear on it (see Figure 5.12).**

Fine Tune Clip Start   Fine Tune Clip End

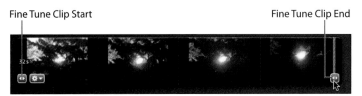

5.12 The Fine Tuning buttons appear when you position the mouse pointer over a clip on the Storyboard.

2. **Click the Fine Tune Clip Start button or the Fine Tune Clip End button to display an orange handle for trimming the start or end of the clip.**

3. **Click and drag the handle to the left or right, as appropriate.**

Genius

To quickly change the beginning or end of a clip by only a few frames, move the mouse pointer toward the end you want to affect. Press Option+left arrow to move the end to the left or Option+right arrow to move the end to the right.

Figure 5.13 shows an example of trimming the end of a clip. The readout shows the number of frames you moved the clip end and the current length of the clip.

You can also display the orange handle for fine-tuning a clip by holding down ⌘+Option while you point to the clip's start or end. If you

5.13 Click and drag the orange handle to fine-tune the start or end of a clip.

deselected the Show Fine Tuning buttons check box in iMovie's Preferences, you need to use this technique because the Fine Tuning buttons won't appear when you point to a clip.

Splitting a clip into two or three pieces

Often, you'll need to split a clip into two so that you can use different parts of it easily in different sections of your movie. Or you may want to insert another clip — for example, a cutaway — between the different parts of the clip to add visual interest.

From the Storyboard, you can split a clip into either two pieces (a beginning piece and an end piece) or three pieces (a beginning piece, a middle piece, and an end piece). Here's what to do:

1. **In the Storyboard, select the part of the clip that you want to split off from the rest.** You can split a clip into two parts by selecting either the beginning or the end, or split it into three parts by selecting a section in the middle.

2. **Choose Clip ⇨ Split Clip or press ⌘+Shift+S.** iMovie splits the clip into the required number of parts.

Cropping a video

To get the best effect in your video, you may need to crop a clip so that only part of it appears on the screen. Cropping applies to an entire clip rather than just part of it, but you can split off the part you want to crop into a separate clip by using the technique just described.

Note

You can crop a frame down to 50 percent of the original dimensions. As you'd imagine, quality suffers when you crop an image because the remaining data must appear at a larger size to occupy the whole frame. But you can usually get good results if you crop standard-definition video only a modest amount. And if you have high-definition video, you can crop up to that 50 percent limit and still retain good quality.

Here's how to crop a clip:

1. **Click the clip in the Event browser or on the Storyboard.** iMovie displays the clip in the viewer.

2. **Click the Crop button on the toolbar.** iMovie displays the cropping and rotation buttons in the viewer.

3. **Click the Crop button in the upper-left corner of the viewer.** iMovie displays green cropping handles and a frame in the viewer (see Figure 5.14) and adds a red dot to the playhead on the clip.

4. **Click and drag a corner handle to resize the cropping area proportionally.** iMovie stops you at the 50 percent limit of size and height if you drag that far.

5. **If necessary, reposition the cropping area by clicking and dragging anywhere in the rectangle.** The mouse pointer becomes a hand when it's in the cropping area.

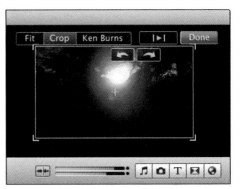

5.14 Click and drag the green cropping handles to select the part of the frame you want to keep. The green cross shows the middle of the cropping area.

6. **Check the effect of the cropping in either of these ways:**

   - Click and drag the red dot on the Playhead to skim through the crop.
   - Click the Play button in the viewer to play the clip.

7. **Click Done to apply your cropping.**

Genius

Cropping is an effect that you apply to the clip rather than a change that you make to it, so you can change the cropping if you need to. Just open the clip for cropping again, and choose the cropping effect you want. If you want to get rid of the cropping, click the Fit button.

Adjusting color

One of the neatest things that iMovie can do is adjust the color of your video clips. So if you find that a precious clip is overexposed or underexposed, or if the color balance makes everyone's otherwise healthy face look green, iMovie may be able to save the day.

To adjust the color of a clip, follow these steps:

1. **In the Event browser or the Storyboard, click the clip whose colors you want to adjust.** As usual, if you click the clip in the Event browser, the color adjustments apply to all projects that use the clip. If you click the clip on the Storyboard, the adjustments apply only to the current project.

2. **Click the Inspector button on the toolbar and then click the Video tab in the Inspector window (see Figure 5.15).** iMovie also adds a playhead with a red dot to the clip.

3. **Click and drag the playhead dot to select a frame that gives you a good view of the colors you want to adjust.**

4. **If you want to use iMovie's automatic best guess at the color adjustments needed, click the Auto button.** If you

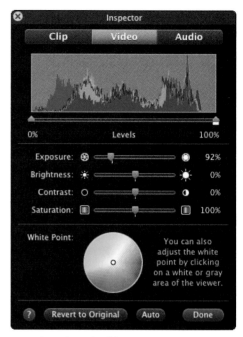

5.15 The Video tab of the Inspector window lets you correct the exposure, brightness, contrast, saturation, and color balance of your video clips.

don't like the effects, click the Revert to Original button to restore the previous color balance. If you do like them, either adjust them further as described next, or simply skip the remaining steps in this list.

Note

Like cropping, color adjustments apply to the whole of a clip rather than part of it, so if only a part of a clip needs adjustment, you will need to split it off into a separate clip, as described earlier in this chapter.

5. **If necessary, use the histogram at the top of the Video tab to change the overall color balance:**

   - Click and drag the black slider to the right to add black tones to the clip.

   - Click and drag the white slider to the left to add white tones to the clip.

Genius The histogram shows how the colors in the selected video frame are distributed between pure black (at the left end, 0 percent) and pure white (at the right end, 100 percent). The red, green, and blue show the individual red, green, and blue color channels in the image.

6. **To adjust the exposure of the clip, click and drag the Exposure slider.** The scale goes from 0 percent to 100 percent, but generally you'll need to make only small changes to improve the clip's look considerably.

7. **To adjust the brightness of the clip, click and drag the Brightness slider.**

8. **To increase or decrease the contrast, click and drag the Contrast slider.**

9. **To boost or lower the intensity of the colors, click and drag the Saturation slider.**

Genius If you want to adjust the red, green, and blue levels separately, you need to add the Red Gain slider, Green Gain slider, and Blue Gain slider to the Video tab of the Inspector window. To do so, choose iMovie ⇨ Preferences, click the General tab in the iMovie Preferences window, select the Show Advanced Tools check box, and then click the Close button (the red button at the left end of the title bar).

10. **To correct the clip's white balance, set the white point by clicking the appropriate color on the color wheel or clicking a white or gray area of the frame in the viewer.** You may need to try several colors to find one that gives the look you want.

11. **When you're satisfied with the effect you produced, click Done to close the Inspector window.**

Genius Getting color adjustments right can be a ticklish process you don't want to repeat unnecessarily. When you apply color adjustments to one clip, you can apply the same adjustments to another clip by copying them and pasting them. Control+click or right-click the clip you fixed and choose Copy, and then select the target clip and choose Edit ⇨ Paste Adjustments ⇨ Video. Repeat this trick for other clips as needed.

Rotating video

Another effect that iMovie lets you apply to a clip is rotation. Again, this applies to the whole clip rather than part of it, so you may need to split a clip into smaller clips to separate the footage you want to rotate.

To rotate a clip, follow these steps:

1. **Click the clip in the Event browser or on the Storyboard.** iMovie displays the clip in the viewer.

2. **Click the Crop button on the toolbar (or press C).** iMovie displays the cropping and rotation buttons in the viewer.

3. **Click the Rotate Counterclockwise button or the Rotate Clockwise button in the viewer.** Each click gives you a 90-degree rotation in that direction.

4. **If necessary, crop the video to make it the right aspect ratio in its new orientation.**

5. **Click Done to apply the rotation and any cropping.**

Restoring a clip to how it was before

Because iMovie's editing is nondestructive, you can always restore a clip to the way it was before. To restore a clip, open the tool you used to edit it, and then remove the change you made. For example

- **Remove cropping.** Click the clip, and then click the Crop button to display the cropping and rotation buttons. Click the Fit button to fit the video back to the frame, and then click Done.

- **Remove color adjustments.** Click the clip, click the Inspector button, click the Video tab, click the Revert to Original button, and then click Done.

- **Remove rotation.** Click the clip, click the Crop button to display the cropping and rotation buttons, and then click the rotation button needed to put the clip the right way around again. Change the cropping as well if necessary. Click Done to apply the change.

Deleting your rejected footage

Video tends to hog hard drive space, and even with today's ever-larger hard drives, creating and editing movies can run you out of space quickly. You can reclaim disk space by deleting your rejected footage, as described here, or use iMovie's Space Saver feature (described next) to attack the problem even more aggressively.

Genius

The reason iMovie doesn't automatically delete your rejected footage is that you may need it again. For example, you may need to lengthen a clip by using some of the rejected footage, or you may simply have rejected some valuable footage by accident when working quickly.

Here's how to delete your rejected footage:

1. **In the Event Library, click the Event from which you want to remove the footage.** You can select several Events if necessary. For example, select a month (or even a year) to work with all the Events it contains.

2. **Open the Show pop-up menu and choose Rejected Only to make iMovie display only the rejected clips (see Figure 5.16).**

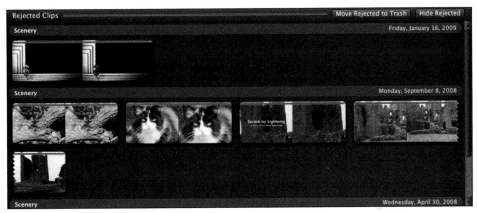

5.16 Review your rejected clips before clicking Move Rejected to Trash.

3. **Review the clips to make sure there's nothing valuable.** Depending on how many clips are involved, you may want to play them all or simply glance at the filmstrips and skim any clips you don't recognize.

4. **Click Move Rejected to Trash in the Event browser or choose File ⇨ Move Rejected Clips to Trash.** iMovie displays the Move Rejected Clips to Trash dialog (see Figure 5.17) to make sure you understand what's happening.

5.17 Confirm your decision to trash the rejected clips from the Event.

5. **Click Move to Trash to move the clips to the Trash.** iMovie changes the selection in the Show pop-up menu to Favorites and Unmarked.

6. **When you're ready to empty the Trash, click the Trash icon on the Dock, and then click the Empty Trash button.**

Reclaiming hard drive space with Space Saver

If you deleted your rejected footage (as just described) but you need more space, try the Space Saver feature. Space Saver provides a way to grab all the frames that you haven't used or made into favorites — and then deletes them.

Caution Don't run Space Saver casually because it's important you understand what the command does before you use it to delete footage you'll later regret losing. Usually, the right time to run Space Saver is when you finish creating a project and need to get rid of all the extra space it consumes on your Mac's hard drives.

Here's how to run Space Saver:

1. **Select the Event you want to strip of unused video.** You can select several Events if you want.

2. **Choose File ⇨ Space Saver.** iMovie displays the Space Saver dialog (see Figure 5.18).

> Reclaim space on your hard disk by moving rejected clips to the trash.
>
> Reject entire clips if any portion is:
> ☑ Not added to any project
> ☑ Not marked as Favorite
> ☐ Not marked with a keyword
>
> (Cancel)   (Reject and Review)

5.18 Use the Space Saver feature to reclaim valuable space on your Mac's hard drive by disposing of clips you're not using.

3. **In the Reject entire clips if any portion is area, make sure that only the check boxes you need are selected:**

- **Not added to any project.** Select this check box if you want iMovie to get rid of any clips that you haven't made part of any project.

- **Not marked as Favorite.** Select this check box if you want iMovie to dispose of any clips you haven't marked as favorites.

- **Not marked with a keyword.** Select this check box if you want iMovie to dispose of any clips you haven't marked with one or more keywords.

4. **Click Reject and Review.** iMovie closes the dialog and switches the Show pop-up menu to Rejected Only, marking the clips with the red bar across the top that means they're rejected.

5. **Skim or play the clips to make sure there's nothing you want to keep.**

6. **Click Move Rejected to Trash at the right end of the Rejected Clips bar.** iMovie displays the Move Rejected Clips to Trash dialog (shown earlier) to confirm the decision.

7. **Click Move to Trash to move the clips to the Trash.** iMovie changes the selection in the Show pop-up menu to Favorites and Unmarked.

8. **When you're ready to empty the Trash, click the Trash icon on the Dock, and then click the Empty Trash button.**

Genius

If you realize you've rejected vital footage, choose Edit ⇨ Undo Move Rejected Clips to Trash immediately in iMovie. If it's too late for that, but you haven't yet emptied the Trash, quit iMovie, open the Trash folder and go spelunking in the iMovie Temporary Items folders you'll find in it. You can click and drag the items named clip and the date and time (for example, clip-2011-02-01 19;57;42.mov) to the Event's folder in the ~/Movies/iMovie Events folder to restore the clips. Click and drag the contents of the iMovie Thumbnails folder in the iMovie Temporary Items folder in the Trash to the iMovie Thumbnails folder inside the Event. Restart iMovie.

Finding out where a clip lives

When you place many clips on the Storyboard, you may need to find out which Event a particular clip belongs to. To do so, Control+click or right-click the clip on the Storyboard and choose Reveal in Event Browser.

iMovie can also show you a clip's file in the Finder, which is useful when you want to duplicate a clip or share it with someone else. Just Control+click or right-click the clip on the Storyboard or in the Event browser and choose Reveal in Finder. iMovie opens a Finder window showing the folder containing the clip.

Adding Still Photos to a Movie

As its name suggests, iMovie is primarily designed for working with movie footage, but the application also makes it easy to use still photos in your movies. Completely still photos tend to lack visual excitement compared with moving pictures, but iMovie lets you easily apply the Ken Burns Effect to add life and movement to your still photos.

Preparing your photos for use in iMovie

To get your photos ready for use in iMovie, you'll normally want to import them into iPhoto, as described in Chapter 1. Use iPhoto's tools for rotating your photos, editing them, cropping them, and adjusting the colors as necessary.

Genius

If you need to use a photo differently in iMovie than in iPhoto, duplicate the photo in iPhoto (press ⌘+D), and then change the duplicate so that it's suitable for iMovie.

Importing a photo into iMovie

To import a photo into iMovie from iPhoto, you use the Photos browser pane. Click the Photos browser button (see Figure 5.19) to open the Photos browser pane. You can also choose Window ⇨ Photos or press ⌘+2.

After you open the Photos browser pane (see Figure 5.20), use its controls to navigate to the photo you want.

Photos browser   Titles browser

Music and sound   Transition
effect browser   browser

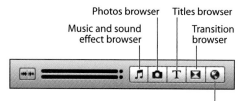

Maps, backgrounds, and
animation browser

5.19 Clicking the Photos browser button is the easiest way to open the Photos browser pane for inserting a photo in your movie.

Genius

Alternatively, click in the Search box and type a search term. You can click the pop-up button at the left end of the Search box and choose Keywords from the pop-up menu to restrict the search to items you've tagged with a particular keyword in iPhoto. (This is another good reason to tag your photos in iPhoto.) You can also restrict the search by choosing Faces, Places, or Rating from the Search pop-up menu at the bottom of the Photos browser pane.

5.20 Use the Photos browser pane to add photos to iMovie from your iPhoto albums.

Here's how to find the photo you want and insert it in your iMovie project:

1. **In the Albums pop-up menu at the top of the Photos browser pane, choose the album that contains the photo you want.** For example

   - If the photo is in the last set of photos you imported, choose Last Import in the Albums pop-up menu.

   - If you want to see the last year's worth of photos, choose Last 12 Months.

   - If you want to see all the photos from a particular location, choose that location in the Places list.

   - If you want to find photos of a particular person, click Faces.

2. **Select the photo or photos you want.** If necessary, click and drag the Thumbnail Size slider in the lower-right corner of the Photos Browser pane to zoom in on the thumbnails (or zoom out so that you can see more at once).

3. **Click and drag the photo or photos to the Storyboard.** iMovie displays a vertical green line to show where they'll land.

153

Setting the duration for a photo

When you place a photo on the Storyboard, iMovie automatically assigns a 4-second duration to it. Try playing back the part of the movie that contains the photo and see if this is suitable. If not, set the duration like this:

1. **Click the photo to select it.**

2. **Click the Inspector button on the toolbar (or press I).** The Inspector window appears.

3. **Click the Clip tab (see Figure 5.21).**

4. **Type the duration in the Duration box.**

5. **If you want to use this duration for all your photos, select the Applies to all stills check box.**

6. **Click Done to close the Inspector window.** Try playing back the movie around the photo, and make sure the setting is suitable.

5.21 Set the duration (in seconds and frames) for iMovie to display the photo.

Setting cropping and Ken Burns Effect

When you place a still photo on the Storyboard, iMovie automatically applies a Ken Burns Effect to it with a modest amount of zoom — just enough to give that elusive soupçon of visual interest. For some photos, you may want to remove the Ken Burns Effect and simply show the full picture (or a cropped version of it) without panning and zooming. More likely, though, you'll want to set up a custom Ken Burns Effect to highlight the parts of the picture you want your audience to concentrate on.

Here's how to crop a picture or customize the Ken Burns Effect:

1. **Click the photo on the Storyboard to display it in the viewer.**

2. **Click the Crop button on the toolbar to display the cropping tools for still photos (see Figure 5.22).**

3. **To crop the photo without adding the Ken Burns Effect, follow these steps:**

    ○ Click the Crop tab if it's not already selected.

    ○ Click and drag one or more corners of the green cropping frame to select the crop size you want.

    ○ If necessary, click and drag the cropping frame so that it contains the part of the photo you want to use.

    ○ Skip to Step 5 in this list.

4. **To customize the Ken Burns Effect, follow these steps:**

    ○ Click the Ken Burns tab if it's not already selected.

    ○ Click and drag a corner or side of the green Start rectangle to select the photo size to display at the beginning of the pan and zoom. If necessary, click within the Start rectangle and drag it to select a different area of the picture. The green cross shows you where the middle of the Start rectangle is, and the yellow arrow shows you the direction and extent of the pan you'll get.

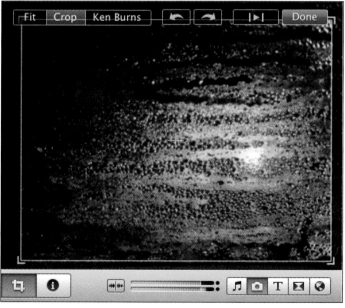

5.22 The cropping tools for still photos.

- Click and drag a corner or side of the red End rectangle to select the photo size to display at the end of the pan and zoom. As with the Start rectangle, click within the End rectangle and drag it to select a different area of the picture. The red cross shows you where the middle of the End rectangle is. Figure 5.23 shows an example.

- Click the Play button to view the effect and judge how well it works.

5. **Click Done to apply the cropping or Ken Burns Effect to the photo.**

Genius

If you need to swap the start position and end position of the Ken Burns Effect, click the Switch Beginning and End button, the little button bearing two curving arrows. And if you need to create a multistage Ken Burns effect, insert two copies of the picture. Set the first pan and zoom on the first copy, and then the second pan and zoom on the second copy. Make sure the start point of the second Ken Burns Effect matches the end point of the first, so there's a smooth transition.

Start   End   Switch beginning
rectangle   rectangle   and end button

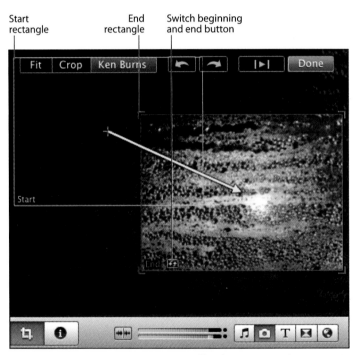

5.23 You can create a custom Ken Burns Effect by resizing and repositioning the green Start rectangle and the red End rectangle. The yellow arrow shows you the direction and extent of the movement.

Exporting a still picture from a video clip

One trick you'll probably want to use when working with still pictures is creating a still picture from a video clip. This trick is great when you've shot a brief amount of compelling movie footage and you want to make the most of it — for example, by using the Ken Burns Effect to zoom and pan over it.

Genius

You can also use your still pictures to create a freeze-frame scene, making the action stop for a moment — or as many moments as you choose — before restarting again. Or you can use a still picture with a Ken Burns Effect, followed by another still picture of the same frame, to create an effect of panning and zooming, then holding on the subject.

Here's how to export a still picture from a video clip:

1. **Either in the Event browser or on the Storyboard, skim through the clip to the frame you want.**

2. **Control+click or right-click to display the context menu, then click the appropriate command:**

   ● **Storyboard.** Click Add Freeze Frame. iMovie creates a still picture from the frame and adds it to the Storyboard, splitting the clip with the still picture.

   ● **Event browser.** Click Add Still Frame to Project. iMovie creates a still picture from the frame and adds it to the end of the Storyboard.

Genius

When you create a still photo from a clip in the Event Library, iMovie automatically applies a small Ken Burns Effect to the still picture, so you'll probably want to customize the effect, as described in the previous section. When you create a still picture from a clip on the Storyboard, iMovie doesn't apply a Ken Burns Effect.

3. **If you created the still picture in the Event browser, move the still picture to where you want it to appear in the project.**

Genius

If you want to use the still picture elsewhere in Mac OS X, Control+click or right-click the picture's clip on the Storyboard and choose Reveal in Finder. iMovie opens a Finder window showing the contents of the Stills folder within the project. You can then copy the picture file to wherever you need it.

How Do I Finish My Movie and Share It?

You Tube™ **Publish your project to YouTube**

Account:	edsempio
Password:	••••••••••••••
Category:	Howto & Style
Title:	Bike Workshop 4: Trueing a Wheel
Description:	Bike expert Rusty Wheeler shows you how to fix a bent bike wheel. All you need is a spoke wrench -- and your bike!
Tags:	bike bicycle workshop fix true wheel straighten

Add... Remove

	iPhone	iPad	▲tv	Computer	YouTube	
Size to publish:						
○ Mobile	●	●			●	480x360 ⓘ
● Medium	●	●	●	●	●	**640x480** ⓘ
○ Large	●	●	●	●	●	720x540 ⓘ
○ HD 720p	●	●		●	●	1280x720 ⓘ
○ HD 1080p				●	●	1920x1080 ⓘ

☐ Make this movie personal

Cancel   Next

With your clips placed in the right order and edited to fit in with each other, your movie is starting to look like a finished product. Now you need to increase its impact by adding titles, transitions, and audio, and polish the movie until you're satisfied with it. It may then feel like it's time to rest on your laurels — but what you should do first is create a trailer and share your movie. iMovie makes it easy to share your movie with iTunes on your Mac or with the world by publishing it to YouTube or your MobileMe Gallery. When you need to use your movie elsewhere, you can export it either as an MPEG-4 movie file or a wide variety of other file formats.

Applying a Theme to a Movie

To make editing your videos as effortless as possible, iMovie includes a variety of themes that you can use to give your movie projects a kick-start. Each theme comes with its own set of titles and transitions that are added automatically, saving you lots of work. iMovie has seven themes: Photo Album, Bulletin Board, Comic Book, Scrapbook, Filmstrip, News, and Sports. If any of these themes is suitable for your project, you can cut down on your production time by applying the theme.

As you saw in Chapter 4, you can choose a theme when you first start your project or go without a theme by choosing the No Theme option. You can change the theme at any point like this:

1. **Open the project for editing on the Storyboard if it's not already open.**

2. **Choose File ⇨ Project Theme, or press ⌘+Shift+J. iMovie displays the Project Themes dialog (see Figure 6.1).**

6.1 Use the Project Themes dialog to switch quickly from one theme to another.

3. **Click the theme you want to use.**

4. **When using a theme, select the Automatically add transitions and titles check box if you want to use the transitions and titles built in to the theme.** When using No Theme, you can add default transitions by selecting the Automatically add check box and choosing the transition type in the pop-up menu.

5. **When you choose not to use automatic transitions in a project that already contains transitions, iMovie expands the dialog (see Figure 6.2), and you use the following options to decide how to handle the ends of clips and the current transitions:**

   ● **Remove transitions and extend clip ends.** Select this option button to make iMovie remove the transitions and extend the clip ends to fill the space that the transitions previously occupied. This option keeps your movie the same length, so it's the best choice if you've already created an audio track synchronized with the movie.

- **Remove transitions and maintain clip durations.** Select this option button if you want to remove the transitions but keep the clips at their current lengths. Choose this option if you don't want to reveal extra footage at the end of clips that was hidden (or partly hidden) by transitions. This option shortens your movie, so you will usually need to rework the audio track.

- **Leave transitions in current locations.** Select this option button if you want to keep your existing transitions but not let iMovie add any other transitions automatically. You can then change the existing transitions manually as needed.

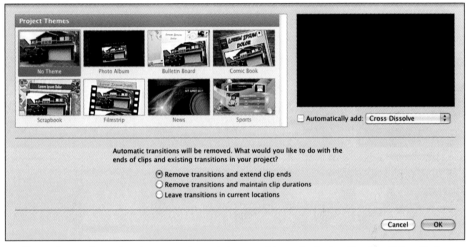

6.2 If your theme change involves removing existing transitions, the Project Themes dialog displays an extra section to let you decide how to deal with them.

6. **Click OK.** iMovie adds the theme's titles and transitions.

Adding Titles to a Movie

Most movies need one or more title screens at the beginning and credits at the end — and many require other text screens strategically placed within the movie.

If your project uses automatic titles as part of its theme, it may already have the titles you need. If your project doesn't use automatic titles, or if you want to supplement the existing titles, you can add titles manually.

161

To start working with titles, open the Titles Browser by clicking the Titles Browser button on the toolbar, choosing Window ⇨ Titles, or pressing ⌘+3. Figure 6.3 shows the Titles Browser as it appears for a project that uses a theme. The top line of titles comes from the theme (in this case, the News theme).

iMovie provides more than 30 styles of titles (plus four extra theme-specific styles if you have a theme applied), so you have plenty of choices. Many of the titles are animated, which can be very effective if used in moderation. (To see a preview of a title's animation effect, hover the mouse pointer over the title thumbnail in the Titles Browser.) In most cases, you'll use the animated titles on their own, such as the Scrolling Credits title style shown in Figure 6.4.

6.3 The Titles Browser pane gives you instant access to all iMovie's various titles.

You can use the static title styles on their own or superimpose them over a clip. For example, the Gradient – Black title style is a classy way to identify what's on-screen (see Figure 6.5) or provide a name for an upcoming video segment.

6.4 Some title styles, such as Scrolling Credits shown here, are best applied on their own.

6.5 You can superimpose titles on existing video clips. This style, Gradient – Black, gives a discreet effect.

Applying the title

To apply a title, simply click it in the Titles Browser and drag it to where you want to place it on the Storyboard. You can either place a title on its own or superimpose it on a clip.

Applying a title on its own

To place the title on its own, follow these steps:

1. **Click and drag the title to the Storyboard so that iMovie displays a vertical green bar between clips where you want to place it (see Figure 6.6).**

6.6 Placing a title between two clips adds to the movie's length and file size.

2. **Drop the title in the Storyboard.**
   iMovie displays the Choose Background window (see Figure 6.7).

3. **Click the background color or pattern you want to use for the title.** iMovie extends the movie by adding enough frames to cover the duration of the title (4 seconds, by default) and displays a title box over the new frames.

4. **Type the title text, as described later in this chapter.**

5. **Change the duration of the title, as described later in this chapter, to suit your needs.**

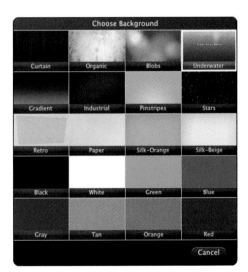

6.7 When you place a title between clips, you get to choose the background color or pattern for the title you're adding.

163

Superimposing a title on a clip

To superimpose the title on a clip, click and drag it to the clip on which you want to place it. You can drag it to the middle of the clip to use the title for the entire clip, to the beginning to use it for the first part of the clip, or to the end to use it for the last part.

As you drag the title, iMovie displays shading on the clip and a time readout so you can see what's covered (see Figure 6.8).

After you drop the title, it appears above the clip in a little balloon (see Figure 6.9), and you can drag the sides of the balloon to extend or shorten the time the title appears. You can fine-tune these settings later as needed. Superimposing a title on a clip works well for most title styles.

6.8 When you drag a title onto a clip, the shaded area and time readout show you where and how long the title will play.

Applying theme titles

As you saw earlier, when you apply a theme to your project you can choose to have iMovie add titles and transitions automatically. When you do this, iMovie adds two titles to your project automatically:

6.9 The title appears as a balloon above the clip. You can drag the ends of the balloon to control when the title plays.

- **Opening title.** This is the name of your project superimposed on the first few seconds of the movie.

- **Closing title.** This displays "Directed By" followed by your user account name, which is superimposed over the last few seconds of the movie.

Genius

If you put a title in the wrong place, you can remove it by Control+clicking or right-clicking it on the Storyboard and then choosing Delete Selection.

iMovie also adds four theme-related title styles to the top of the Titles Browser (look back to Figure 6.1), so you can also add your own theme titles.

Adding the text to the title

When you put the title on the Storyboard, you can edit its text by clicking the title's box on the Storyboard and then working in the viewer. Click to select a line of the placeholder text and then type the text you want.

Most of the title styles include a subtitle. Select that line too and type a subtitle if you want one; if not, just press Delete to delete the subtitle.

6.10 The iMovie Choose Font panel gives you a quick and easy way to apply font formatting to titles when you're not using a theme.

Genius If you're using a theme, iMovie hides the Show Fonts button to encourage you to stick with the theme's fonts. You can change the theme by choosing Text ⇨ Show Fonts (or pressing ⌘+T) and working in the Fonts window, as described later in this chapter.

To change the font used in a movie to which you haven't given a theme, select the part of the title you want to affect, and then click Show Fonts to display the Choose Font panel (see Figure 6.10). The main part of the window is divided into three columns: The left column is the font family; the middle column is the font color; and the right column is the font size. Click the item you want in each column to set the basic font. You can fine-tune the font by clicking the Style buttons (from left to right, Bold, Italic, and Shadow) and Alignment buttons (from left to right, Align Left, Center, Justify, and Align Right).

When you finish using the Choose Font panel, click Done to close it.

Note Remember that you can customize the layout of the Choose Font panel. Choose iMovie ⇨ Preferences, click the Fonts tab, and then customize each of the nine font family choices and the nine font color choices.

If you need more font-formatting options, click System Font Panel in the Choose Font panel window to display the Mac OS X Fonts window (see Figure 6.11). You can then work with the full set of font options like this:

Text strikethrough   Document color

Text underline   Font color

6.11 You can apply a wide range of font formatting to any titles that need it.

● **Font.** Choose a font collection in the Collections box (or simply choose All Fonts), and then choose the font family in the Family box. In the Typeface box, choose the typeface — for example, Regular, Italic, Bold, or Bold Italic. Then choose the size in the Size list, or drag the Size slider beside the Size list; you can also type the font size you want in the Size box.

● **Underline and Strikethrough.** Use the Text Underline pop-up menu and the Text Strikethrough menu if you need to apply these effects.

● **Text Color.** Click the Text Color button to open the Colors window, pick the color, and then click the Close button (the red button) to return to the Fonts window.

● **Style.** Click the Bold button, Italic button, Underline button, or Outline button, as needed.

● **Alignment.** Click the Align Left button, Center button, Justify button, or Align Right button to align the title's paragraph with the margins.

In iMovie the Document Color control in the Fonts window doesn't change the background color of free-standing titles.

Note

- **Line Spacing.** Drag the slider to increase the line spacing. This is especially useful for spacing out scrolling credits.

- **Kerning.** Click the left button to move the selected letters closer together, or click the right button to move them farther apart.

- **Baseline.** Click the left button to move the baseline of the selected letters down, or click the right button to move the baseline up.

- **Outline.** Drag the slider to change the strength of the outline.

To see the effect of the titles you create, you have two choices:

- **In the Fonts window, click Play in the viewer.**

- **In the Choose Font panel, place the mouse pointer near the beginning of the font family box you chose, and then move the pointer to the right.** As you move the pointer, a playback bar appears inside the box, and the viewer displays the title effect. You can use the same technique in any font family box, any font color box, and any font size box.

When you finish working on the text of the titles, click Done.

Changing the duration and timing of the title

As you saw, when you drop a title on a clip, you can set the title's approximate duration by dragging it to the middle, beginning, or end of the clip on which you're placing it. Here's how you can fine-tune the duration and timing of a title:

1. **To change the duration of the title, position the mouse pointer over the beginning or end of the title so that the pointer changes to a two-headed arrow, and then drag to the left or right.** As you drag, iMovie displays the new duration on the left side of the title box.

2. **To change when the title plays, click the title box on the Storyboard and drag it to where you want it.** The playhead on the clip shows where the title will start, and iMovie tells you how far from the beginning of the clip the title will start (see Figure 6.12). Watch the viewer to get a close-up on the frame that the playhead is over.

Genius

You can also use the Inspector dialog to change the duration of a title. Click the title box and the click the Inspector button in the toolbar. In the Inspector dialog, use the Duration text box to type the duration. If you want to override the default fade and fade out times, select the Manual option and then drag the slider to set the fade time you want to use. Click Done to put the new settings into effect.

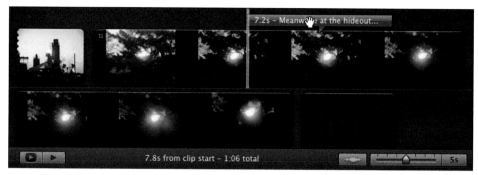

6.12 Click and drag the title to where you want it to start.

Adding Transitions to a Movie

When one clip of your movie ends, the next clip begins. The changeover between the two is called the transition. If you don't apply one of iMovie's transition effects (or let iMovie apply a transition automatically), you get what's called a straight cut — iMovie blips straight from the last frame of the first clip to the first frame of the second clip.

If those last and first frames are similar in contents, a straight cut can work well. If the contents are substantially different, a straight cut can produce a jarring effect. Sometimes, you may want to give the audience that jar, but often, you will want to treat the audience more gently.

To reduce the disjunction of the change between two clips, you can apply one of iMovie's transition effects to the transition between those clips.

To start working with transitions, open the Transitions browser by clicking the Transitions Browser button on the toolbar, choosing Window ⇨ Transitions, or pressing ⌘+4. Figure 6.13 shows the Transitions browser.

6.13 The Transitions browser lets you apply any of iMovie's transitions to your clips in moments. Point to a transition to preview its effect.

Choosing a suitable transition to apply to a clip

The key to using transitions successfully in your movies is to use the right transition at the right time. Table 6.1 explains the various types of transitions that iMovie provides.

Note iMovie provides 24 transitions for use with all projects. If you apply a theme to your project, iMovie adds an extra four transitions to the top of the Transitions browser. You can apply a theme right from the Transitions browser, too: click Set Theme, click the theme you want, and then click OK.

Table 6.1 iMovie's Transitions and When to Use Them

Transition Name	Explanation
Circle Open	Displays a small circle on the first clip that gradually opens to reveal the contents of the second clip. This is a dramatic effect that suggests the second clip is springing from the first.
Circle Close	Draws the first clip gradually into a circle that shrinks down, revealing the second clip, and then disappears. This is a dramatic effect that suggests the first clip is vanishing into the distance.
Cross Blur	Gradually cross fades from the first clip to the second clip, where the second clip starts off blurry and gradually comes into focus. This is useful if you want to obscure the second clip briefly to add tension to the transition.
Cross Dissolve	Gradually cross fades from the first clip to the second clip. This transition is widely useful, and you can make it almost imperceptible by shortening it to ten frames or so.
Cross Zoom	Gradually cross fades from the first clip to the second clip, where the second clip zooms in quickly and then zooms back to its normal size. Use this transition to emphasize speed or the rapid passing of time.
Cube	Uses Apple's widely used rotating-cube effect to switch from the first clip to another. This transition suggests a complete change of focus to something happening separately in parallel. Use Cube with care because it's not subtle.
Doorway	The first clip splits vertically as though opening a double-doorway. The second clip zooms in as though entering the doorway. This is an occasionally useful transition when you need to introduce someone or something.
Fade Through Black	Fades out the end of the first clip to a black screen and then fades into the second clip. This transition is good for suggesting that whatever was happening in the first clip has ended and that the movie's subject is changing.

continued

Table 6.1 continued

Transition Name	Explanation
Fade Through White	Fades out the end of the first clip to a white screen and then fades into the second clip. This transition tends to give a ghostly feeling; use it in moderation if at all.
Mosaic	Divides the first clip into a series of small squares, each of which turns randomly to reveal parts of the second clip, which is then consolidated into the actual scene. This transition is useful for indicating that the second clip is a different aspect of, or the opposite of, the first clip in some way.
Page Curl Left	Curls down the upper-right corner of the frame of the first clip and pulls it down and across to the left, revealing the second clip underneath. This is a dramatic transition that can easily bother the audience, but it can be effective at suggesting a major change if you use it in moderation.
Page Curl Right	This is the same as Page Curl Left, except that it curls down the upper-left corner of the frame of the first clip and pulls it down and across to the right.
Puzzle Left	Three panels containing the second clip slide across the first clip in sequence, entering from different directions and starting from the right (moving to the left).
Puzzle Right	Three panels containing the second clip slide across the first clip in sequence, entering from different directions and starting from the left (moving to the right).
Ripple	Creates a ripple in the middle of the first clip as through you dropped a stone in a still pool. As the ripple spreads outward, it reveals the second clip. Use this transition with care.
Slide Left	The second clip slides across the first clip from the right, moving to the left.
Slide Right	The second clip slides across the first clip from the left, moving to the right.
Spin In	The second clip starts off in a small rectangle set at an angle. The clip gradually grows larger and rotates into place. This is a trick transition that can be effective if you use it in moderation.
Spin Out	This is the same as Spin In, except the first clip transitions out of the scene by shrinking into a small rectangle set at an angle.
Swap	This transition reduces the first clip to a thumbnail and displays it beside a thumbnail of the second clip in a distinctly Cover Flow-like arrangement. The second clip then turns and zooms into the scene. Use this transition if you want the audience to briefly compare the two scenes.
Wipe Down	Gradually wipes down across the first clip from the top, revealing the second clip.
Wipe Left	Gradually wipes left across the first clip from the right, revealing the second clip.
Wipe Right	Gradually wipes right across the first clip from the left, revealing the second clip.
Wipe Up	Gradually wipes up across the first clip from the bottom, revealing the second clip.

Caution

iMovie makes it easy to use transitions, but don't use transitions just because they're there. Before you apply a transition, always ask yourself whether the clips need the transition. If a straight cut works fine, don't embellish it. When you do apply a transition, check that it works as you intended; if not, replace it with another transition, or simply remove it.

Applying a transition between clips

To apply a transition between clips, click the transition type in the Transitions browser, drag it to the Storyboard, and then drop it between the clips you want to affect. iMovie displays a green bar to show where the transition will land, and then displays an icon representing the transition. Each transition type has a different icon, but some of the icons are hard to decipher at first.

Genius

If possible, stick with just one transition type to give your movie a consistent look, or use cross-dissolves and one other type of transition. Using many different types of transitions tends to grate on the audience.

To delete a transition, Control+click or right-click it, and then choose Delete Selection or press Delete. To replace a transition with another transition, click and drag the replacement transition on top of the existing transition, and then click Replace on the pop-up menu that iMovie displays. The replacement transition picks up the duration of the transition it replaces.

Note

If you didn't apply a theme for your project, but you did select the Add automatically check box for transitions in the Properties dialog for the movie project, iMovie automatically adds transitions of the type you choose. If you want to prevent iMovie from doing this, choose File ⇨ Project Properties, deselect the Add automatically check box, and then click OK.

Changing the transition duration

iMovie automatically makes each transition you add to your movie project the length you set in the project's Properties dialog. You can change the duration of a transition like this:

1. **Click the transition on the Storyboard.**

2. **Click the Inspector button in the toolbar.** iMovie displays the Inspector dialog for transitions.

3. **In the Duration box, type the length you want to use for the transition.**

4. **If you want iMovie to use this duration for all your transitions, select the Applies to all transitions check box.**

5. **Click Done.** iMovie applies the change.

Caution iMovie limits any transition to occupying only up to half of a clip (so that you can also put another transition at the other end of the clip). You may find this limiting with short clips because even if you set the exact transition length you want, you won't get it if the clips aren't long enough.

Adjusting the transition with the Precision Editor

When you add a transition between two clips, the increased visual appeal is sometimes offset by having a bit of your footage obscured in some way. For example, if you're using a Fade to Black transition, iMovie increasingly darkens the last few frames of the first clip, and increasingly lightens the first few frames of the second clip. Similarly, if you're using a Cross Blur transition, iMovie slowly blurs the last few frames of the first clip, and slowly focuses the first few frames of the second clip.

If those darkened or blurred frames contain frames you don't want the audience to miss, you can use the Precision Editor tool to adjust exactly where the transition occurs. So, for example, if you want fewer frames at the end of the first clip to be darkened or blurred (or whatever) during the transition, you can shift the transition toward the second clip.

Here's how to adjust a transition with the Precision Editor:

1. **Move the mouse pointer over the transition icon.** The Action button appears below the transition icon.

2. **Click the Action button and then click Precision Editor.** iMovie displays the Precision Editor in the bottom half of the window, as shown in Figure 6.14. This window has the following features:

   - The top filmstrip shows the frames from the first clip.

   - The bottom filmstrip shows the frames from the second clip.

   - The bar in the middle represents the transition.

   - The brightened frames in both filmstrips represent clip footage that appears in the movie.

- The darkened frames in both filmstrips represent clip footage that doesn't appear in the movie.

- In both filmstrips, the diagonal separation of bright and dark within the transition zone represent the progress of the transition. In the top filmstrip, for example, the decreasing brightness indicates the increase of the transition effect (such as darkening or blurring).

- You can use the Playhead to play the filmstrips (move the mouse pointer across the filmstrip) or the transition (move the mouse pointer across the transition bar).

3. **Use any of the following techniques to adjust the transition:**

   - To adjust the position of the transition relative to both clips, move the mouse pointer over the transition bar and then click and drag the bar left or right,

   - To include a particular frame in the transition, click the frame in its corresponding filmstrip.

   - To change just the start point of the transition, click and drag the left edge of the transition bar.

   - To change just the endpoint of the transition, click and drag the right edge of the transition bar.

4. **Click Done.**

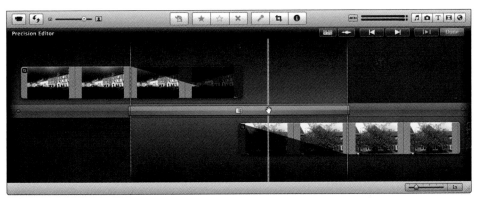

6.14 Use the Precision Editor tool to make frame-by-frame adjustments to transitions.

Adding Audio to a Movie

If you've ever seen a silent movie, you know what a huge difference a soundtrack makes. And though most video footage you shoot includes sound, you'll usually want to work on your movie's audio to make it sound right and give it the impact you need.

Understanding how iMovie handles audio

As well as helping you make the most of the audio recorded in your clips, iMovie lets you add music and sound effects to your movie:

- **A clip's own audio plays along with the clip.** You can change the audio's volume or timing, or suppress it altogether.

- **Music plays from the start of the movie and continues to the end.** Music can either be a single song or a playlist of songs that you assemble in iTunes.

- **A sound effect or song plays at the point of the clip to which you attach it.** If you move the clip, the sound effect goes along.

You can also use a song as a sound effect by attaching it to a clip rather than adding it to the movie as a whole. You can find more about this in the next section.

To add either music or sound effects, open the Music and Sound Effects browser by clicking the Music and Sound Effects browser button on the toolbar, choosing Window ⇨ Music and Sound Effects, or pressing ⌘+1. Figure 6.15 shows the Music and Sound Effects browser.

Adding music and sound effects to a movie

Here's how to add music and sound effects to a movie:

1. **In the Music and Sound Effects browser, choose the item that contains the music or sound effect you want:**

   - **GarageBand.** Choose GarageBand to see the songs you've composed in GarageBand.

   - **iTunes.** Choose iTunes to see all the songs in iTunes.

   - **A playlist or playlist folder.** Choose a particular playlist or playlist folder in iTunes to see only the songs in that playlist or the playlists in the folder.

   - **iMovie Sound Effects.** Choose this item to see iMovie's wide range of sound effects — everything from an alarm and a dog barking to a walrus roar and whale sounds.

   - **iLife Sound Effects.** Choose this item to see the hundreds of sound effects available to the iLife applications. Choose one of the folders — Ambience, Animals, Booms, Foley (extra sound effects usually added after a movie has been shot), Jingles, Machines, People, Sci-Fi, Sports, Stingers, Textures, Transportation, and Work – Home — to see only the effects that folder contains.

6.15 The Music and Sound Effects browser lets you quickly place sound effects from iMovie and iLife and songs from GarageBand and iTunes in your movie.

2. **Find the song or sound effect you want.** If necessary, click in the Search box and start typing a word to find matching items.

3. **To play a song or sound effect, click it, and then click the Play button in the lower-left corner of the Music and Sound Effects browser.** Alternatively, double-click the song or sound effect. Click the Play button or press spacebar to stop playback.

4. **Click the song or sound effect and drag it to the Storyboard:**

   - **Music.** To apply the song or sound effect as background music, drop it in open space on the Storyboard. You can easily see when it's in the right place, as iMovie displays a green border around the area in the Storyboard that will be affected and applies green shading to everything within the border (see Figure 6.16).

6.16 The green border and shading indicates that iMovie will apply the sound effect or song as music to the whole movie.

- **Sound effect.** To apply the song or sound effect as a sound effect attached to a clip, drag it over the clip, move the playhead to where you want the sound to start, and then drop the song or sound effect. The sound effect appears as a box under the clip (see Figure 6.17).

6.17 A sound effect you attach to a clip appears as a box under the clip.

Note

If you want to remove music or a sound effect, Control+click or right-click it and choose Delete Selection. You can also click the item and then press Delete.

Changing when the music starts

Once you add music to a project, iMovie keeps it in place even if you edit the movie. This is handy if you're editing the movie to suit the music, but if you want the music to suit the movie, you may need to change when the music starts. To do so, follow these steps:

1. **Make sure the music isn't selected on the Storyboard.** If it is selected, click outside its left or right border to deselect it.

2. **Click the name of the music at the top of the Storyboard (scroll up if necessary) and then drag to the right.** iMovie changes the green shading to purple and lets you move the beginning of the music (see Figure 6.18).

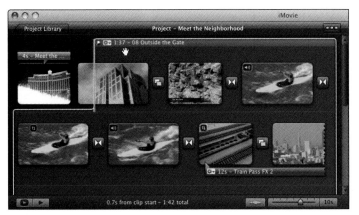

6.18 Click and drag the name of the music to the right to change the music's starting point.

3. **When the mouse pointer reaches the frame at which you want the music to start, release the mouse button.**

To change when a sound effect plays, click its box on the Storyboard and drag it until its pointer and the playhead reach the frame where you want the effect to start.

Trimming a song or sound effect

When you need to trim a song or sound effect quickly, you can do so like this:

1. **Click the sound effect's box to select it.**

2. **Move the mouse pointer over the left end or right end of the box so that the mouse pointer turns to a double-headed arrow.**

3. **Click and drag to shorten the sound effect from the end you drag.**

For greater control, or when you need to trim a music track rather than a sound effect, use the Clip Trimmer pane like this:

1. **Click the Action button that appears on the left side of the music track or sound effect and then click Clip Trimmer.** iMovie displays the Clip Trimmer pane (see Figure 6.19).

177

6.19 Use the Clip Trimmer pane to trim a music track down to the right length.

2. Click and drag the left handle or right handle to trim the beginning or end. Click the Play button to check your trimming.

3. Click Done to close the Clip Trimmer pane.

Adding a voiceover

Many movies need a voiceover — spoken words that help set the scene, explain what's happening, or bridge show-stopping gaps in the plot that you can no longer patch with footage. Here's how to add a voiceover to your movie:

1. Click the Voiceover button on the toolbar (the microphone button) or press O to open the Voiceover window (see Figure 6.20).

2. In the Record From pop-up menu, choose the microphone or sound source you want to use. For example, choose Built-in Microphone if you're recording through your Mac's microphone.

3. Speak into the microphone at the volume you'll use. Drag the Input Volume

6.20 Choose the recording source and set the input volume in the Voiceover window.

slider as needed to put the volume bars about three-quarters of the way across to the right, but not so far that you get the red LEDs at the right end all the time.

4. **If you're recording in a noisy environment, you may need to adjust the Noise Reduction slider to get good results.** This slider allows you to tell the microphone to try to filter out background noises so that it picks up your voice clearly.

5. **Select the Voice Enhancement check box if you want iMovie to try to improve the sound of your voice.** Experiment with this feature and see if you like the effect; if not, turn it off by deselecting the check box.

6. **Select the Play project audio while recording check box if you need to hear the project's audio as you speak your narration.** You'll need to wear headphones to prevent your microphone from picking up the audio and recording it into the voiceover.

7. **In the Storyboard, skim to the point at which you want to start recording the voiceover.**

8. **When you're ready to begin, click where you want to start.** The viewer prompts you to get ready and then counts down from 3 to 1, showing you the 3 seconds of footage before you clicked.

9. **Speak the voiceover, and then press spacebar to stop.** iMovie displays a purple bar called Voiceover Recording under the clips (see Figure 6.21).

10. **Repeat Steps 7 to 9 if you need to record more voiceovers.**

6.21 iMovie displays the voiceover as a purple bar under the clip or clips to which it's attached.

11. **When you finish recording, click the Close button (the X button) to close the Voiceover window.**

Genius You can make voiceovers overlap if need be. And you can trim a voiceover either by clicking it and dragging one of its end handles or by clicking its action button, clicking Clip Trimmer, and then working in the Clip Trimmer pane.

Viewing the audio waveforms

When you need to work in detail with audio, you may find it helpful to display the audio waveforms along with the clips, sound effects, voiceovers, and other items.

To display the audio waveforms for the items on the Storyboard (see Figure 6.22), click the Show/hide audio waveforms button at the bottom of the Storyboard.

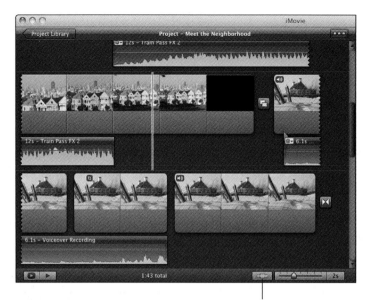

Show/hide audio waveforms button

6.22 Click the Show/hide audio waveforms button when you want to display
the audio waveforms.

Similarly, to display the waveforms for the clips in the Event Browser, click the Show/hide audio
waveforms button at the bottom of the window. Each Show/hide audio waveforms button
appears to the left of the corresponding Frames per thumbnail slider (one for the Storyboard, the
other for the Event browser).

When you no longer need to see the audio waveforms, click the appropriate Show/hide audio
waveforms button again.

Adjusting audio volume and fading

When you add music, sound effects, or a voiceover to your movie, you usually need to adjust one
or more of the audio clips to make sure the parts you want to hear are audible. You can also adjust
the audio that's part of the video clip, which is useful when you need to boost it, reduce it, or suppress it altogether.

To adjust an audio clip's volume, fading, and normalization, follow these steps:

1. **Click the audio clip you want to adjust.** For example, click a Voiceover Recording clip
    or the music clip. To work with the audio in the video track, click the video clip.

2. **Click the Inspector button on the toolbar or press I to display the Inspector window with the Audio tab displayed (see Figure 6.23).**

3. **Drag the Volume slider to increase or decrease the volume.** You can mute the track altogether by dragging the slider all the way to the left.

4. **Apply ducking if the track needs it.** Ducking means reducing the volume of the other tracks while this track plays, and then restoring their volume. To set ducking, follow these steps:

   ● **Drag the Reduce volume of other tracks to slider to the left or right.** iMovie automatically selects the Reduce volume of other tracks to check box for you. (You can select it first manually if you prefer.)

   ● **Listen to the effect to see if your track is audible over its competition.** Increase or decrease the ducking as needed.

6.23 Use the Audio tab in the Inspector window to change the volume on an audio clip.

5. **If you want to create a gradual fade-in instead of using iMovie's automatic rapid fade-in, select the Manual check box in the Fade In area.** Drag the slider to the right to set the number of seconds and frames the fade-in occupies. The maximum setting is 5 seconds.

6. **If you want to create a gradual fade-out instead of using iMovie's automatic rapid fade-out, select the Manual check box in the Fade Out area.** Drag the slider to the right to set the number of seconds and frames the fade-out occupies. As with the fade-in, the maximum setting is 5 seconds.

7. **If the audio suffers from background noise, try selecting the Reduce background noise by check box and experimenting with the slider in different positions.** Listen to the result and see if there's an improvement.

8. **If you want to apply equalization to the audio clip, select the Equalizer check box, open the pop-up menu, and choose the equalization to use.** For example, choose Voice Enhance equalization if you want to give the movie's vocals a boost.

181

Note

If none of the equalizations suits the audio, create a custom equalization by dragging the ten sliders to different positions. The leftmost slider affects the lowest frequencies (bass), and the rightmost slider the highest frequencies (treble). Drag a slider up above the midpoint (the zero mark) to get more of that frequency; drag a slider below the midpoint to get less of that frequency.

9. **If your audio was recorded at different volumes, try clicking the Normalize Clip Volume button to even it out.** If you don't like the result, click Remove Normalization.

10. **To work with another clip, click it, and then repeat Steps 3 to 9.**

11. **When you finish working with audio, click Done to close the Inspector window.**

Genius

If you mess up a clip's audio by working on the Audio tab of the Inspector window, click Revert to Original to restore the clip to its original state.

Creating a Trailer for a Movie

When you create a movie, you'll likely want to get as many people as possible to see it. One great way to drum up an audience is to create a powerful and professional-looking trailer for the movie, just like the professional studios do for their movies, and then share the trailer on the Internet.

To create a movie trailer, follow these steps:

1. **Choose File ⇨ New Project to display the New Project dialog.** You can also press ⌘+N, or click the New Project button in the Project Library.

2. **In the list box on the left, scroll down so that you can see the full list of movie trailers (see Figure 6.24).**

3. **Click a trailer to display a preview in the box on the right.** iMovie displays brief details for the trailer: the number of cast members, the duration, and a synopsis of the approach and what it's suitable for.

4. **After you choose the trailer, set up the other details of the project as usual:**

   - Type the name in the Name text box.

   - Choose the aspect ratio — Widescreen (16:9) or Standard (4:3) — in the Aspect Ratio pop-up menu.

   - Choose the frame rate in the Frame Rate pop-up menu. As with movie projects, your choices are 30 fps – NTSC, 25 fps – PAL, or 24 fps – Cinema.

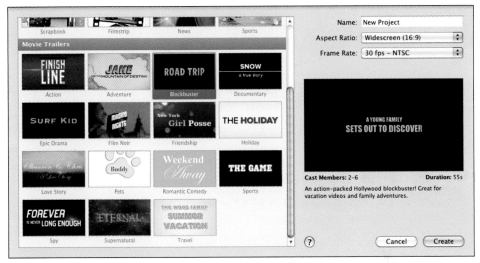

6.24 In the Movie Trailers list in the New Project dialog, click the trailer for which you want to see a preview and details.

5. **Click Create to close the New Project dialog and create the movie trailer project.**
   iMovie opens the project for editing, putting the Outline tab at the front of the Storyboard (see Figure 6.25).

6.25 On the Outline tab, fill in the details of the movie, release date, cast, and other information.

6. **Fill in the movie's name and release date, the cast members, the studio, and the credits.** Click the Add button (+) to add another cast member, or click the Remove button (−) to remove an existing cast member.

7. **Click the Storyboard tab to bring it to the front, and then fill in the text and clips you want (see Figure 6.26):**

   - Click each text bar in turn, and then type the text you want. Some bars contain a single text item, while others contain two text items, one for each line on the screen.

   - After you type the text in a text bar, it displays a curling counterclockwise arrow that you can click to restore the placeholder text.

   - Click the first photo placeholder, and then in your Event Library click a frame showing the type of content the placeholder mentions — for example, Landscape for a scenery shot or Group for a group of people. iMovie automatically selects the next placeholder for you so that you can move right along. If you get the wrong item in a placeholder, just click it again, and then click the right frame.

6.26 On the Storyboard tab, type the text to use for the captions, and add a clip to each placeholder.

8. **When you finish filling in the text and photo placeholders on the Storyboard, iMovie displays the Trailer Complete dialog, as shown in Figure 6.27).** Click Watch Trailer if you want to see how the trailer looks in the viewer. If you want to watch the trailer full screen, click Done, and then click the Play trailer full-screen button in the upper-right corner of the Storyboard area (or press ⌘+G).

As your trailer plays, you'll almost certainly find that some of the clips you chose don't work in their contexts or that you have other clips that are more suitable or will give greater punch.

You can replace clips or change the text by working on the Storyboard tab. You can also click a clip and use the icons that appear to make adjustments to it — for example, turning on its audio.

6.27 Click Watch Trailer in the Trailer Complete dialog if you want to watch the trailer in the viewer.

To get a breakdown of the shots the trailer uses, click the Shot List tab (see Figure 6.28). On this tab, you can replace a shot by clicking the placeholder and then clicking the replacement clip in the Event Library. And as with the Storyboard, you can click a clip and use the icons that it displays to make adjustments to it.

6.28 Use the Shot List tab to get an overview of the shots in the trailer and to replace any that don't work.

After adjusting the trailer, play it again — full screen for best effect — and keep working on it until it gives the message and impact you want.

Sharing and Exporting a Movie

Watching your movie (or trailer) on your Mac is great with your family, but you'll probably want to share it with other people, too.

iMovie lets you share your movies quickly and easily in five ways:

- **iTunes.** You can add a movie to iTunes so that you can watch it in iTunes;, on an iPad, iPhone, or iPod; or on an Apple TV.
- **iDVD.** You can burn your movie to a DVD using the iDVD application.
- **Media Browser.** You can publish a movie to iLife's Media Browser so that you can use it in iDVD or iWeb.
- **YouTube and other major online sites.** You can publish a movie straight from iMovie to major video-sharing sites on the Web. YouTube is the biggest site, but you can also post your videos to Facebook, to Vimeo, or to CNN iReport.
- **MobileMe Gallery.** If you have a MobileMe subscription, you can publish a movie straight from iMovie to your Gallery on MobileMe so that visitors to your MobileMe site can view it.

If you want to turn your movie into a file you can use on other sites, you can export your movie in three ways:

- **Export Movie.** This command lets you quickly save the movie as an MPEG-4 file using standard settings.
- **Export using QuickTime.** This command gives you more control over the exported movie. You can choose exactly the settings you need, and you can save it in any of various file formats. For example, you can create a movie file in the AVI format to share with Windows users.
- **Export Final Cut XML.** This command lets you create a version of the movie that you can bring into Final Cut Express or Final Cut Pro, Apple's more powerful video-editing applications.

Understanding the essentials of sharing

When you share a movie, you decide which size or sizes to use for it. iMovie offers five sizes; for some types of sharing, you choose a single size, but for others, you can use multiple sizes. Table 6.2 explains the five sizes iMovie offers, their resolutions, and the devices on which they work.

Table 6.2 iMovie's Sizes and Resolutions for Exporting Movies

Name	Standard Resolution (pixels)	Widescreen Resolution (pixels)	iPod	iPhone	iPad
Mobile	480 × 360	480 × 272		x	x
Medium	640 × 480	640 × 360	x	x	x
Large	720 × 540	960 × 540		x	x
HD 720p	1280 × 720	1280 × 720		x	x
HD 1080p	1920 × 1080	1920 × 1080			
Name	Standard Resolution (pixels)	Widescreen Resolution (pixels)	Apple TV	Computer	YouTube
Mobile	480 × 360	480 × 272		x	x
Medium	640 × 480	640 × 360	x	x	x
Large	720 × 540	960 × 540	x	x	x
HD 720p	1280 × 720	1280 × 720		x	x
HD 1080p	1920 × 1080	1920 × 1080		x	x
Name	Standard Resolution (pixels)	Widescreen Resolution (pixels)	Facebook	Vimeo	iReport
Mobile	480 × 360	480 × 272	x	x	x
Medium	640 × 480	640 × 360	x	x	x
Large	720 × 540	960 × 540	x	x	x
HD 720p	1280 × 720	1280 × 720	x	x	x
HD 1080p	1920 × 1080	1920 × 1080		x	

Seeing where you exported a movie

Given these various ways of exporting a movie, it can become difficult to keep track of which copies of the movie you put where. Luckily, iMovie automatically tracks the various copies you export and keeps you up to date with a clear readout at the top of the Storyboard.

Figure 6.29 shows the Storyboard for a video that has been shared to iTunes and published to both MobileMe and YouTube. You can click the pop-up menu to display options for viewing the movie, starting an e-mail giving a friend the URL of a movie, republishing the movie, or removing it from the site.

6.29 The Storyboard shows you where you published a movie and provides a pop-up menu for viewing and sharing it.

187

iMovie also places icons to the right of the movie project's name in the Project Library, showing that you've shared the movie (the beam icon) and which sizes you created for it (the four rounded rectangles). Figure 6.30 shows an example. A white rectangle indicates a size you've created, and a gray rectangle indicates a size you haven't created yet.

6.30 The Project Library shows you which projects you've shared and the sizes you've created for them.

Updating a movie you already published

If you change a movie project after publishing it to iTunes, MobileMe, or YouTube, iMovie displays the Shared or Finalized Project dialog, as shown in Figure 6.31, to warn you that the published project is now out of date. Click OK to continue making the edit, or click Undo if the warning has made you change your mind.

6.31 When you change a movie you've already shared, iMovie reminds you that you need to share it again.

iMovie then displays a yellow triangle with an exclamation point and an out-of-date notice at the top of the Storyboard (see Figure 6.32). The yellow triangle icon also appears on the project's sharing icon in the Project Library.

When you finish updating the movie, republish it to the sites on which you've published it. In most cases, the easiest way to do this is to click the site's button on the Storyboard screen and then click the Republish or the Publish command.

iMovie displays the dialog for publishing the movie (you see these dialogs shortly) but reapplies the settings you chose the first time. Make any changes, and then click the button to publish the movie.

Sharing a Movie to the Media Browser

If you want to use your movie in iWeb or iDVD, share it to the Media Browser like this:

6.32 These yellow exclamation icons remind you that the published version of the movie is out of date.

1. **Choose Share ⇨ Media Browser to display the Publish your project to the Media Browser dialog, as shown in Figure 6.33.**

6.33 In the Publish your project to the Media Browser dialog, choose the sizes you want to be able to use in your iWeb and iDVD projects.

2. **Select the check box for each size you want to create.**

3. **Click Publish.**

Publishing a movie to iTunes, iPad and iPhone (or iPod), or Apple TV

If you want to be able to watch your movie in iTunes, on your iPad or iPhone (or iPod), or on an Apple TV, export it to iTunes like this:

1. **Choose Share ⇨ iTunes.** iMovie displays the Publish your project to iTunes dialog (see Figure 6.34).

Publish your project to iTunes
Choose sizes based on where you will view your movies.

	iPod	iPhone	iPad	Ꭶtv	Computer		
Sizes: ☐ Mobile		●	●			480x272	ⓘ
☐ Medium	●	●	●	●	●	640x360	ⓘ
☑ Large		●	●	●	●	960x540	ⓘ
☑ HD 720p		●	●		●	1280x720	ⓘ
☐ HD 1080p					●	1920x1080	ⓘ

Cancel   Publish

6.34 When you publish a project to iTunes, create multiple sizes to ensure the movie looks good on the different devices you use.

2. **Choose the sizes you want to create.**

   - Usually you'll want to select the the Medium check box and the Large check box so that you can watch the movie on an iPhone or iPad, an Apple TV, or your Mac.

Genius

The iPhone 4 uses 960×640-pixel resolution, and the iPad uses 1024×768 resolution. If you're using either of these devices, the Large size will look much better than the Medium size or the Mobile size.

   - iMovie creates a separate movie file for each, adding the size to the project's name — for example, Our New Arrival – Mobile and Our New Arrival – Medium — so that you can distinguish the files.

3. **Click Publish.**

When iMovie finishes creating the files, it automatically launches or activates iTunes so that you can check out the movies. Click Movies in the sidebar to see the list of movies.

Publishing a movie to YouTube, Facebook, Vimeo, or CNN iReport

iMovie makes it easy to publish a movie to four major sites for sharing videos online:

- YouTube (www.youtube.com)
- Facebook (www.facebook.com)
- Vimeo (www.vimeo.com)
- CNN iReport (http://ireport.cnn.com)

Here are the essentials of publishing a movie to these sites:

- **Set up an account.** If you don't already have an account with the site, go to its Web site, and then follow the instructions for creating an account.

- **Publish a movie to the site.** Click the project in the Project Library or open it on the Storyboard, and then choose Share ⇨ YouTube, Share ⇨ Facebook, Share ⇨ Vimeo, or Share ⇨ CNN iReport, as appropriate. Choose the account you want to use, and then follow the prompts.

- **Remove a movie from the site.** Open the project on the Storyboard. Click the site's button on the Shared to bar at the top, and then click the Remove from command — for example, Remove from YouTube. Follow the prompts to remove the movie.

Publishing a movie to your MobileMe Gallery

If you have a MobileMe subscription, you can easily publish a movie to your MobileMe Gallery.

First, if you're not currently signed in to your MobileMe account, sign in before publishing your movie. Click System Preferences in the Dock, click MobileMe, click Sign In, and then type your MobileMe credentials.

Now follow these steps in iMovie:

1. **Select the movie project in the Project Library or open it on the Storyboard.**

2. **Choose Share ⇨ MobileMe Gallery.** iMovie displays the Publish your project to your MobileMe Gallery dialog, as shown in Figure 6.35.

3. **Improve the title in the Title box if necessary.**

4. **Type a description of the movie in the Description box.**

5. **In the Sizes to publish area, select the check box for each size you want to publish.**

6. **In the Viewable by pop-up menu, choose who may view the movie:**

   - **Everyone.** Anyone on the Web can view the album.

   - **Only me.** You keep the album to yourself — good for personal or work photos.

   - **Edit Names and Passwords.** To add the name of a person or group and assign a password, click this item, and work in the dialog that appears. Click OK when you finish.

7. **If you want to hide the movie on your Gallery page, select the Hide movie on my Gallery home page check box.**

8. **Select the Allow movie to be downloaded check box if you want people to be able to download the movie rather than just watch it online.**

> **Publish your project to your MobileMe Gallery**
>
> Title: Meet the Neighborhood
>
> Description: Take a two-minute tour of our neighborhood, seeing the sights and meeting the key families who live here.
>
> | | iPod | iPhone | iPad | ᴬtv | Computer | MobileMe | |
> |---|---|---|---|---|---|---|---|
> | Sizes to publish: ☑ Tiny | | ● | | | | ● | 176x144 ⓘ |
> | ☑ Mobile | | ● | ● | | | ● | 480x360 ⓘ |
> | ☑ Medium | ● | ● | ● | ● | ● | ● | 640x480 ⓘ |
> | ☐ Large | | ● | ● | ● | ● | ● | 720x540 ⓘ |
>
> Viewable by: Everyone ⬍
>
> ☐ Hide movie on my Gallery home page
> ☑ Allow movie to be downloaded
>
> (Cancel) (Publish)

6.35 You can put up to four different sizes of movie on your MobileMe Gallery. This allows visitors to download the size they want.

Genius

Hiding a movie so that it doesn't appear on your MobileMe Gallery page is good for when you need to share different movies with different people. Instead of needing to password-protect a movie to keep out people you don't want to see it, you can simply prevent the movie from appearing, and give the movie's URL to the people you want to watch it.

9. **Click Publish.** iMovie prepares the movie sizes you chose and publishes them to your Gallery, and then displays a dialog telling you it has done so.

10. **Click Tell a Friend to start an e-mail message announcing your movie, click View to view your Gallery, or click OK to close the dialog.**

Putting a movie on a DVD

iMovie gives you two ways to publish a movie to a DVD:

● **Media Browser.** Choose Share ⇨ Media Browser to publish the movie to iLife's Media Browser. Then switch to iDVD and pull in the movie from the Media Browser.

● **Publish to iDVD.** Choose Share ⇨ iDVD to publish the movie straight to the iDVD application.

See Chapter 12 for the details on using iDVD to create a DVD.

Exporting a movie quickly to an MPEG-4 file

If you want to export a movie quickly to a Mobile, Medium, or Large size MPEG-4 file using iMovie's preset settings, creating a file that will play on almost any type of computer, follow these steps:

1. **Select the movie project in the Project Library or open it on the Storyboard.**

2. **Choose Share ⇨ Export Movie or press ⌘+E.** iMovie displays the Export As dialog shown in Figure 6.36.

6.36 The quick way to create a file containing a movie is to choose Share ⇨ Export.

3. **In the Export As box, iMovie enters the project's name.** Edit this name or type a new name as necessary.

4. **In the Where pop-up menu, choose the folder in which to store the exported file.** If necessary, expand the dialog so that you can see the sidebar.

5. **In the Size to Export area, select an option button —Mobile, Medium, or Large — as appropriate.** Table 6.2 (earlier in this chapter) explains the sizes.

6. **Click Export.** iMovie exports the movie to the file and saves it in the folder you chose.

Exporting to another file format

When you need a file format other than MPEG-4, or when you need to control exactly how iMovie exports the file, you can export to a QuickTime file instead. Here's what to do:

1. **Select the movie project in the Project Library or open it on the Storyboard.**

2. **Choose Share ⇨ Export using QuickTime.** iMovie displays the Save exported file as dialog shown in Figure 6.37.

```
                    Save exported file as...

        Save As: Service Sampler.mov          [▼]

         Where: [▣ Movies                  ⬍]

  Export:  [ Movie to QuickTime Movie      ⬍]   ( Options... )
  Use:     [ Default Settings              ⬍]

                                    ( Cancel )   ( Save )
```

6.37 The Export using QuickTime command lets you choose from a wide variety of export formats.

3. **In the Save As box, iMovie enters the project's name.** Edit this name or type a new name as necessary.

4. **In the Where pop-up menu, choose the folder in which to store the exported file.** If necessary, expand the dialog so that you can see the sidebar and navigate to other folders.

5. **In the Export pop-up menu, choose the format you want.** Table 6.3 explains your options.

Genius

QuickTime's Sound To export formats are great for grabbing the audio from a movie so that you can use it elsewhere.

6. **If the Options button is available instead of being dimmed, you can click it to choose options for the export format.** For example, if you choose the Movie to QuickTime Movie export format, you can choose options like this:

- Click Options to display the Movie Settings dialog.

- To change the video settings, click the Settings button in the Video box, and then choose compression, motion, data rate, and encoding settings in the Video Compression Settings dialog.

- To apply a special effect such as Lens Flare, click the Filtering button, and then choose settings in the Filtering dialog.

Table 6.3   Export Options Using QuickTime

Export Format	Explanation
Movie to 3G	Creates a movie in the 3GP format, streaming the movie to 3G mobile phones.
Movie to Apple TV	Creates a movie in the MPEG-4 format. This gives you the same result as choosing Share ⇨ Export Movie and choosing the Medium size (which is easier). The movie's resolution is 640×480 pixels.
Movie to AVI	Creates a movie in the AVI format, which is widely used on Windows. You can choose the quality and compression (if any).
Movie to DV Stream	Creates a movie in a DV format. You can choose whether the movie is formatted for NTSC or for PAL.
Movie to FLC	Creates a movie in the FLIC animation format. You can choose the frame rate and whether the movie uses Windows Colors or Mac Colors.
Movie to Image Sequence	Creates an image file for each frame of the movie. You can choose from various image formats (such as JPEG).
Movie to iPhone	Creates a movie in the MPEG-4 format suitable for viewing on the iPhone or iPod touch. This gives you the same result as choosing Share ⇨ Export Movie and choosing the Mobile size. The movie's resolution is 480×360 pixels.
Movie to iPhone (Cellular)	Creates a movie in the 3GP format suitable for watching as a stream on the iPhone. The movie's resolution is 176×132 pixels.
Movie to iPod	Creates a movie in the MPEG-4 format suitable for viewing on any iPod or on a TV to which it's connected. The movie's resolution is 640×480 pixels, the same as the Movie to Apple TV export format, but it uses a lower bit rate and so has a smaller file size.
Movie to MPEG-4	Creates a movie in the MPEG-4 format. This is the same as choosing Share ⇨ Export Movie, except you can click the Options buttons to set a wide variety of movie options, including the image size, frame rate, and audio format.
Movie to QuickTime Movie	Creates a movie in the QuickTime format. You can choose from a wide variety of settings to get the resolution and quality you need.
Sound to AIFF	Exports the soundtrack from the movie to a file in the AIFF format, an uncompressed, full-quality format used widely on the Mac.
Sound to AU	Exports the soundtrack from the movie to a file in the AU format. This file format is less widely used than AIFF or WAV.
Sound to Wave	Exports the soundtrack from the movie to a file in the WAV format, an uncompressed, full-quality format used widely on Windows.

- To change the resolution of the video, click the Size button, and then choose settings in the Export Size Settings dialog.

- To use a different sound format or quality, click the Settings button in the Sound box, and then choose settings in the Sound Settings dialog.

- If you want to be able to stream the movie across the Internet, select the Prepare for Internet Streaming check box, and then choose Fast Start, Fast Start – Compressed Header, or Hinted Streaming. Fast Start is usually the best choice for general use. Hinted Streaming is for use with QuickTime Streaming Server.

- Click OK to close the Movie Settings dialog and return to the Save exported file as dialog.

7. **Click Save.** iMovie exports the file in the format you chose.

Exporting to a Final Cut XML file

If you have Final Cut Express or Final Cut Pro, Apple's more powerful video-editing applications, you may want to bring into it movies that you've created in iMovie so that you can develop them further.

To do this, you can use the Export Final Cut XML command. But before you do, it's vital that you're clear on what you get and what you don't get:

- **Video.** You get the video footage, but iMovie removes any color adjustments you made.

- **Audio.** You get the audio tracks, but iMovie removes any voiceovers, sound effects, and music tracks.

- **Transitions.** iMovie replaces all your custom transitions with Cross Dissolves.

- **Titles.** You lose all the titles.

- **Cropping and Ken Burns Effects.** iMovie removes these as well.

That may sound as though there's not much left. But if what you're looking to do is get your edited video into one of the Final Cut applications so that you can reedit it there, you get just about enough.

Here's how to export your movie project to a Final Cut XML file:

1. **Click the movie project in the Project Library or open it on the Storyboard.**

2. **Choose Share ⇨ Export Final Cut XML.** iMovie displays the Export FCP XML dialog, as shown in Figure 6.38.

Export FCP XML

Save As: Service Sampler – XML

Where: ▦ Movies

☐ **Use flattened audio from thumbnail movies**

Notes about the exported XML file:

- All transitions will be represented by Cross Dissolves.
- Titles, voiceovers, sound effects and music tracks are not exported.
- Cropping/Ken Burns and color adjustments are not exported.
- Green Screen and Picture in Picture clips are not exported.

(Cancel)   (Save)

6.38 When you export a movie to Final Cut XML, you lose transitions, voiceovers, cropping, and more — but you do transfer the footage.

3. **In the Save As box, type the name you want to give the file.** iMovie suggests the name XML File, so you'll normally want to change it.

4. **In the Where pop-up menu, choose the folder in which to store the exported file.** If necessary, expand the dialog so that you can see the sidebar.

5. **Select the Use flattened audio from thumbnail movies check box if you want to include the rendered audio.** Deselect this check box if you plan to render the audio in Final Cut (which gives you more control over how it sounds).

6. **Click Save.** iMovie exports the file. You can then import it into Final Cut.

How Do I Set Up a Virtual Studio in GarageBand?

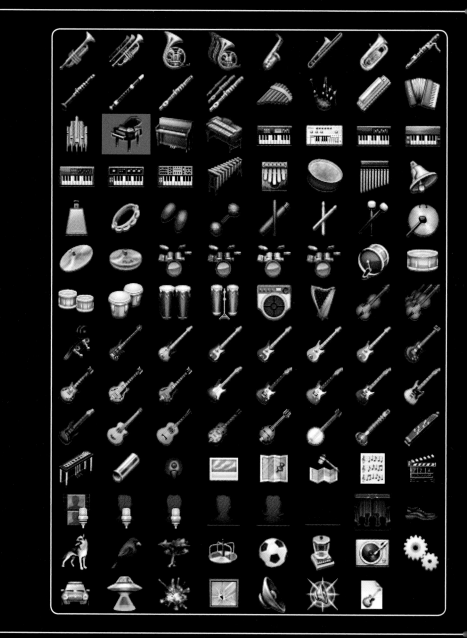

GarageBand gives you all the tools you need to create professional-quality music on your Mac. But because of its power and complexity, GarageBand has a steep learning curve and takes some getting used to. This chapter shows you how to come to grips with GarageBand, assemble and configure your computerized music studio, use the Magic GarageBand feature to quickly create a customized backing track containing exactly the type of music you want to play along to, and even have GarageBand teach you how to play songs.

Understanding What You Can Do with GarageBand

GarageBand lets you create original music quickly and easily by using your Mac on its own or with musical instruments.

GarageBand comes with a library of prerecorded audio loops for many different instruments, from rock music standards such as drums, bass, and guitars (lead and rhythm) to instruments such as woodwind, brass, and organs. You can arrange these loops to play back in the order you want, repeat them as needed, and even change their tempo and pitch. You can use the Magic GarageBand feature to quickly whip together a backing track from loops that work with each other.

You can connect a MIDI keyboard to your Mac and use its keys to play either keyboard-based Software Instruments (such as pianos or synthesizers) or instruments such as guitars or drum kits. You can play along to tracks you build out of prerecorded loops, record your performances, and choose the best of them.

You can connect a physical musical instrument such as a guitar or bass to your Mac (usually through an external audio interface) and play along with a backing track. You can record what you play and manipulate it to make it sound better.

You can connect one or more microphones to your Mac (again, usually through an external audio interface) so that you can add vocals or other instruments you cannot connect directly to your Mac. For example, you can record an acoustic guitar, a flute, or a drum kit through one or more microphones. You can record these tracks, too, and improve them in GarageBand.

You can mix your loop-based tracks and your recorded tracks, adding effects as needed to give you a professional-quality result. You can then export the resulting song to iTunes or to a CD.

If you want to improve your playing, you can use the Learn to Play feature to take lessons in instruments such as piano and guitar and the How Did I Play? feature to track your progress as you play live with GarageBand. You can download guitar lessons, piano lessons, and lessons from individual artists who teach you how to play particular songs of theirs. Last but not least, you can unleash the full power of GarageBand on the tiny task of creating a ringtone for the iPhone.

Understanding Real and Software Instruments

GarageBand uses two kinds of instruments: Software Instruments and Real Instruments.

Software Instruments are synthesized instruments whose sounds GarageBand creates on the fly as needed. You play Software Instruments using one of GarageBand's on-screen keyboards (discussed later in this chapter) or an external MIDI keyboard connected to your Mac.

Real Instruments are physical instruments that you connect to your Mac — for example, a guitar or bass that you connect via an audio interface, or a microphone you connect to record vocals, drums, or another acoustic instrument.

Where things get confusing is that GarageBand contains Real Instrument loops as well as Software Instrument loops. Real Instrument loops are recordings of real instruments playing, whereas Software Instrument loops are sounds generated by software — as it were, recipes that tell your Mac how to put together the right sounds.

Real Instrument loops appear in blue in the GarageBand interface, and Software Instrument loops appear in green. You can edit Software Instrument loops much more extensively than you can edit Real Instrument loops.

Note GarageBand also lets you create podcasts and add chapter markers to movies for DVDs. Chapter 11 shows you how to create podcasts. Chapter 12 explains how to add chapter markers to movies.

Creating and Saving a Song Project

The first time you launch GarageBand by clicking the GarageBand icon on the Dock or (if the icon doesn't appear there) double-clicking the icon in the Applications folder, GarageBand displays the opening screen shown in Figure 7.1.

Note The next time you open GarageBand, it automatically loads the project you were working on the last time you quit the application. If you closed the project before quitting GarageBand, the application displays the opening screen so that you can decide between opening an existing project and starting a new project.

7.1 When you open GarageBand, the application displays this screen to let you choose which feature to use.

Create and save your song project like this:

1. **If the New Project button in the left panel isn't selected, click it so that you see the available instruments (such as Piano, Electric Guitar, and Voice) and features (such as Songwriting and Podcast).**

2. **Click the instrument you want to use — for example, Keyboard Collection — and then click Choose.** GarageBand displays the New Project from Template dialog (see Figure 7.2).

7.2 In the New Project from Template dialog, name your song; choose where to save it; and set the tempo, signature, and key.

Note

Chapter 11 discusses how to use GarageBand to create podcast episodes and distribute them via iWeb.

3. **In the upper part of the dialog, name your song, and choose where to save it.** As usual, you can click the arrow button to the right of the Save As box to reveal the dialog's navigation area.

4. **Set the tempo for the song by dragging the Tempo slider to adjust the number in the bpm box.** See the nearby sidebar for advice on choosing the tempo, signature, and key. You can also type the number directly in the bpm box if you find that easier than dragging the Tempo slider.

5. **Choose the time signature for the song in the Signature pop-up menu.**

Caution

GarageBand wraps each song into a package file that contains all the track information and any audio files that you record into the song. The result is that GarageBand song files that include recorded audio can be large, so don't try to save them on any storage device that's short of space.

6. **Choose the key in the Key pop-up menu, and then choose major or minor in the pop-up menu to the right of it.**

7. **Click Create.** GarageBand closes the New Project from Template dialog and displays your project.

Choosing the Tempo, Signature, and Key for Your Song

If (like most people) you haven't composed music before, you may not be familiar with tempos, signatures, and keys:

- **Tempo.** The tempo is the number of beats per minute. You can set from an ultraslow 40 bpm to a super-high-energy 240 bpm. GarageBand suggests 120 bpm to start.

- **Signature.** The signature or time signature sets the relationship between beats and measures in the song. Your choices are 2 / 2, 2 / 4, 3 / 4, 4 / 4, 5 / 4, 7/ 4, 6 / 8, 7 / 8, 9 / 8, or 12 / 8. The number to the left of the slash

continued

continued

> is the number of beats in each measure; the number to the right of the slash is the length of the note that gets one beat. For example, in the widely used 4 / 4 time signature, there are four beats per measure, and each quarter note receives one beat.

- Key. The key is the central note in the musical scale for the song. Your choices are C, Db (D flat), D, Eb, E, F, F# (F sharp), G, Ab, A, Bb, or B. You can also choose between major and minor keys.

Unless you already have a firm idea of the song you're composing, it's hard to know which tempo, signature, and key will work best. In this case, try accepting GarageBand's default values: a tempo of 120 beats per minute, the 4 / 4 time signature, and the C major key.

You can change the tempo, time signature, and key easily when you're working with GarageBand's Real Instruments and Software Instruments in the project, so you don't have to get them exactly right when creating the song. What's important is to fix these settings before you start recording your own audio because GarageBand can't change the tempo and key on these.

Getting Up To Speed with the GarageBand Interface

After you create your first project, the GarageBand window should look something like Figure 7.3, which uses the Keyboard Collection instruments. GarageBand starts the project with a track for the instrument you chose, or a track for each instrument in the collection, but you can delete any track — or change it to another instrument — as needed.

These are the main elements of the GarageBand window:

- **Tracks column.** You place a track in this column for each Software Instrument or Real Instrument you want to play or record. The track header shows the instrument type and contains controls for recording the track, listening to it, changing its volume, and panning it. The track header for the instrument you've currently selected appears in green so you can easily pick it out.

- **Playhead.** The triangle in the Timeline and the red line down across the tracks indicate the current play position. The playhead moves as you play back the tracks. You can also move it by dragging or by using the Transport controls.

- **Timeline.** This is the area where you arrange loops, tracks, and sounds so that they start when you want them to and play for the required length.

- **Zoom slider.** Drag this slider to zoom in on the Timeline so you can see it in more detail, or to zoom out to see more of your project at once.

- **New Track button.** Click this track to open the dialog box for adding a new Software Instrument track or Real Instrument track.

- **Loop Browser.** In this pane, you pick prerecorded audio loops to place in the song.

- **Loop Browser button.** Click this button to display or hide the Loop Browser.

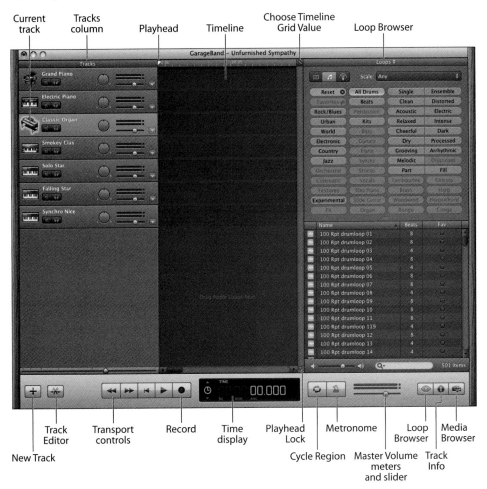

7.3 When you create a song project, GarageBand looks something like this. The track or tracks depend on the instrument or feature you chose in the New Project from Template dialog.

- **Track Info button.** Click this button to display or hide the Track Info pane, which you use for working with Software Instruments and Real Instruments.

- **Media Browser button.** Click this button to display or hide the Media Browser, which you use to select audio clips, photos, and movies, just like in most of the other iLife applications. You use the Media Browser when creating podcasts rather than when creating songs; see Chapter 11 for details.

- **Track Editor button.** Click this button to display the Track Editor, which you use to edit the audio in a track.

- **Record button.** Click this button to start or stop recording.

- **Transport controls.** Use these buttons to move the playhead to where you want it.

- **Time display.** This readout displays details of the time, measures, chord, or project. To switch among the four available sets of information, either click the up and down arrows at the left end, or click the icon on the left and choose from the pop-up menu.

- **Master Volume slider.** Drag this slider to control the master volume of the song. You use the controls in the Mixer column to set the volume level for an individual track.

- **Volume meters.** These meters display the output level for the song as a whole. Each track has its own volume meters that show only that track's output level.

- **Playhead Lock button.** Click this button to lock or unlock the playhead in the Timeline from the playhead in the Track Editor. By unlocking the two playheads, you can work with a different part of the song in the Timeline than in the Track Editor, which can be handy.

- **Choose Timeline Grid Value button.** Click this button to change the note value shown in the Timeline grid. For many projects, it's best to use the default setting, Automatic, which lets GarageBand change the note value automatically as you zoom in and out.

- **Cycle Region.** Click this button to turn on the cycle region, which you use to make a part of the song play in a loop so that you can work with it while ignoring the rest of the song.

- **Metronome.** Click this button to turn on the metronome, which plays a click track to help you keep time.

Using the on-screen keyboard and Musical Typing

To play Software Instruments on your Mac, you'll most likely want to connect an external musical keyboard, as discussed later in this chapter. This gives you the greatest flexibility and lets you play almost as if you were using a full-size instrument.

If you don't have a musical keyboard, or for times when you can't take a musical keyboard with you (for example, when you travel), GarageBand provides an on-screen keyboard that you can play either with the mouse or by pressing the keys on your Mac's keyboard.

Using the on-screen keyboard

To display or hide the on-screen keyboard, choose Window ⇨ Keyboard or press ⌘+K. Figure 7.4 shows the on-screen keyboard.

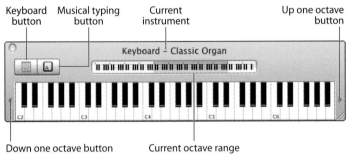

7.4 The on-screen keyboard lets you play any Software Instrument using your mouse.

The on-screen keyboard is easy to use, but it has a couple of hidden features:

- **Choose the instrument.** Click the Software Instrument track you want to play. The Keyboard window's title bar shows the instrument.

- **Play a note.** As you'd guess, you click the key. But the farther down the key you click, the harder you strike it. So if you want to play a note gently, click near the top of the key.

- **Change the octave range.** Click the gray button at the left end to move down an octave, or click the gray button at the right end to move up an octave. Or simply drag the blue-shaded area on the miniature keyboard at the top.

- **Resize the keyboard.** Drag the sizing handle in the lower-right corner of the Keyboard window to stretch out the keyboard or to shrink it back down. Drag the handle all the way to the right to display the entire keyboard so that you don't need to use the octave arrows.

Using Musical Typing

If you're handy with the mouse, you can play the on-screen keyboard pretty well in a pinch — one note at a time. But what you may find easier is to play using your Mac's keyboard. GarageBand calls this feature Musical Typing.

To use Musical Typing, click the Software Instrument track you want to play with the keyboard, and then choose Window⇨ Musical Typing or press ⌘+Shift+K. GarageBand displays the Musical Typing window (see Figure 7.5).

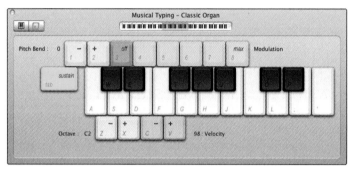

7.5 The Musical Typing keyboard lets you play piano — or any other Software Instrument — using your Mac's keyboard instead of an external keyboard.

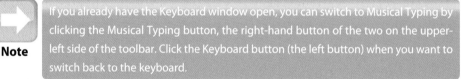

Note If you already have the Keyboard window open, you can switch to Musical Typing by clicking the Musical Typing button, the right-hand button of the two on the upper-left side of the toolbar. Click the Keyboard button (the left button) when you want to switch back to the keyboard.

The title bar shows the instrument you're currently playing. You can switch the keyboard to play another Software Instrument by clicking that instrument's track header in the main GarageBand window.

The Musical Typing keyboard is easy to use:

- **Play a note.** Press the note shown on the key.

- **Change octave.** Click the piano keyboard at the top of the window to pick an octave, or drag the blue shaded area to the left or right. You can also press Z to move down an octave or X to move up an octave.

- **Sustain a note.** Hold down Tab to sustain the note you're playing.

- **Change velocity.** Press C to reduce the velocity or V to increase it.

- **Add pitch bend.** Press 1 to lower the pitch or 2 to raise it. Keep holding down the key for as long as you want to bend the pitch.

- **Add modulation.** Press the number keys 4 through 8 to add modulation (the higher the number, the more modulation). To turn modulation off, press 3.

If you prefer, you can click the buttons on the Musical Typing keyboard instead of (or as well as) pressing the keys.

Using the Loop Browser

To make the best use of the space available in the window, GarageBand makes the Loop Browser, the Track Info pane, and the Media Browser share the same area. That means you can display only one of them at a time.

To add audio loops to your projects, you use the Loop Browser. Click the Loop Browser button to display the Loop Browser on the right side of the window. You can then click one of the category buttons in the top part of the Loop Browser to display the matching loops in the list at the bottom. For example, Figure 7.6 shows the Loop Browser open with the Guitars button clicked, so the list at the bottom displays all the guitar loops.

7.6 Open the Loop Browser and then click a category button to see a list of matching loops. Click a loop to listen to it; click again to stop, or click another loop to start it.

Click the loop you want to hear, or drag it to the Track list to create a new track that uses that loop. GarageBand adds the loop to the track as a region, a section of the track.

Genius

You can increase the depth of the Loop Browser so that it shows more category buttons by clicking the two-bar handle below the category buttons and dragging downward.

Meeting the Track Editor

To display the Track Editor across the bottom of the GarageBand window, click the Track Editor button. You can then click a region to open it for editing in the Track Editor (see Figure 7.7) or double-click a region to bring it to the leftmost position in the Track Editor.

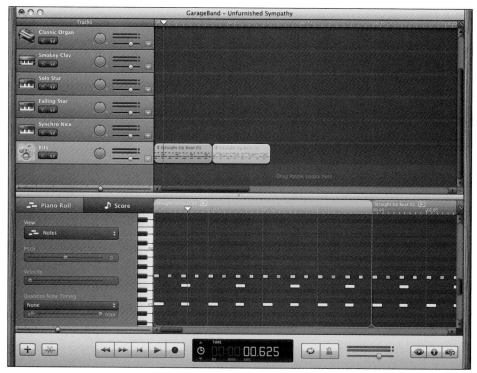

7.7 Opening a region for editing in the Track Editor. Hide the Loop Browser, Track Info pane, or Media Browser to give the Track Editor more space.

Genius

You can increase the depth of the Track Editor so that it shows a wider range of notes by dragging upward the bar that divides it from the upper part of the window. The bar has a circular handle in the middle, but you can drag any part of the bar.

Meeting the Track Info pane

You use the Track Info pane to check and change the settings for a selected instrument track or for the master track (which controls the song as a whole). To display or hide the Track Info pane, click the Track Info button or press ⌘+I. Figure 7.8 shows the Track Info pane as it initially appears for a Real Instrument track, Male Rock Vocals. Click the Browse tab to choose among the different instruments that GarageBand provides, and select the input source and recording level for Real Instrument tracks.

7.8 The Track Info pane appears on the right side of the GarageBand window.

211

You can click the Edit tab at the top of the Track Info pane to display the Edit tab (see Figure 7.9), which you use to set effects for the track.

The other GarageBand component that occupies the same part of the GarageBand window as the Loop Browser and the Track Info pane is the Media Browser. You use the Media Browser to add photos, audio clips, and movies to podcasts, so I leave this component until Chapter 11 (which covers creating podcasts).

Connecting Your Audio Instruments

You can make great music in GarageBand by using its audio loops, but to get the most out of GarageBand you need to connect your own instruments.

Connecting a MIDI keyboard

The first essential is a MIDI keyboard. If you buy a MIDI keyboard that connects via USB (such as the M-Audio KeyStation models that the Apple Store sells), you connect the keyboard via a single USB cable and don't even need to use a power supply because the keyboard gets power from the USB cable. Other MIDI keyboards connect to a MIDI controller, which you then connect to your Mac via USB.

When you connect a keyboard or other MIDI instrument, GarageBand lets you know instantly by displaying a dialog telling you that the number of MIDI inputs has changed and how many there now are. Figure 7.10 shows an example of this dialog.

7.9 Click the Edit tab of the Track Info pane when you need to set effects manually.

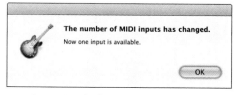

7.10 GarageBand tells you when the number of MIDI inputs changes — for example, when you connect a MIDI keyboard to your Mac.

Genius

If possible, connect your MIDI keyboard directly to a USB port on your Mac rather than to a USB hub connected to your Mac.

Connecting a microphone

To record live instruments such as drums, acoustic guitar, or vocals, you need to use one or more microphones. If your Mac has a built-in microphone, you can use that in a severe pinch, but for high-quality results you should use an external microphone that you can position exactly where you need it. Choose a microphone designed for recording music rather than a general-purpose microphone.

If you're using a single microphone, you can connect it directly to your Mac's audio input socket. To use two or more microphones, you need to use an audio interface, which is discussed next.

Connecting an audio interface

When you need to connect other instruments or audio equipment to your Mac so that you can direct their output into GarageBand as input, you need to use an audio interface — an electronic box that accepts the input from the instrument or audio kit, processes it as needed, and then passes it along to your Mac. You can get Mac-compatible audio interfaces that connect via either USB or FireWire; USB interfaces are usually easier.

Genius

When choosing an audio interface, figure out how many audio inputs you need, including high-impedance (for instruments) and lower-impedance (for lower-powered devices) inputs. Decide whether you need audio outputs (for example, for playback through an amplifier) as well as the USB output, and whether you need "phantom" power that will allow you to use a dynamic microphone.

For most audio interfaces, you need to install a driver to enable Mac OS X to recognize the interface. After you install the driver, you typically manage the audio interface either through a custom panel in System Preferences or via a custom application provided by the interface's manufacturer. Figure 7.11 shows an example of a control panel in System Preferences.

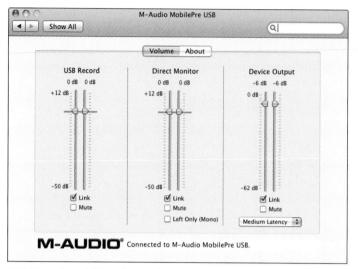

7.11 Managing a USB audio interface via a custom control panel in System Preferences

Setting Preferences to Suit the Way You Work

To enable yourself to work as fast and smoothly as possible in GarageBand, it's a good idea to spend a few minutes setting the application's preferences to suit the way you work. Even if you choose not to change the default settings at first, knowing which preferences you can change will be helpful when you find you do need to alter GarageBand's behavior.

Start by pressing ⌘+, (⌘ and the comma key) or choosing GarageBand ➪ Preferences to open the Preferences window.

Setting General preferences

If GarageBand doesn't display the General preferences (see Figure 7.12) at first, click the General button to display them.

- **Cycle Recording.** Select the Automatically merge Software Instrument recordings when using the cycle region check box when you want to loop through a section of a Software Instrument track and add what you play to what's already there. This technique is useful for creating complex parts. For example, when recording a drum beat, you can play the bass drum on the first pass, add the snare drum on the second pass, add the hi-hat and cymbals on the third pass, and have all of them merged into a single track. The alternative is to have GarageBand record each pass through the region as a separate take; you can then select the take you want to keep.

General

General Audio/MIDI Loops Advanced My Info

Cycle Recording: ☑ Automatically merge Software Instrument
recordings when using the cycle region
Combines multiple passes when recording to create
drum beats and other layered parts.

Audio Preview: ☐ Render an audio preview when saving
An audio preview lets you audition GarageBand projects
in the Finder, Time Machine, and other applications, but
takes longer each time you close a project.

(Reset Warnings)

7.12 GarageBand's General preferences let you choose whether to use cycle recording and whether to create an audio preview of your projects.

- **Audio Preview.** Select the Render an audio preview when saving check box if you want GarageBand to create a preview that you can listen to from the other iLife applications or from the Finder. Creating this preview is usually a good idea, but it means that each time you close a project in GarageBand, saving the file takes a little longer because of creating the preview. Saving an audio preview increases the project's file size as well, but the difference is negligible given how useful the preview is.

- **Reset Warnings.** Click this button to reset GarageBand's warning messages to their default settings. Normally, you won't want to do this because it causes all the warning dialogs you've suppressed to start springing out of the woodwork again.

Note If you don't select the Render an audio preview when saving check box in General preferences, GarageBand prompts you to decide whether to create a preview until you tell it to stop prompting you. So normally it's best to select the check box.

Setting Audio/MIDI preferences

Next, click the Audio/MIDI tab to display the Audio/MIDI preferences (see Figure 7.13), and then choose settings:

- **Audio Output.** In this pop-up menu, choose where you want to direct GarageBand's output. Select System Setting to use the output selected on the Output tab in Mac OS X's Sound preferences in System Preferences. Select Built-in Audio or Built-in Output (depending on your Mac) to use your Mac's speakers or output jack. If you have connected an audio interface, you can select it from this pop-up menu to send the audio to the interface (and then to whichever amplifier or speakers you've connected to it).

- **Audio Input.** In this pop-up menu, choose which audio input GarageBand should use. Select System Setting to use the input selected on the Input tab in Mac OS X's Sound preferences in System Preferences. Select Built-in Microphone to use your Mac's built-in microphone, or Built-in Audio to use the input jack. If you have connected an audio interface, select it from this pop-up menu.

7.13 In Audio/MIDI preferences, choose your Mac's inputs and outputs, decide how to optimize GarageBand's playback, and set the keyboard sensitivity.

- **MIDI Status.** This readout shows how many MIDI devices GarageBand has detected. You can't change it directly, only by plugging in or unplugging MIDI devices. Use this readout to make sure GarageBand is aware of all the MIDI devices you're using.

- **Keyboard Sensitivity.** Drag the slider to choose how sensitive GarageBand should treat your keyboard as being. Finding the best setting for yourself depends on the keyboard and your playing style, so you'll probably need to experiment with this setting. Start with the slider at the Neutral position (in the middle), and then drag toward the Less end or the More end as needed.

Setting Loops preferences

Now click the Loops tab to display the Loops preferences (see Figure 7.14), and then choose settings for working with loops:

- **Keyword Browsing.** Select the Filter for more relevant results check box if you want to return only search results that are within two semitones of the song key you're using. This setting is useful when you've installed many loops and need to narrow your search results.

7.14 In Loops preferences, choose how to browse loops, whether to convert Software Instruments to Real Instruments when you add them to the Timeline, and whether to share your loops.

- **Keyword Layout.** Click Reset to reset the keyword layout to its default after you customize it.

- **Adding Loops to Timeline.** Select the Convert to Real Instrument check box if you want GarageBand to automatically convert Software Instrument loops to Real Instrument loops when you add them to the Timeline. Real Instrument loops take less processor power to play than Software Instrument loops, so converting Software Instrument loops to Real Instrument loops can be a good move if your Mac is struggling to play a song. You can override this setting by Option+dragging a loop to the Timeline.

- **My Apple Loops.** Select the Available to *Your Username* Only option button if you want to keep your selection of Apple loops to yourself. Select the Share with all users on this Mac option button if you want to share the loops with others. Two things to note here: First, this setting applies only to extra loops you add, not to GarageBand's main set of loops (which are available to all users of your Mac). Second, only administrator users can make this choice; standard users can't.

- **Loop Browser.** Select the Display original tempo and key check box if you want the Loop Browser to display the Tempo column and the Key column, showing these two pieces of information about each loop. Give this option a try to see if you find it useful; many people do, but others prefer to keep the Loop Browser stripped down to the essentials.

Setting Advanced preferences

Click the Advanced tab to display the Advanced preferences (see Figure 7.15), and then choose settings that suit you:

- **Auto Normalize.** Select the Export projects at full loudness check box if you want GarageBand to automatically adjust the volume on projects you export. Unlike the normalization in iTunes that tends to wreck the dynamic range of songs, GarageBand's normalization is usually a good idea because it enables you to export songs at around a standard volume even if you've mixed them at a lower volume.

- **Audio Resolution.** In this pop-up menu, select Good, Better, or Best, as appropriate. Good resolution records and exports at standard CD audio quality (16-bit), which is enough for any projects you plan to put on CD. Better resolution records at 24-bit quality and exports at 16-bit, allowing you to keep higher-quality versions in GarageBand than you're outputting. Best resolution both records and exports at 24-bit quality; use this for songs you'll distribute at higher quality than CDs.

Genius

The disadvantage to using Better or Best audio resolution is that your GarageBand files take up one-and-a-half times as much space because the quality is higher.

- **Movie Thumbnail Resolution.** For your movie and podcast projects, select the Low option button or the High option button to control the resolution of the movie thumbnail image that GarageBand creates. High-resolution thumbnails make your files larger.

7.15 Advanced preferences let you normalize projects automatically and choose resolution for audio and for movie thumbnails.

Setting My Info preferences

Finally for the preferences, click the My Info tab (see Figure 7.16) and set the information you want to use to tag your songs and podcasts in iTunes:

- **iTunes Playlist.** This setting tells iTunes which playlist to place your songs in. If the playlist doesn't exist yet, iTunes creates it when you export the first song from GarageBand.

- **Artist Name.** This setting tells iTunes which artist name to assign to the song.

7.16 In the My Info preferences, provide the information for tagging your songs and podcasts in iTunes.

- **Composer Name.** This setting tells iTunes what to write in the Composer tag.
- **Album Name.** This setting controls the album name that iTunes applies.

Kick-Starting a Song with Magic GarageBand

Have you ever needed to put together a backing track in a minute so that you can play along and develop an idea you've had on the guitar or piano?

If so, you can use Magic GarageBand to quickly create a custom backing track from generic ingredients. The "magic" part is that GarageBand automatically picks sequences of instrumental loops that work together, quickly creating a viable custom backing track for the combination of instruments and musical genres you choose.

Here's how to get started with Magic GarageBand:

1. **Press ⌘+N or choose File ➪ New to display the GarageBand opening screen.** If you have a project open that contains unsaved changes, GarageBand prompts you to save them.

2. **Click the Magic GarageBand button in the left panel to display the Magic GarageBand music choices.**

3. **Click the icon for the music genre you want to create: Blues, Rock, Jazz, Country, Reggae, Funk, Latin, Roots Rock, or Slow Blues.** To preview the type of music, move the mouse pointer over an icon and click the Play icon on the Preview button that appears; click the Stop icon (which replaces the Play icon) to stop the preview.

4. **Click the Create button.** GarageBand displays the Magic GarageBand screen and loads a standard set of instruments for the musical genre you chose. Figure 7.17 shows the selection you get for Rock.

5. **Choose your instrument from the My Instrument pop-up menu on the left.** You can choose Keyboard, Line In, or a microphone. From the same menu, you can turn the monitor on (so that you hear the instrument through GarageBand) or off (so that you hear the instrument only through your other audio equipment).

Genius

In the lower part of the My Instrument pop-up menu, the Monitor On item automatically applies feedback protection to the monitoring to help you avoid creating a feedback loop to rival The Who in their prime. The Monitor On (no feedback protection) item removes the feedback protection; use this setting with care.

7.17 Magic GarageBand loads a standard set of instruments for music of the genre you choose.

6. **Tune your instrument (or your voice).**
   Click the tuning-fork icon to the right of the My Instrument pop-up menu, and then use the controls that appear to make sure GarageBand agrees the note you're playing or singing is what you intend. Click the icon again when you finish tuning.

7. **Click the icon for the subtype of instrument you're using.** For example, for Keyboard, choose Grand Piano, Electric Piano, or Arena Run. You can also click the Customize button to display a window containing a wider selection of choices (see Figure 7.18); click the instrument you want, and then click Done.

Pianos and Keyboards

Boldt Vibraphone
Electric Piano
Grand Piano On Stage
Grand Piano Punchy
Grand Piano
Smokey Clav
Smooth Clav
Swirling Electric Piano
Whirly

Cancel   Done

7.18 Use this dialog to select from a wider range of instruments than appear in the main Magic GarageBand window.

221

8. **Decide whether to create a snippet or an entire song by moving the switch on the bottom of the window frame to Snippet or Entire Song.** Entire Song usually gives better results because you can hear more of the music. If you choose Snippet, click the section of the song in the gray bar: Intro, Verse 1, Chorus, Verse 2, or Ending.

From here, you pick a sound for each instrument you want to include, and knock out any instruments you don't need. Exactly how you proceed depends on the genre of music you're creating, your musical skills, and what kind of music you like. But here's an example of setting up a rock backing track to which you will add a lead guitar line.

Note

You can simply start the music playing by clicking the Play button and working from there, but many people find it easier to start with a single instrument as described in this example.

1. **Silence all the instruments except the one you want to start with.** Click each instrument to display its name, click the disclosure triangle to the left of the name to display a set of controls, and then click the Mute button on the left (see Figure 7.19).

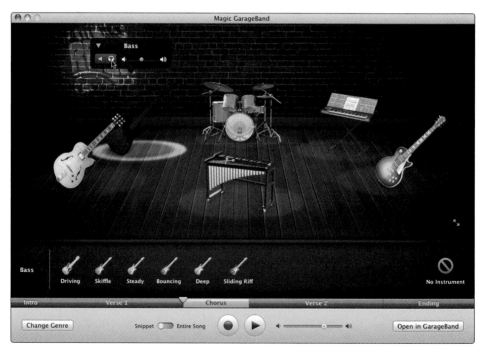

7.19 It's usually easiest to start by silencing most of the instruments so that you can gradually build up the sound you want. You can play along on your instrument to help choose the right backing tracks.

Note Instead of silencing an instrument, you can get rid of it. Click the instrument, and then click the No Instrument button on the toolbar. The instrument disappears, leaving an empty spotlight on the boards as its placeholder.

2. **When you've silenced all the instruments except the one you want to start with, click the Play button, and then click the toolbar button for the style you want.** Drag the instrument's volume control if you need to increase or decrease the volume.

3. **Click the instrument you want to add next, turn off its muting, and then click the toolbar button for the style.**

4. **Repeat Step 3 as needed to add each other instrument you want to the song and choose the style you want it to play.** To focus on one instrument, you can click its Solo button (the button that shows a pair of headphones).

5. **When you're satisfied with your choices, click Open in GarageBand to create the project.** Magic GarageBand pulls together the files, and then displays the song in the GarageBand window. Figure 7.20 shows an example.

7.20 When your song appears in the main GarageBand window, you can customize it manually to get exactly the structure and sound you're looking for.

Genius

You can change an instrument's style at any point by clicking the instrument, and then clicking the style you want.

Note

To switch to another genre, you can click Change Genre at any time.

From here, you can adjust the song as needed. For example

- **Rename it.** Magic GarageBand gives the song a generic name based on the genre. To rename it, choose File ⇨ Save As.

- **Customize your instrument.** Double-click the track header for your instrument to open the Track Info pane, click the Edit tab, and then pick your preferred settings.

- **Change some of the loops.** If you find that a particular section doesn't fit the song you're trying to create, you can change it or simply delete it. See Chapter 8 for details.

- **Add other tracks as needed.** See Chapter 8 for details.

Improving Your Instrument Playing with GarageBand

One of GarageBand's most exciting features is Learn to Play, which gives you lessons in instruments such as piano and guitar right through GarageBand. GarageBand includes the first couple of basic lessons, and you can download further basic lessons for free from the Lesson Store. The Lesson Store also sells artist lessons, in which artists give you a walkthrough of how to play a particular song.

Getting started with Learn to Play

To get started with Learn to Play, simply choose File ⇨ New (or press ⌘+N), and then click the Learn to Play button on the left of the opening GarageBand screen. Click the lesson you want, and then click Choose. GarageBand opens the lesson full screen (see Figure 7.21) and starts teaching you.

7.21 GarageBand's Learn to Play feature helps you get up to speed on piano or guitar — and even teaches you how to play popular songs.

Practicing with the How Did I Play? feature

To play along and have GarageBand track your progress with its How Did I Play? feature, move the mouse pointer over the left end of the instruction area, and then click Play on the pop-up panel that appears. GarageBand switches to Play mode. Click the Record button to start recording your playback. GarageBand automatically tracks your results, showing the notes you hit correctly in green and the notes you get wrong in red (see Figure 7.22).

Click the History button to display a screen showing a history of your progress. Click the Done button when you're ready to resume practice.

Getting more lessons for Learn to Play

To get more lessons for Learn to Play, choose File ➪ New (or press ⌘+N), and then click the Lesson Store button on the left of the opening GarageBand screen. Click the Guitar tab to find guitar lessons, the Piano tab to find piano lessons, or the Artist tab to find lessons by particular artists (see Figure 7.23).

7.22 The How Did I Play? feature scores the notes you play against those you should be playing, enabling you to keep track of your progress.

7.23 The Lesson Store provides guitar lessons and piano lessons by popular artists.

How Do I Record a Song in GarageBand?

With your music studio set up on your Mac as described in Chapter 7, you're ready to record an original song. If you want to begin by assembling tracks from loops, start at the beginning; if you want to start using the Arrangement Track to structure your song, or if you're ready to record either Software Instrument or Real Instrument tracks, jump straight into the middle of the chapter. And if you've wondered how to create your own custom Software Instruments or jot down the lyrics in a song project, go to the end of the chapter to find out.

Creating a New Track

If you've come straight from Chapter 7 and already have GarageBand running with a music project open — either a new project from exploring GarageBand or a project you've kick-started using Magic GarageBand — you're ready to start. Otherwise, start a new project like this:

1. **Launch GarageBand from the Dock or from the Applications folder.**
2. **If GarageBand opens the previous project you were working on, choose File ⇨ New to close it and display the GarageBand opening screen.**
3. **In the left column, click the New Project button.**
4. **Click the instrument or instrument collection you want to use.** For example, click Piano.
5. **Click Choose.** GarageBand displays the New Project from Template dialog.
6. **Type the song name; choose the tempo, signature, and key; click Create.**

This chapter starts off with a new project that uses the default settings from the New Project from Template dialog: 4 / 4 time signature at 120 beats per minute and the C major key.

When you start most new projects, GarageBand gives you a single track for the instrument you chose. For example, if you choose Piano in the New Project from Template dialog, GarageBand gives you a Grand Piano track to start off with. For other projects, such as Keyboard Collection, GarageBand starts you off with multiple tracks.

To pick a different type of instrument, double-click the track header to open the Track Info pane with the Browse tab selected. You can then change the instrument to another Software Instrument, as described later in this chapter.

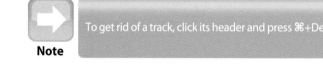

Note To get rid of a track, click its header and press ⌘+Delete or choose Track ⇨ Delete Track.

Beginning to add a track

Here's how to add a new track to your music project and choose the instrument for it:

1. **Click the New Track button in the lower-left corner of the GarageBand window, or choose Track ⇨ New Track, or simply press ⌘+Option+N.** GarageBand displays the dialog shown in Figure 8.1, prompting you to choose between a Software Instrument track, a Real Instrument track, or an Electric Guitar track.

Software Instrument	Real Instrument	Electric Guitar
For Instrument sounds created by GarageBand and playable using a USB, MIDI, or onscreen keyboard.	For audio recordings such as voice, guitar, bass, or any instrument that can be captured by a microphone.	For audio recordings of electric guitar using built-in GarageBand amps and stompbox effects.

▶ Instrument Setup

⑦   Cancel   Create

8.1 The first step in adding a new track is to choose a Software Instrument track, a Real Instrument track, or an Electric Guitar track.

2. Click the track type you want to add:

- **Software Instrument.** Click this button if you want to add a track consisting either of Software Instrument loops or of a Software Instrument that you play using either one of GarageBand's on-screen keyboards (see Chapter 7 for details) or an external musical keyboard you connect via USB.

- **Real Instrument.** Click this button to add a track that you use either to play Real Instrument loops or to record a real instrument such as an electric guitar or bass, a vocal track, or any other track that uses an external microphone (for example, a piano, an acoustic guitar, or a woodwind instrument).

- **Electric Guitar.** Click this button to add a track specifically for electric guitar. This option enables you to use GarageBand's built-in amplifiers and stompbox effects.

Genius

GarageBand can't actually tell which instrument you've plugged in, so you can put other instruments through an Electric Guitar track if you want to use its effects on them.

3. If you want to change the instrument's setup, click the Instrument Setup disclosure triangle to reveal the hidden part of the dialog (see Figure 8.2), and then choose settings:

- **My instrument is connected with.** In the upper pop-up menu, select the means of connection — System Setting (using the setting in System Preferences's Sounds pane), Built-in Input, Built-in Microphone, or an external audio interface you've connected. In the lower pop-up menu, select Mono 1 for a mono input on channel 1, Mono 2 for a mono input on channel 2, or Stereo 1/2 for a stereo input using both channels.

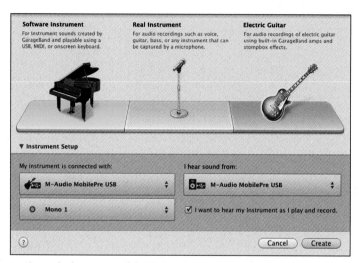

Note For a Software Instrument track, only the I hear sound from pop-up menu is available in the extra section of the dialog for adding a track.

8.2 Open the lower part of the dialog if you need to specify the way the instrument is connected

- **I hear sound from.** In this pop-up menu, choose the audio output you're using — System Setting (using the setting in System Preferences's Sounds pane), Built-in Output, or an external audio interface you've connected.

- **I want to hear my Instrument as I play and record.** Select this check box if you want GarageBand to play the instrument's sound back through whichever output you've chosen in the I hear sound from pop-up menu. Usually, you'll want to select this check box unless you're listening to the instrument using a means that bypasses GarageBand — for example, headphones plugged into an external audio interface.

4. **Click Create.** GarageBand adds the track and displays the Track Info pane. You can now choose settings for the Software Instrument track (as discussed in the next section), the Real Instrument track, or the Guitar Track.

Setting up a Software Instrument track

Use the Track Info pane (see Figure 8.3) to set up a Software Instrument track like this:

1. **In the left column, click the instrument category you want — for example, Drum Kits.** The list of available instruments (or kits, for drums) appears in the right column.

8.3 Choose the instrument category and the specific instrument for a Software Instrument track on the Browse tab of the Track Info pane.

2. **In the right column, click the instrument you want — for example, Rock Kit.** GarageBand applies the instrument. If an instrument is grayed out, you may need to install extra GarageBand files from your iLife install DVD or from Software Update.

3. **Test the instrument's sound by playing your keyboard.** Use either the Onscreen Keyboard, the Musical Typing keyboard, or your external musical keyboard. If you don't like the sounds, you can either choose another instrument by repeating Steps 2 and 3, or change its sound as described later in this chapter.

4. **If you want to change the icon for the instrument, click the instrument icon near the bottom of the Track Info pane, and then choose an icon on the pop-up panel.**

5. **Click the Track Info button if you're ready to hide the Track Info pane again.** (If you have enough screen space, you can leave the Track Info pane open if you prefer.)

Setting up a Real Instrument track

Here's how to set up a Real Instrument track in the Track Info pane (shown in Figure 8.4):

1. **If you will play an instrument through this track instead of playing loops, connect the instrument, as described in Chapter 7.** If the instrument is already connected, you're set.

2. **In the left column, click the category of loop or instrument you will play through this track — for example, Bass.** The list of available effects appears in the right column.

3. **In the right column, click the effect you want to apply to the instrument — for example, Edgy Rock Bass for a bass.**

4. **For a musical instrument or microphone, make sure the Input Source pop-up menu shows the source you want.** This is the setting you chose when adding the track; you can change it here if necessary (for example, if you plug your guitar into a different input).

5. **For a musical instrument or microphone, you can use the Monitor pop-up menu to change the monitoring of the input.** Select Off, On, or On (no feedback protection), as needed; the On setting has feedback protection. If you're planning to use

8.4 On the Browse tab of the Track Info pane for a Real Instrument, choose the instrument type, the effect you want, and the input source and recording level if you're using an instrument rather than loops.

this Real Instrument track only for GarageBand's Real Instrument loops, make sure the Monitor pop-up menu is set to Off.

Genius

Turn GarageBand's monitor off if you put the musical instrument through an audio interface that lets you monitor it outside the Mac. For example, if your audio interface can drive an amplifier, you can monitor the instrument through the amplifier rather than through GarageBand.

6. **For a musical instrument or microphone, drag the Recording Level slider to set the recording level.** Select the Automatic Level Control check box if you want GarageBand to set the level for you. If these settings aren't available, you'll need to control the input volume manually on your audio interface.

7. **Click the Track Info button if you're ready to hide the Track Info pane again.**

Caution

Avoid using GarageBand's Automatic Level Control if possible. GarageBand doesn't know how loud you're going to play, so it will need to adjust the level as the input volume changes. You'll get much better results by setting the Recording Level control manually to a level that allows your loudest playing without distortion but that doesn't adjust automatically for quieter passages.

Setting up an Electric Guitar track

Here's how to set up an Electric Guitar track in the Guitar Track pane:

1. **If you haven't already connected the guitar, connect it as described in Chapter 7.**

2. **In the pop-up menu at the top of the pane, choose the sound on which you want to base this guitar track.** For example, choose Classic Crunch, Seventies Metal, or Woodstock Fuzz. GarageBand displays an amplifier with the effects pedals used for the sound. Figure 8.5 shows an example.

3. **To switch to a different amplifier, move the mouse pointer over the amplifier, and then click either the Previous button or the Next button that GarageBand displays.** GarageBand changes the amplifier. Test the setting, and decide whether to change it again.

4. **To change one of the existing settings, click the effects pedal you want to change, and then use your mouse to change the knobs, switches, and other controls.**

5. **To change the pedals used for the sound, click the Edit button to the right of the pop-up menu that shows the sound's name.** The Guitar Track pane shows the selection of available pedals (see Figure 8.6). Drag a pedal up to a space on the stage to add it, or drag a pedal down off the stage to remove it. Click Done when you finish.

8.5 In the Guitar Track pane, choose the basic sound, and then customize it as needed while you play.

8.6 You can add or remove effects pedals to produce exactly the sound you want.

Genius

To swap the positions of two of the pedals you're using, drag one from its current position to the other pedal's position. GarageBand swaps the pedals for you.

6. **If you've customized the sound, save the changes.** Click Save Setting, type a name for the new sound in the Save Instrument dialog, and then click Save. You can then reapply your sound quickly by choosing it from the My Settings section at the bottom of the pop-up menu.

7. **Click the Track Info button if you're ready to hide the Track Info pane again.**

Browsing and Auditioning Loops

The quick way to build a track is by using GarageBand's prerecorded loops of music. These loops, which are called Apple Loops, contain chunks of music that you can assemble into the order you want to create a track. GarageBand lets you change the tempo and pitch of loops, so you can make them sound substantially different to suit the needs of a song.

To work with loops, you use the loop browser, which lets you audition loops, add them to your song, and view their original tempo, key, and duration.

Start by opening the loop browser in one of these ways:

- **Click the loop browser button.**
- **Press ⌘+L.**
- **Choose Control ⇨ Show loop browser.**

Figure 8.7 shows the loop browser in its normal view with the Guitars button

Musical view

Column view | Podcast sounds view

Preview volume slider | Drag down to reveal more buttons

Results list

8.7 The loop browser open in Musical Button view.

237

clicked. The icons that appear in green indicate Software Instrument loops and work only in Software Instrument tracks. The icons that appear in blue indicate Real Instrument loops and work only in Real Instrument tracks.

Choosing a view and finding loops

You can find loops in three easy ways in the loop browser:

- **Musical Button view.** Click a button to display the list of loops tagged with that keyword — for example, Guitars. Click another button to narrow the selection further.

- **Column view.** Click the keyword type in the first column, click the category in the second column, and then click the keyword in the third column (see Figure 8.8). The results then appear in the results list.

- **Searching and sorting.** To search, click in the Search box, type one or more keywords, and then press Return. To sort the loops you find, click a column heading.

8.8 Column view enables you to browse the loops by genres, instruments, moods, or favorites.

Genius

You can swap the positions of any two buttons in Musical Button view by clicking a button, dragging it onto another button, and dropping it there. You can also change a button by Control+clicking or right-clicking it and choosing the item you want it to bear.

Note

The loop browser also has Podcast Sounds view, which shows only jingles, stingers, sound effects, and favorites. See Chapter 11 for coverage of Podcast Sounds view.

Auditioning a loop by itself

To audition a loop by itself, click it in the list in the loop browser. GarageBand starts playing the loop repeatedly until you stop it by clicking again, by clicking another loop to start that loop playing, or by dropping the loop on a track in the song (as discussed next).

Genius

When you audition a loop and find you like it, select its check box in the Fav (Favorites) column. You can then find it quickly by clicking the instrument type (for example, Bass) and then clicking the Fav column heading to bring your favorites to the top. In Column view, you can click Favorites in the first column to browse by favorites.

Adding a loop to your song

When you find a loop you want to use in your song, drag the loop from the Results List to the Track List:

● **To use an existing track, drop the loop on that track.** GarageBand displays a black vertical bar that shows the bar at which you place the loop's start (see Figure 8.9). If you need to change the settings for the track, double-click its header and work in the Track Info pane, as described earlier in this chapter.

8.9 When you add a loop to an existing track, the black vertical bar shows where the loop's region will begin.

● **To create a new track, drop the loop below the last track you used in the Track List.** GarageBand automatically creates a new track of the right type (Software Instrument or Real Instrument) for the loop you dropped.

239

When you add a loop like this, GarageBand creates a region containing the loop. The region is a copy of the loop that you can adjust without changing the original version of the loop.

If the region ends up in the wrong track bar, click it and drag it to where you want it.

Playing back the song

When you place one or more loops in your song, listen to it so that you can judge how the loops work together.

1. **Move the playhead to where you want to start playback.** For example, click the Go to Beginning button in the transport controls (see Figure 8.10) to move the playhead to the beginning of the song.

2. **Click the Play button to start playback.**

3. **Click the Play button again when you want to stop playback.**

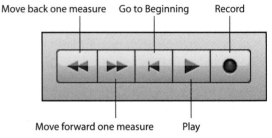

Move back one measure   Go to Beginning   Record

Move forward one measure   Play

8.10 Use the transport controls to play back the song.

Repeating, shortening, and extending regions

Next, adjust the duration of the region as needed for your song:

⦿ **Repeat the region.** To make the region play back more than once, position the mouse pointer over the upper part of the region's right border so that the pointer changes to a curling arrow. Drag the border to the right as far as you want the region to repeat. GarageBand shows a notch at the end of each full repetition (see Figure 8.11), so you can easily end the region right at the end of a repetition if you need to.

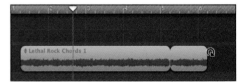

8.11 Drag the upper part of a region's right border to the right to repeat the region. The notches at the top and bottom indicate complete repetitions of the loop.

240

Note

You can't shorten a region that you've repeated. Instead, reduce the length of the last repetition by dragging to the left with the curling arrow.

 Shorten a region. To play only part of the region, position the mouse pointer over the lower part of the region's right border so that the pointer changes to a bracket with two arrows. Drag to the left to shorten the region (see Figure 8.12).

8.12 Drag the lower part of a region's right border to the left to shorten the region.

Genius

You can also extend a Software Instrument region by dragging the lower part of its right border to the right. Extending the region is different from looping it because you add empty air to the end of the region. This sounds pointless, but it lets you join two regions together, as described next. You can't extend a Real Instrument region.

Joining two or more regions into a single region

After you adjust two or more regions so that they play just right in sequence, you can join them together so that you can repeat the sequence more easily in another part of the song.

Here's how to join adjacent regions:

1. **Select the regions you want to join.** Click the first region, and then Shift+click each other region in turn.

2. **Choose Edit ⇨ Join or press ⌘+J.** GarageBand joins the regions together and gives the joined region the name that the first region had.

Splitting a region in two

Other times, you may need to split a region into two parts. Splitting is especially useful with regions you record and then find you want to use in separate parts, but you can also split GarageBand's prerecorded regions if you want. Follow these steps:

1. **Position the playhead where you want to split the region.**

2. **Click the region you want to split.**

3. **Choose Edit ⇨ Split or press ⌘+T.** GarageBand splits the region and gives each new region the same name.

4. **Rename the regions to indicate the change.** This step is optional, but if you don't rename the regions, it's easy to get confused by their having the same name but different contents.

Auditioning a loop with your song

Auditioning a loop by itself lets you focus on how it sounds, but often you'll be able to judge its suitability better by listening to how it sounds with the rest of your song so far. You can do this easily:

1. **Move the playhead to just before the part of the song where you want to try out the loop.**

2. **Click the Play button to start playback.**

3. **When playback reaches the bar before where you want to hear the loop, click the loop in the results list.** GarageBand starts playing the loop when the new bar begins.

4. **Drag the Preview Volume slider as needed to change the loop's volume.** For example, you may need to increase its volume so that you can hear it more clearly over the other tracks.

Auditioning multiple loops with the cycle region

If you need to audition several loops, turn on the cycle region so that GarageBand repeatedly plays back the part of the song you want to hear. Follow these steps:

1. **Click the Cycle Region button (the button with two gray arrows to the right of the time display) to turn on the cycle region.** GarageBand changes the arrows to blue and displays a golden bar below the Timeline indicating the extent of the cycle region.

2. **To change the region, position the mouse pointer over the start or finish, and then drag the region to where you want it (see Figure 8.13).**

8.13 Drag either end of the yellow cycle region to tell GarageBand which part of the song to repeat.

3. **Move the playhead to where you want to start play, and then click the Play button.**
   GarageBand starts playing the cycle region and loops back to the start when it reaches the end.

Note When you turn on the cycle region, clicking the Go to Beginning button in the transport controls moves the playhead to the beginning of the cycle region rather than the beginning of the song.

4. **Click the first loop you want to play.**
   When you're ready to start the next loop, click it. Click the Play button when you want to stop playback.

Switching to another loop in the same family

Two arrows that appear in the upper-left corner of the loop's region means the loop is part of a family of loops, a group of loops that are related to each other.

You can switch quickly to another loop in the same family by clicking the arrows and then choosing the loop from the pop-up menu (see Figure 8.14).

✓ 100 Rpt bass Cmaj 01
100 Rpt bass Cmaj 02
100 Rpt bass Cmaj 03
100 Rpt bass Cmaj 04
100 Rpt bass Cmaj 05
100 Rpt bass Cmaj 06
100 Rpt bass Cmaj 07
100 Rpt bass Cmaj 08
100 Rpt bass Cmaj 09
100 Rpt bass Cmaj 10
100 Rpt bass Cmaj 11
100 Rpt bass Cmaj 12
100 Rpt bass Cmaj 13
100 Rpt bass Cmaj 14
100 Rpt bass Cmaj 15
100 Rpt bass Cmaj 16

8.14 Click the pair of arrows in the upper-left corner of a loop to switch quickly to a related loop.

Genius Switching loops like this can give strange effects, but it's well worth a try, especially because you can switch back to the previous loop in moments.

Filtering loops

To cut down on the number of results in the results list, you can filter the results by scale type. To do so, open the Scale pop-up menu at the top of the loop browser and choose Major, Minor, Neither, or Good For Both. Filtering by scale is helpful with harmonic loops such as bass lines or melodies; don't use it for rhythmic loops such as drums, where it won't help.

To turn off filtering by scale type, choose Any in the Scale pop-up menu.

Note You can filter loops further by selecting the Filter for more relevant results check box in Loops preferences (choose GarageBand ➪ Preferences, and then click Loops). This setting restricts the display to loops within two semitones of the song key and is useful when you have many loops in your GarageBand library.

Adding loops to your collection

GarageBand comes with plenty of loops to get you started, but if you get heavily into GarageBand, you'll want to add further loops. You can add other people's prerecorded loops as described here, or you can create your own custom loops, as described next.

You can add loops to GarageBand in three ways:

- **Run an installation routine.** If you buy one of the GarageBand Jam Packs from the Apple Store (http://store.apple.com), run the installation routine to install the loops.

- **Add individual loops or folders of loops to the loop browser.** Open a Finder window to the folder that contains the individual loops or the folders of loops. Select the loops or the folders you want to add, drag them to the loop browser, and drop them there. GarageBand displays the Importing Loops dialog while it imports the loops and categorizes them.

- **Add a loop to a song.** Instead of adding one or more loops to the loop browser, you can insert a single loop directly in a song. When you do this, the loop doesn't appear in the loop browser, so you can use it only in the song to which you added it. Chances are you won't want to do this often, but when you do, open a Finder window to the folder that contains the loop, drag the loop to the existing track in which you want to use it in the GarageBand window, and then drop it. To create a new track using the loop, drop the loop below the last track in the track list.

Creating your own loops

One of the best things about GarageBand is that you can create your own loops from either Real Instrument or Software Instrument recordings you make. You're getting a bit ahead of yourself here because you probably haven't made any recordings yet, but when you have, come back to this section and try making a loop.

Follow these steps to create a loop:

1. **Record the loop and edit it as necessary to make a region the right length for the loop.** Use the editing techniques described in this chapter and in Chapter 9.

2. **Click the region in the Timeline to select it.**

3. **Choose Edit ⇨ Add To Loop Library to display the dialog shown in Figure 8.15.**

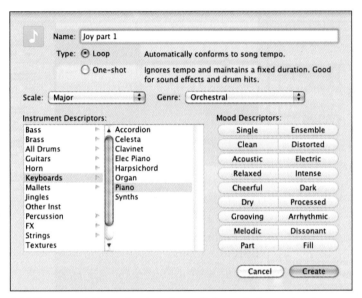

8.15 You can quickly create a loop from a Software Instrument region or a Real Instrument region.

4. **Type the name you want to give the loop in the Name box.** GarageBand suggests the instrument's name, but giving it a more descriptive name is better. Name your loops consistently (for example, Storming Electric Lead 1, Storming Electric Lead 2) to make them appear next to each other in the results list.

5. **In the Type area, choose whether to create a loop or a one-shot sound:**

    - **Loop.** This is what you'll normally create — a region that GarageBand automatically manipulates to make it match the song's tempo.

    - **One-shot.** This is a sound file that you want to always play back at the tempo at which you recorded it — for example, a cymbal smash, a guitar riff that you want to use only at a specific tempo, or a sound effect that always needs to play at the same speed.

6. **Open the Scale pop-up menu and choose with which scales you want to use the loop or sound: Any, Minor, Major, Neither, or Good For Both.** This setting controls when the loop appears when you filter the loops by the Scale pop-up menu in the loop browser.

7. **Open the Genre pop-up menu and choose the genre: None, Rock/Blues, Electronic, Jazz, Urban, World, Cinematic, Orchestral, Country/Folk, Experimental, or Other Genre.** Specifying the genre lets you browse the loops by genre, which can save time.

8. **In the Instrument Descriptors box, click the instrument type on the left, and then click the specific instrument on the right.** For example, choose All Drums on the left and Kick on the right.

9. **In the Mood Descriptors area, click the button for each descriptor you want to apply to the loop.** When you click a button, it turns blue; click it again if you want to turn it off. The buttons are arranged in opposing pairs by row, so clicking one button in a pair turns off the other button if it's on. For example, Single and Ensemble are opposites, so you can select only one of them at once.

10. **Click Create to close the dialog and add the loop to GarageBand's library.**

Working with the Arrangement Track

If your song follows a normal pattern, it will have several components that repeat one or more times, either identically or with variations. GarageBand lets you break up your song into different sections that you can copy and repeat as needed. For example, you can divide your song into an intro section, a verse section that repeats, a chorus section that repeats, a bridge between some of the repetitions, and an ending.

To define and manipulate the different sections of the song, you create what GarageBand calls arrangement regions in the Arrangement Track. An arrangement region acts as a vertical section of the Timeline — you choose how many beats or bars it lasts — and gives you a way of grabbing all the loops you've positioned in that part of the Timeline. You can then move or copy all the contents of the arrangement region at once.

Setting up arrangement regions

First, set up arrangement regions within the Arrangement Track like this:

1. **Display the Arrangement Track at the top of the Timeline by choosing Track ⇨ Show Arrangement Track or pressing ⌘+Shift+A.** The Arrangement Track appears as a gray bar below the beat ruler with a single button — the Create a new Arrangement region button — on it (see Figure 8.16).

Arrangement track

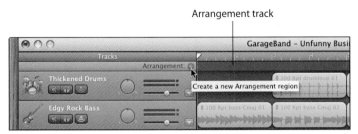

8.16 The Arrangement Track appears below the beat ruler.

2. **Click the Create a new Arrangement region button to create a new arrangement region.** GarageBand adds an eight-bar region and names it "untitled."

3. **If you need to change the start position of the arrangement region, drag the bar so that its beginning is in the appropriate place.**

Note If you move the first arrangement region from the beginning of the song, GarageBand automatically creates a new arrangement region at the beginning of the song to occupy whatever space is available.

4. **To change the duration of the arrangement region, drag its right border to where you want the region to end.**

5. **Rename the arrangement region by double-clicking the "untitled" name, typing the new name, and then pressing Return.** Make sure the arrangement region is selected before you double-click; if it's not, the double-click won't register correctly.

6. **To create a new arrangement region, click the Create a new Arrangement region button.** GarageBand adds the new arrangement region after the one you just renamed. Adjust the new arrangement region and rename it as before.

Moving and copying arrangement regions

After you create arrangement regions, you can quickly rearrange your song by dragging them in these ways:

● **Copy an arrangement region.** Option+drag the arrangement region to where you want the copy. GarageBand creates a copy and adds "copy" to the original name. Rename the copy with a more descriptive name.

● **Move an arrangement region.** Drag the arrangement region to where you want it. GarageBand moves the other arrangement regions out of the way as you drag (see Figure 8.17).

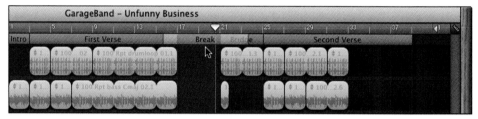

8.17 Drag an arrangement region to move its section of your song to another position.

● **Swap the positions of two arrangement regions.** Drag one of the arrangement regions and drop it on the other arrangement region. GarageBand swaps the two arrangement regions over.

● **Overwrite an arrangement region with another arrangement region.** ⌘+drag the arrangement region and drop it on the arrangement region you want to overwrite.

Joining and splitting arrangement regions

You can join two or more arrangement regions like this:

1. **If the arrangement regions aren't adjacent, drag one or more of them so that they are.**

2. **Click the first arrangement region, and then Shift+click each other arrangement region to select all the ones you want to join.**

3. **Choose Edit ➪ Join or press ⌘+J to join the regions.** GarageBand gives the joined arrangement region the name of the first arrangement region. Rename it if necessary.

Similarly, you can split an arrangement region into two arrangement regions:

1. **Position the playhead where you want to split the arrangement region.**

2. **Choose Edit ➪ Split or press ⌘+T.** GarageBand splits the arrangement region and gives each new arrangement region the same name.

3. **Rename one or both of the arrangement regions as needed.** Leaving both with the same name is a recipe for confusion.

Changing the Song's Tempo, Signature, and Key

When you first create the song project, you choose the tempo, the time signature, and the key for it. But often, as you assemble the song, you realize that you need to change one or more of these elements.

GarageBand makes it easy to change the tempo, the time signature, and the key. However, it's important that if you do need to make one of these changes, you do so before you record any Real Instrument tracks into your song. This is because GarageBand can't change the tempo, time signature, and key of audio you record in Real Instrument tracks.

To change the tempo, time signature, or key, choose Project in the LCD Mode pop-up menu at the left side of the display. You can then use the Key pop-up menu, the Tempo pop-up menu, or the Signature pop-up menu (see Figure 8.18) to make the change.

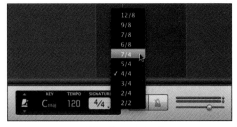

8.18 You can quickly change the key, tempo, or time signature using the Project LCD.

Recording Software Instruments and Real Instruments

GarageBand's wide selection of Software Instruments lets you play everything from grand piano to bass and drums using your musical keyboard, the Onscreen Keyboard, or the Musical Typing keyboard. This is great for composing music, but what's even better is adding a real musical instrument or a vocal part to your GarageBand song. This section shows you how to do both.

You can record either Software Instruments or Real Instruments in a single take or in multiple takes. With Software Instruments, you can also combine multiple passes through a cycle region into a single recording.

Preparing to record a Software Instrument

Start by getting your keyboard and the Software Instrument track ready like this:

1. **Get your keyboard ready.** Connect your musical keyboard via USB if it's not already connected. Or, if you're using the Onscreen Keyboard or the Musical Typing keyboard, display that keyboard.

2. **Add a Software Instrument track for the instrument you want to play, as described earlier in this chapter.** If your song already contains a Software Instrument track for the instrument, click that track's header to activate it.

3. **Position the playhead where you want to start playing.** For example, click the Go to Beginning button to move the playhead to the beginning of the song.

Preparing to record a Real Instrument or Electric Guitar

Follow these steps to get a musical instrument ready for recording:

1. **Connect your instrument to your Mac, as discussed in Chapter 7.** For example, plug your electric guitar into an audio interface connected via USB to your Mac, and check that the Audio Input pop-up menu in GarageBand's Audio/MIDI preferences is set to use that audio interface.

2. **Add a Real Instrument track of the appropriate type to the song, as discussed earlier in this chapter.** Choose the right input source in the Input Source pop-up menu in the Track Info pane, and choose whether to turn the monitor off, on, or on without feedback protection. For an electric guitar, add an Electric Guitar track.

3. **Play your instrument, and set the recording level.** Look at the level meter in the Mixer column for the track you're recording. You need to have the green LEDs and some of the orange LEDs lighting up while the input plays, but not have all the red on constantly or you'll get distortion. To adjust the recording level, drag the Recording Level Slider in the Track Info pane for the track or change the volume on the instrument or the audio interface.

4. **If you want to change the track's name, double-click the default name in the track header, type the new name, and then press Return.**

Genius

To give yourself a heads-up of when to start playing, turn on the count-in feature by choosing Control⇨ Count In or pressing ⌘+Shift+U. GarageBand then gives you a one-bar count-in when you click the Record button. The count-in works only when the metronome is turned on (choose Control⇨ Metronome or press ⌘+U).

Recording in a single take

The straightforward way of recording a track is by using a single take, either for part of the song or (if you prefer) for the whole song. Follow these steps:

1. **Click the Record button to start recording.** Alternatively, press R.

2. **Play your part on the keyboard (for a Software Instrument) or on the musical instrument (for a Real Instrument).**

3. **Click the Record button to stop recording, or click the Play button to stop both recording and playback.**

Caution   Before recording multiple takes with Software Instruments, make sure that you deselect the Automatically merge Software Instrument recordings when using the cycle region check box in the General preferences. If this check box is selected, you will create a single layered part instead (as discussed next). This setting doesn't apply to Real Instruments.

Recording multiple takes with cycle recording

If you prefer, you can record multiple takes for the same part of the song by turning on the cycle region. This works for both Software Instrument tracks and Real Instrument tracks.

Here's how to record multiple takes:

1. **Click the cycle region button to turn on the cycle region.** Drag the ends of the cycle region so that it will repeat the part of the song you want to record.

2. **Click the Record button to start recording.**

3. **Play your part on the keyboard or musical instrument.** When the Playhead reaches the end of the cycle region, it loops back to the start of the region. GarageBand starts recording a new take, so you can just keep playing.

8.19 The yellow icon shows how many takes you've recorded for the region.

4. **Click the Record button to stop recording, or click the Play button to stop both recording and playback.** The yellow icon in the upper-left corner of the recorded region shows how many takes you've recorded (see Figure 8.19).

Now play back the song and decide which take you want to keep. You can switch from take to take by clicking the icon and choosing the take from the pop-up menu (see Figure 8.20).

8.20 Use the pop-up menu to switch from one take to another and to delete the takes you don't want to keep.

Creating a layered part with cycle recording

With Software Instruments, the alternative to recording multiple takes with cycle recording is to use multiple passes through the same region to build a layered part. Each time GarageBand loops through the cycle region, it merges the new notes you play with those you recorded on previous passes.

This technique is especially useful for creating drum parts because it lets you record using several passes rather than a single pass. For example, you can record hi-hat and bass drum on the first pass, snare drum and ride cymbal on the second pass, tom-toms on the third pass, and extra cymbals and percussion on subsequent passes. You end up with a single region that contains all the drums instead of having a separate region for each pass.

Here's how to create a layered part:

1. **Choose GarageBand ⇨ Preferences.** Select the Automatically merge Software Instrument recordings when using the cycle region check box in the General preferences, and then close the Preferences window.

2. **Click the Cycle Region to turn on the cycle region.** Drag the ends of the cycle region so that it repeats the part of the song you want to record.

3. **Click the Record button to start recording.**

4. **Play your first pass on the keyboard.** When the playhead reaches the end of the cycle region, it loops back to the start of the region. Start your second pass, and repeat with as many passes as you need. As you play, GarageBand merges all the notes into the same region. Figure 8.21 shows this process on the Rock Kit track.

8.21 Creating a layered part by playing multiple passes through the same cycle region

5. **Click the Record button to stop recording, or click the Play button to stop both recording and playback.**

After you finish recording, listen to the track. If you need to add further to it, you can do so by simply starting recording again and playing the additions.

Recording multiple tracks at once

Record button

8.22 Click to place a red dot on the Record button for each track you want to record with multitrack recording.

At first, GarageBand is set to record a single track at once. When you're working on your own, this is usually the best way to proceed unless you're a live-action, one-man band.

When you need to record two or more tracks at once, choose Track⇨Enable Multitrack Recording or press ⌘+Option+R to turn on multitrack recording. When you do this, GarageBand displays a Record button at the left end of the buttons on each track's track header (see Figure 8.22). Click the Record button for each track you want to record so that the Record button shows a red dot.

Note Each track you record must have its own input channel — otherwise GarageBand doesn't know which track receives the input. And if you have connected only a single MIDI keyboard to your Mac, you can record only a single Software Instrument track at once.

When you want to turn off multitrack recording, choose Track⇨Disable Multitrack Recording or press ⌘+Option+R again.

Creating Custom Software Instruments

GarageBand comes with a great set of Software Instruments that you can use straight out of the box, but if you want to make your music sound special, you can build your own Software Instruments. The process is quick and easy, especially if you start from an existing Software Instrument, as this section shows you how to do.

Follow these steps to create a custom Software Instrument from an existing Software Instrument:

1. **Click the New button, or press ⌘+Option+N, to display the dialog for creating a new track.**

2. **Select the Software Instrument option button, and then click Create.** GarageBand creates a new Grand Piano track and displays the Track Info pane showing its settings.

3. **Switch to the instrument on which you want to base your new instrument.** In the left list box, select the category of instrument — for example, Guitars. In the right list box, select the instrument itself — for example, Big Electric Lead.

4. **Click the Edit tab to display the settings for the instrument you chose.** Figure 8.23 shows an example.

5. **Play the instrument using your musical keyboard (or one of GarageBand's keyboards) and see how it sounds.** Continue to play as you make changes so that you can judge their effects.

8.23 Use the controls on the Edit tab of the Track Info pane to create a new custom Software Instrument that sounds just the way you want it to.

6. **If you want to make sweeping changes, change the sound generator used to create the sound.** In the Sound Generator area, choose the generator from the upper pop-up menu and the sound from the lower pop-up menu. You can also click the picture under the Sound Generator text and use the dialog that appears to customize the sound of the instrument. The dialog contains different controls depending on the instrument; Figure 8.24 shows an example of the Guitar dialog. Click the Close button (the red button) to close the dialog when you finish.

7. **Adjust or remove the effects already applied to the instrument:**

   - To adjust an effect, choose a different sound in the pop-up menu below its name.

   - To edit the sound in the pop-up menu, click the picture button to its left, and then work in the dialog that appears. Figure 8.25 shows the Amp Simulation dialog for adjusting guitar sounds. Click the Close button (the red button) to close the dialog when you finish.

   - To turn an effect off, click the green light on the left side of the picture button so that the light goes off.

8. **Add other effects as needed:**

   - Click one of the unused buttons in the Effects area, and choose the effect from the pop-up menu that appears.

   - Choose a sound or setting in the pop-up menu below the name of the effect you added.

   - If necessary, edit the sound or setting by clicking the picture button and working in the resulting dialog.

9. **To make your custom instrument easy to recognize in the track list, click the Browse tab, click the icon button at the bottom, and choose a distinctive icon from the panel.**

10. **Click Save Instrument at the bottom of the Details pane, type a descriptive name in the Save Instrument dialog, and then click Save.**

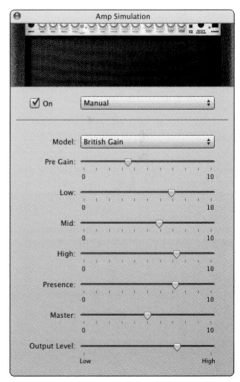

8.24 To change the overall sound of an instrument, open its dialog and adjust the controls.

8.25 Configuring the amplifier simulation effect for a guitar.

Normally, you'll want to keep the Software Instruments you create, but if you decide you no longer need one, you can delete it by clicking it in the Track Info window and then clicking Delete Instrument. GarageBand confirms the deletion (see Figure 8.26); click Remove to get rid of the instrument.

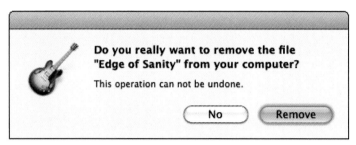

Do you really want to remove the file "Edge of Sanity" from your computer?

This operation can not be undone.

No   Remove

8.26 GarageBand confirms that you want to delete a custom Software Instrument from your Mac.

Keeping Notes with GarageBand's Notepad

When you write a song, you often need to jot down ideas, lyrics, or notes about the instruments and settings you use. GarageBand provides a handy Notepad for taking notes within a project.

To open the Notepad, choose Window ➪ Notepad or press ⌘+Option+P. With the Notepad window open (see Figure 8.27) you can write down whatever you need.

You don't need to save the contents of the Notepad separately because GarageBand automatically saves the notes in the project file.

Notepad

Colors   Fonts

** get Sue to sing the intro|

There isn't much that you can say
You had it once
Threw it away

You asked for more
I gave you all
You set me up
You watched me fall

8.27 Use the Notepad window to jot down lyrics, notes, and ideas for the project.

How Can I Make My Song Sound Great and Then Share It?

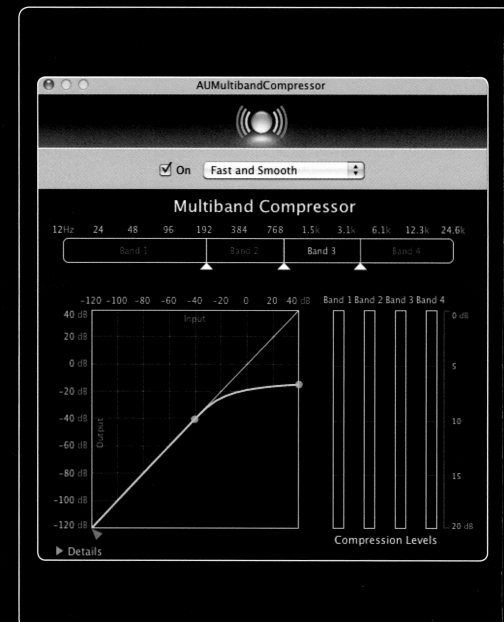

Recording a song is half the battle won, but if you want to grab your listeners by the ears and not let them go, you need to edit and mix the song as well. GarageBand provides powerful tools for editing both Software Instrument tracks and Real Instrument tracks to remove unwanted parts and change the pitch. You can then mix the song by changing the volume, panning, and effects of both individual tracks and the master track that controls the song's overall sound. When the song is finished, you can use it in the other iLife applications directly from GarageBand; but what you'll probably want to do is export the song to iTunes, give it a full set of tags, add lyrics and artwork, and then share the song with friends or the world via the Internet. You may also want to create a ring tone from the song for your iPhone.

Editing a Song

To edit a song, you need to pick out the tracks you want to work on, either individually or together. You can then open a track in the Track Editor and edit it. You can change Software Instrument tracks extensively, even changing the pitch and velocity of individual notes; for Real Instrument tracks, including Electric Guitar tracks, your options are more limited, but you can move sections of audio, delete them, and change the track's tuning or timing.

Muting and soloing tracks

When you edit a song, you often need to focus on a single track or just a handful of tracks. You can do this by using GarageBand's Mute and Solo controls, which appear in the track header (see Figure 9.1).

To mute a track so that you hear the other tracks without it, click the track's Mute button once to turn on muting. Click a second time to turn off muting again.

To solo a track so that you hear that track without the others, click the Solo button. Click the Solo button a second time to turn off soloing.

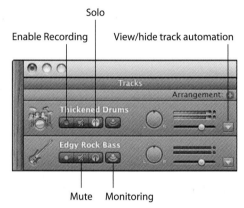

9.1 Use the buttons in the track header to mute and solo tracks so that you can hear exactly what you need to.

Genius

If you need to listen to several tracks but not all of them, you can either solo each of those tracks or mute all the other tracks. Either approach works, so take your pick.

Editing Software Instrument tracks

Recording Software Instrument instruments is pretty wonderful because you can either record multiple takes (and choose the best) or record a single take using multiple passes. But what's even better is that you can edit a region you've recorded, adjust the notes it contains, and even change their length and velocity.

Opening a region for editing in the Track Editor

To open a region for editing, double-click the region in the Timeline. Figure 9.2 shows a Software Instrument region open for editing in Piano Roll view, the view in which GarageBand first opens the region. The other view is Score view, and you meet it shortly.

Selected region is open for editing

Selected track is soloed   Region name   Drag here to expand the Track Editor

Zoom slider   A green note is one you've selected

Lighter notes are struck with greater velocity than darker notes

Block length indicates how long the note plays

9.2 A Software Instrument region open for editing in the Track Editor in Piano Roll view.

Editing individual notes in Piano Roll view

Here's how to edit individual notes in Piano Roll view:

- **Select multiple notes.** Either drag a selection box around the notes (see Figure 9.3), or click the first note, and then Shift+click each of the other notes.

- **Copy a note.** Option+click the note and drag it to where you want the copy.

- **Change the pitch.** Select the note, and then drag it up or down. As you drag, GarageBand plays the note you've reached.

- **Change the velocity.** Select the note, and then either drag the Velocity slider or type a new value in the Velocity box.

261

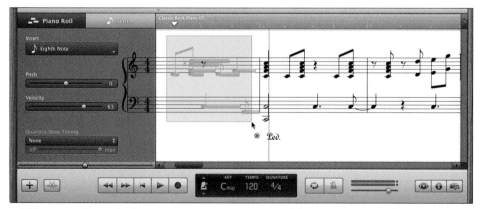

9.3 Selecting multiple notes in Piano Roll view in the Track Editor.

- **Change the length.** Select the note, and then drag the right end of its length bar to the right or to the left.

- **Add a note.** ⌘+click where you want to place the note. Drag the right edge of the note to change the length as needed, and change the velocity by dragging the Velocity slider or typing in the Velocity box.

Editing individual notes in Score view

Score view shows notes as they appear on sheet music, with musical note symbols placed on staves to indicate their timing and pitch. Here's how to edit individual notes in Score view:

- **Select multiple notes.** Either drag a selection box around the notes (see Figure 9.4), or click the first note and then Shift+click each of the other notes.

9.4 When you select multiple notes in Score view, GarageBand displays the length of each note as a box attached to its note character.

● **Copy a note.** Option+click the note head and drag it to where you want the copy.

● **Change the pitch.** Select the note, and then press Up Arrow or Down Arrow. Alternatively, drag the note head up or down. As you move the note, GarageBand plays the note you've reached.

● **Change the velocity.** Select the note, and then either drag the Velocity slider or type a new value in the Velocity box.

● **Change the length.** Select the note, and then drag the right end of its length bar to the right or to the left.

● **Add a note.** Open the Insert pop-up menu and choose the note length you want (for example, Eighth Note), and then ⌘+click where you want to place the note.

● **Change the note value.** Control+click or right-click the existing note you want to change, and then choose the note value from the menu that appears (see Figure 9.5).

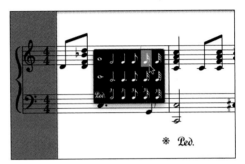

9.5 Changing the length of an existing note in the region.

Changing the timing for a track

If you've recorded a Software Instrument track that's not perfectly in time, you may be able to fix it by using the Quantize Note Timing feature. Follow these steps:

1. **Set the song playing so that you can judge the effect the timing change produces.**

2. **Open the track in the Track Editor by double-clicking one of the track's regions in the Timeline.**

3. **Open the Quantize Note Timing pop-up menu at the bottom of the pane and choose the note value you want to use.** For Software Instrument tracks, this menu offers a wide range of choices, from 1/1 Note through 1/64 Note, from 1/4 Triplet through 1/32 Triplet, and from 1/8 Swing Light through 1/16 Swing Heavy.

4. **Drag the Quantize Note Timing slider to adjust the timing.** Listen to the effect the change produces, and adjust it if necessary.

Changing the modulation, pitchbend, sustain, expression, or foot control

To make your tracks sound more lively, you can change the modulation, pitchbend, sustain, expression, or foot control for a region. If you recorded this controller information by using the controls on your keyboard, you can edit the existing movements of the controls. If not (for example, because your keyboard doesn't have a foot control), you can add controller information manually using your mouse.

To change the controller information, follow these steps:

1. **Set the song playing so that you can judge the effect of the changes you make.**

2. **Open the track in the Track Editor by double-clicking one of the track's regions in the Timeline.**

3. **In the View pop-up menu, choose the controller you want to work with.** The controller information appears in the Track Editor. Figure 9.6 shows an example of changing the pitchbend on a track.

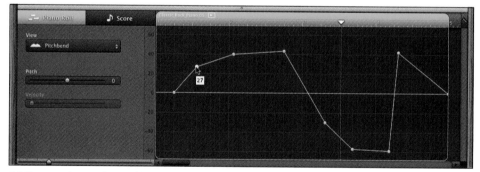

9.6 You can change the pitchbend of a track by choosing Pitchbend in the View pop-up menu and moving the control points.

4. **Adjust the curve as needed:**

   * **Remove unneeded control points, the points at which the curve changes.** Click a control point and press Delete to delete it.

   * **Change the value of a control point.** Drag the control point up or down.

   * **Alter when a change occurs.** Drag a control point to the left or right.

   * **Draw a new line.** ⌘+click an empty area in the control track. You can then drag the control points for the line.

264

Editing Real Instrument tracks

What's even neater than editing the notes in a Software Instrument track is being able to edit the regions in a Real Instrument track — either a region you create from a loop or one you record using a musical instrument. You can edit out mistakes (or mis-takes) and sew together your best performances to produce a seamless track.

Selecting the audio you want to edit

Here's how to select the audio you want to edit in a Real Instrument track:

1. **Double-click the region you want to edit to open it for editing in the Track Editor.**

    Figure 9.7 shows the Track Editor with a Real Instrument region ready for editing.

Playhead

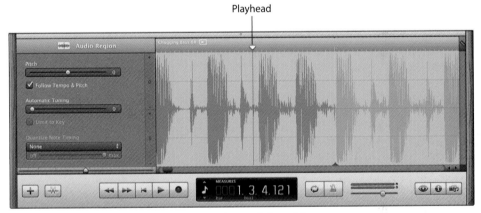

9.7 The Track Editor with a Real Instrument region ready for editing.

2. **Drag the Zoom slider in the Track Editor to zoom in or out so that you can see as much of the region as you need to.**

3. **Move the mouse pointer into the region in the Track Editor below the zero (0) line so that it appears as a cross.** Anywhere below the zero line is fine; anywhere above the zero line means you're using the Flex Time feature, which you learn about later in this chapter.

4. **Drag left or right to select the section you want.** Figure 9.8 shows an example.

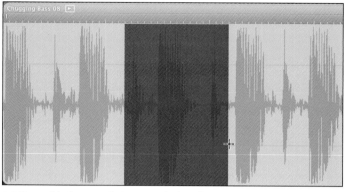

9.8 Drag with the cross-hair pointer below the zero line to select a section of a Real Instrument region in the Track Editor.

Changing the tuning for a track

If you record a Real Instrument track that's in time but not fully in tune, try using the Automatic Tuning feature to fix the tuning like this:

1. **Set the song playing so that you can judge the effect that the tuning change produces.**

Caution

Changing the tuning can save a track, but you need to understand the limitations. First, tuning works accurately only on regions that contain single notes rather than chords. Second, changing the tuning affects all the regions in the track, not just a single region.

2. **Open the track in the Track Editor by double-clicking one of the track's regions in the Timeline.**

3. **Drag the Automatic Tuning slider to the right from the leftmost position (in which it is off).** Listen to the effect the change produces, and adjust it if necessary.

4. **If you want to restrict the tuning to the project's key instead of using the 12-note chromatic scale, select the Limit to Key check box.** Again, listen to the effect of the change and decide whether you want to keep it.

Changing the timing for a track

If you record a Real Instrument track that's not perfectly in time, you may be able to fix it by using the Auto Quantize feature. Follow these steps:

1. **Set the song playing so that you can judge the effect that the timing change produces.**

2. **Open the track in the Track Editor by double-clicking one of the track's regions in the Timeline.**

3. **Open the Auto Quantize pop-up menu at the bottom of the pane and click the note value you want.** For example, choose 1/8 Triplet or 1/8 Note rather than 1/16 Note.

Changing the timing for part of a track

If you recorded a Real Instrument track that has parts in time and parts out of time, you can use the Flex Time feature to fix the timing problems. Flex Time lets you move notes in Real Instrument regions so that they play when you need them to. You can also use Flex Time to extend a note or shorten a note.

To use Flex Time, follow these steps:

1. **Set GarageBand to cycle through the part of the song you want to adjust:**

   - Turn on the cycle region by clicking the Cycle Region button on the toolbar so that it displays two blue arrows.

   - Move the cycle region to the part of the song you want to work on. Drag the cycle region to the right place, and then drag the ends of the cycle region if you need to lengthen or shorten the cycle region.

2. **Click the Real Instrument region you want to change, and then click the Track Editor button on the toolbar to display the Track Editor (assuming the Track Editor isn't already open).**

3. **In the upper part of the Track Editor (above the zero line), click the note you want to change, and then drag to the left or right as needed.** Figure 9.9 shows an example of using Flex Time to change a Real Instrument region. GarageBand displays a different-colored outline around the area that it is changing.

Flex Time button

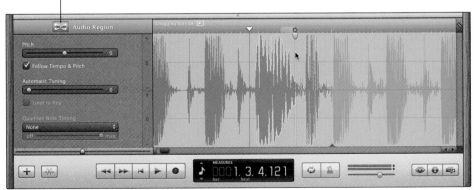

9.9 Click and drag in the upper part of the Track Editor to change a note's timing using the Flex Time feature.

4. **Listen to the effect of the adjustment, and change it again on the next iteration through the cycle region if needed.** Keep making the changes until the region sounds the way you want it to sound.

Genius

You can turn off Flex Time by clicking the Flex Time button at the top of the Audio Region pane. When Flex Time is off, this button shows a waveform on a rectangular white background. When Flex Time is on, this button shows the waveform on a bow-tie-shaped white background.

Editing an audio file outside GarageBand

When GarageBand's editing capabilities aren't enough to fix a problem with a Real Instrument region you've recorded, you can use an external audio editor to fix the problem instead.

GarageBand saves your recorded Real Instrument regions within a package file, so you need to use the Finder to open the package and locate the region file like this:

1. **Close the project file in GarageBand.**

2. **Open a Finder window to the folder that contains the song.** For example, open a window to the ~/Music/GarageBand folder.

3. **Control+click or right-click the song and choose Show Package Contents.** Mac OS X opens a new Finder window showing the files contained in the song's package.

4. **Open the Media folder to locate the audio file containing the region.**

5. **Control+click or right-click the audio file, highlight Open With, and then choose the audio editor.**

6. **When you finish editing the audio, save the file:**

   - If you save the file under the same name, GarageBand simply loads the new version of the file when you open the project.

   - If you save the file under a different name, you must replace the version that's in the Timeline with the new version. This extra step is often a good idea in case editing the file doesn't produce exactly the result you want; if this happens, you can return to the original file (or try editing it again).

Making other tracks match a timing track

When you record, you often get some tracks out of time with others — especially if you have several people playing together (or otherwise) with more enthusiasm than skill. When this happens, you can use GarageBand's Groove Track feature to fix the timing problems. You designate the

Genius

If your song includes a rhythm track you've created using loops, consider using that track as the groove track.

track with the correct timing as the groove track, and GarageBand automatically adjusts the timing of the other tracks to match the timing of the groove track.

To use the Groove Track feature, move the mouse pointer to the left side of the track header for the track you want to use as the groove track, and then click the star button that appears (see Figure 9.10).

GarageBand displays the Analyzing audio for Groove Tracks dialog (see Figure 9.11). Select the Don't show again check box if you don't need to see this dialog again, and then click Continue.

9.10 To set the song's groove track, click the star to the left of the icon in the track's header.

After GarageBand analyzes the audio (which can take a few minutes), GarageBand displays a check box next to each of the other tracks (see Figure 9.12). Leave a track's check box selected to have GarageBand adjust the track's timing using the groove track. Deselect the check box to make the track play with its original timing.

9.11 Click Continue in the Analyzing audio for Groove Tracks dialog to go ahead with creating the groove track.

9.12 Deselect the check box for any track that doesn't need adjusting to the groove track's timing.

Locking a track

When you finish setting up a track, you can lock it to prevent yourself from changing it inadvertently. Locking is often helpful, but GarageBand doesn't display the lock buttons at first, so you need to choose Track⇨Show Track Lock to display them (see Figure 9.13).

To lock the track, click the Lock button in the track header so that the button glows green. Click the Lock button again to remove the locking.

Lock button

9.13 Choose Track⇨Show Track Lock to display the lock buttons so that you can lock one or more tracks against accidental editing.

Genius

Locking a track has a second advantage as well as preventing editing: It tells GarageBand that you're not planning to work with the track for the time being, so GarageBand renders the track to the hard drive. This gives GarageBand more processing power to devote to playing the other tracks.

Mixing a Song

To mix the tracks of your song into the arrangement you want, you use GarageBand's mixer controls (see Figure 9.14). These allow you to adjust the volume and control the left-right panning of each track automatically as the track plays. You can also add other automation curves to a track to control other effects, such as echo, reverberation, or the intensity and speed of a tremolo effect.

Track volume level meters   Track volume slider

Track pan   Hide/view track automation

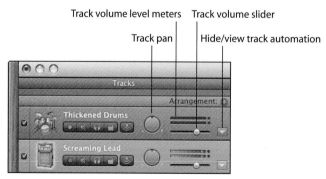

9.14 The mixer's deceptively simple controls can make all the difference to the sound of a track.

Adjusting the volume of individual tracks

GarageBand lets you adjust the volume either for the whole of a track or for parts of it. By using both techniques, you can set the track's volume exactly the way you need it.

Start by using the Track Volume slider to set the relative volume of the track. When you add the track, GarageBand sets the slider to 0 decibels (dB), which means the track's loudness is not increasing or decreasing.

To reduce the track's volume, drag the slider to the left; to increase the volume, drag it to the right. GarageBand displays a tooltip showing the decibel measurement you're setting (as shown in Figure 9.15), but normally you'll do better to rely on your ears to judge whether the track is as loud as you want it.

9.15 Changing a track's volume using the Track Volume slider.

That sets the track to play at the same level. Often, you'll want finer control than this. For example, you may want to fade into the song rather than start with a bang, fade out to a whimper, or play parts of the track at a lower volume so that other tracks can come to the fore.

To make different parts of a track play at different volumes, use the track's volume curve like this:

1. **If the Automation track isn't displayed, click the View/Hide Track Automation button on the track header to display it.** Figure 9.16 shows the Automation track with the Track Volume automation curve displayed and turned on.

On/off   View/hide track automation   Automation track   Automation line   Control point

9.16 The Automation track displays a single automation effect at a time — Track Volume, Track Pan, or another automation effect you add.

2. **In the Automation Parameters pop-up menu, choose Track Volume if it's not already selected.** The line along the Automation track shows the volume level. Unless you've set

271

a volume curve already, this line will be horizontal, maintaining a steady volume. You can increase the volume by dragging the first control point up or decrease it by dragging down. This first control point controls the overall volume of the track until you create a volume curve, so dragging it has the same effect as moving the Track Volume slider for the track: The line remains straight, and moves up or down as you drag.

3. **To create a volume curve, place control points on the volume line like this:**

- Set the song to cycle through the section you're working with so that you can hear the effects of the changes you make. Start playback.

Note

When you create an automation curve for a track, GarageBand automatically turns on that automation parameter and displays the green On light (for a Software Instrument track) or blue On light (for a Real Instrument track) when that parameter is selected in the Automation Parameters pop-up menu. You can turn the automation parameter off by clicking the On light so that it goes off.

- Click where you want to place a control point. Each control point appears as a blue dot for a Real Instrument track or a green dot for a Software Instrument track (see Figure 9.17).

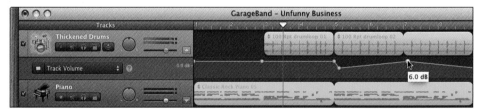

9.17 Dragging a control point to create a volume curve on an Automation track.

- Drag a control point up to increase the volume at that point, or drag it down to decrease the volume.

- To change when a control point alters the volume, drag the control point to the left or right along the volume curve.

- To delete a control point, drag it along to the next control point, which swallows it without comment.

4. **When you finish setting the volume curve, click the View/Hide Track Automation button to hide the Automation track again.** If you're going to change panning (discussed next) or automation (discussed later in this chapter), you may want to leave the Automation track displayed.

Controlling panning

To control the left-right placement of the sound on tracks, use the panning controls. These let you position different tracks where you want them around the panorama of the song, so that the tracks sound as though they're coming from different directions. For example, you may choose to place your drum track, lead instrument, and vocals centrally and pan the backing tracks to the left and right.

You can set a track panning position for the track as a whole, or you can create a custom panning curve that moves the track to different pan positions at different points in the Timeline as needed. For example, you can make your edgy guitar line move from one side of the mix to the other — and then back again.

Genius

Go easy on the panning — you seldom need to pan a track all the way to the left or the right. Doing so can make the song sound stretched and odd. Many tracks need only a single panning position rather than weaving left and right through the mix like the highway patrol in pursuit on the interstate.

To set a track panning position for the track as a whole, click the Track Pan knob and drag downward to pan to the left or upward to pan to the right.

To create a custom panning curve for the track, follow these steps:

1. **If the Automation track isn't displayed, click the View/Hide Track Automation button on the track header to display it.**

2. **In the Automation Parameters pop-up menu, choose Track Pan.**

    *   The line along the Automation track shows the panning for the track, with panning to the left appearing above the 0 mark (with positive values) and panning to the right appearing below the 0 mark (with negative values).

273

- Until you set a custom pan curve for the track, the panning line is horizontal, maintaining a steady position that you set by dragging the Track Pan knob.

- You can adjust the panning for the whole track by dragging the first control point up (to pan to the left) or down (to pan to the right). This first control point controls the overall panning of the track until you create a custom panning curve, so dragging the control point has the same effect as dragging the Track Pan knob: The line remains straight, and you pan the whole track.

3. **To create a panning curve, place control points on the track like this:**

- Set the song to cycle through the section you're working with so that you can hear the effects of the changes you make. Start playback.

- Click where you want to place a control point. Each control point appears as a blue dot for a Real Instrument track or a green dot for a Software Instrument track.

- Drag a control point up to pan to the left at that point, or drag it down to pan to the right.

- To change when a control point alters the panning, drag the control point to the left or right along the panning curve.

- To delete a control point, drag it along to the next control point.

4. **When you finish setting the panning curve, click the View/Hide Track Automation button to hide the Automation track again.** If you're going to change automation (discussed next), you may want to leave the Automation track displayed.

Adding automation parameters to a track

A volume curve and custom panning curve can make a big difference to a track's sound, especially when you set them for most or all of the tracks in the song. But GarageBand also lets you add other automation curves to each track as needed. You can add an automation curve for visual equalization (to control, say, bass frequency or treble gain), echo, reverberation, or any of the other effects you apply to the track.

Adding an automation parameter

Here's how to add an automation parameter to a track:

1. **If the Automation track isn't displayed, click the View/Hide Track Automation button on the track header to display it.**

2. **In the Automation Parameters pop-up menu, choose Add Automation to open the Add Automation dialog.** Figure 9.18 shows the Add Automation dialog for a guitar track with several effects.

3. **If the category for the automation parameter is collapsed, click the disclosure triangle to expand it.** For example, click the sideways triangle next to Echo & Reverb to display the Echo and Reverb automation controls.

4. **Select the check box for each automation parameter you want to give a custom curve.**

5. **Click OK to close the Add Automation dialog.** If you selected a single automation parameter, GarageBand displays the Automation track for it. If you selected more than one, Garage Band displays the Automation track for the first parameter. To choose a different parameter, open the Automation Parameters pop-up menu and choose the automation parameter you want to change first (see Figure 9.19).

6. **Add control points and position them as described earlier in this chapter.**

7. **Work with other automation parameters as needed, or click the View/Hide Track Automation button on the track header to hide the Automation track again.**

Removing an automation parameter

If you need to remove an automation parameter from a track, open the Add Automation dialog, expand the category if necessary, and deselect the check box for the automation parameter. GarageBand prompts you to confirm the decision. Click Continue in the You are about to remove automation dialog, and then click OK to close the Add Automation dialog.

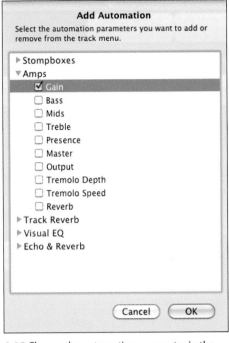

9.18 Choose the automation parameter in the Add Automation dialog.

9.19 Choose the automation parameter for which you want to create an automation curve.

275

Setting up the master track

After you arrange the volume and panning for the individual tracks within the song and apply such effects as are needed, you're ready to do the same for the master track. This is the track that controls the volume, panning, automation, and effects for the song as a whole.

Deciding how to arrange the master track

Given that the master track controls the overall sound of the song, you normally need to treat it differently than the individual tracks. Here are two things you normally need to do to the master track:

1. **Choose track info settings for the master track.** GarageBand comes with a stack of preset settings for different types of track, and you can customize them as needed.

2. **Set a volume curve for the master track to control the overall volume of the song and to implement any fade in, fade out, or volume changes that apply throughout the song.**

Here are two things you may need to do to the master track:

1. **Create a master pitch curve for the song (varying the pitch as the song plays) or a master tempo curve (so that some parts of the song play faster than others).**

2. **Apply automation parameters to control the effects used for the track.** For example, you may need to change the amount or color (feeling) of echo in different parts of the track.

Genius

You may want to apply effects to the master track when creating different mixes of a song. Usually, you do this after you create the song's normal mix.

By contrast, you seldom need to set a panning curve for the master track. If you already panned the individual instruments to where they belong in the mix, you won't need to pan the whole track unless you're trying to disorient the listener.

Similarly, you will normally do best to go easy on the effects you apply to the master track, because these effects build on the effects you already applied to the individual tracks.

Displaying the master track

The master track is normally hidden until you display it by choosing Track⇨Show Master Track or pressing ⌘+B. The master track appears at the bottom of the Track List, separated from the other tracks by an open space (see Figure 9.20).

9.20 The master track appears at the bottom of the track list and has no Mixer controls.

Setting track info for the master track

What you normally need to do first is set track info for the master track. The track info lets you quickly switch the overall feel of your song, so it's great for creating different edits of the song.

To set the track info for the master track, follow these steps:

1. **Double-click the track header for the master track to display the Track Info pane with the Master Track button selected (see Figure 9.21).**

2. **In the left list box, click the sound category you want — for example, Pop or Stadium Rock.** The list of available sounds appears in the right box.

3. **In the right list box, click the sound you want.** For example, if you choose Stadium Rock, you have choices such as Stadium Rock Basic, Large Arena, and Stadium Empty.

4. **Play the song and make sure the effect is what you want.** If not, choose another sound and test it.

5. **If you want to fine-tune the sound, click the Edit tab to display the effects used (see Figure 9.22).**

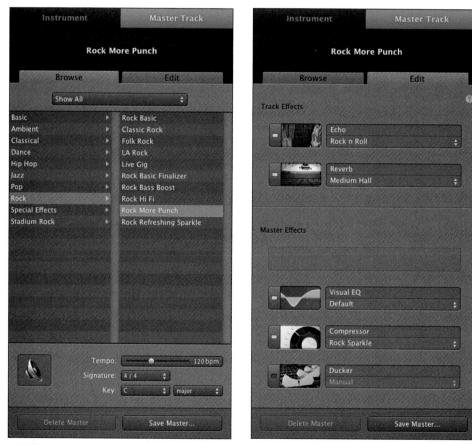

9.21 The master track lets you quickly change the overall feel of the song.

9.22 Use the Edit tab in the Master Track info pane to fine-tune the effects for your song.

Note From the Master Track info pane, you can also adjust the song's tempo, time signature, or key. Usually, you'll want to fix these elements earlier in the process of creating your song because changing them now can wreck the whole song. But sometimes you need to tweak a setting to make the song sound the way you want it to.

6. **Change or remove any of the effects applied to the master track using the techniques explained earlier in this chapter.** For example, choose a different preset for the Echo effect, or click the picture to the left of the Reverb effect and use the resulting Reverb window to set the reverb time, color, and volume you want.

7. **If necessary, add another effect in an empty row in the Master Effects list.** For example, you may want to apply the AUMultibandCompressor effect. This offers preset compressions such as Fast and Smooth, Sub Control, and Gentle, or you can click the Edit button and use the AUMultibandCompressor dialog (shown on the opening page of this chapter) to create custom multiband compression.

8. **If you customized the sound in a way you want to be able to use again for other songs, save the master track settings as a preset.** Click Save Master, type a descriptive name in the Save Master dialog, and then click Save.

Creating a volume curve for the master track

After choosing the effects for your master track, create a volume curve for it like this:

1. **On the master track's track header, open the Automation Parameters pop-up menu and choose Master Volume to display the volume curve (unless it's displayed already).**

2. **Set control points as described earlier in this chapter to create the volume curve you want.** For example, create a swift fade in at the beginning of the track and a gradual fade out at the end.

Genius GarageBand can create a fade out for you automatically. Just click the track and then choose Track ⇨ Fade Out. But because GarageBand doesn't know your music, you should always listen to the effect and customize it as necessary.

Changing the tempo during the song

Many songs work well at a standard tempo, but for others, you can add variation and aural excitement by changing the tempo during the song. For example, you may want to speed up the tempo during the climax of a song or wind it down toward the end.

Note If you've locked any of the tracks in the song, you must unlock them before you can make changes to the master pitch or tempo. (Changes to the master volume are okay because they affect only the volume of the song as a whole, rather than changing individual tracks.) If one or more tracks is locked when you try to change the master pitch or tempo, GarageBand prompts you to unlock them; click the Unlock All button to do so.

To change the tempo during the song, create a custom Master Tempo curve like this:

1. **On the master track's track header, open the Automation Parameters pop-up menu and choose Master Tempo from it.** GarageBand displays the Master Tempo track.

2. **Set control points as usual to create the tempo curve you need.** Drag a control point upward to increase the tempo or downward to decrease it; GarageBand displays the bpm value as you drag. Figure 9.23 shows an example of a tempo curve that makes a section of a song faster before gradually returning to the previous tempo. The change appears minor in the Timeline, but the listener hears a dramatic difference.

9.23 Creating a custom Master Tempo curve to add variation to a song.

Changing the master pitch of the song

Besides letting you change the pitch of a region or track, GarageBand also lets you change the master pitch of the song. This basically means grabbing all the regions that it makes sense to shift and moving them up or down the musical scale. GarageBand doesn't change drum tracks or Real Instrument regions you've recorded.

As with the other Automation tracks, you can either change the pitch for the whole song or create an automation curve that changes the pitch for only the parts of the song that you specify. Here's what to do:

1. **Open the Automation Parameters pop-up menu and choose Master Pitch from it.** GarageBand displays the Master Pitch track.

2. **If you want to change the pitch of the entire song, drag the first control point (which GarageBand creates automatically) up or down.** When you drag the first

control point, the automation curve remains straight, so the pitch changes evenly throughout the whole song.

3. **If you want to change the pitch of parts of the song, set control points as for any other automation curve.** Drag a control point upward to increase the pitch or downward to decrease it. GarageBand displays a tooltip showing the number of musical half-steps by which you're moving the control point (for example, +1 or -2).

Adding automation to the master track

You can add automation to the master track by using the same techniques as for the other tracks:

1. **Open the Automation Parameters pop-up menu and choose Add Automation to display the Add Automation dialog.**

2. **Select the check box for each automation parameter you want to add, and then click OK.**

3. **Open the Automation Parameters pop-up menu and choose the parameter you want to work with.**

4. **Add control points and create an automation curve for the parameter.**

For the master track, GarageBand offers four echo automation parameters rather than the one echo automation parameter that's available for other tracks:

- **Echo Time.** This parameter controls how long each echo lasts (whether it is faster or slower than the previous echo).
- **Echo Repeat.** This parameter controls how many times the echoes repeat.
- **Repeat Color.** This parameter controls whether the echoes are dark, with each repetition sounding duller than the previous one, or bright, with each repetition sounding thinner than the previous one.
- **Echo Volume.** This parameter controls how loud the echoes are.

By working with the different echo parameters, you can produce a wide variation of echo effects that enhance the song.

Sharing a Song

When you finish a song, you'll probably want the world to know about it. GarageBand makes it easy to export a song to iTunes, share it with other people on the Internet, or put it to use in a slide show, a movie, or a DVD. You can also create a ring tone to use on your iPhone.

Exporting a song to iTunes

If you want to listen to your song using iTunes, put it on your iPad or iPhone, or burn it to CD, export the song to iTunes like this:

1. **Choose Share ⇨ Send Song to iTunes to open the Send your song to your iTunes library dialog (see Figure 9.24).**

2. **Change the text in the iTunes Playlist, Artist Name, Composer Name, and Album Name boxes as needed.** Garage Band imports what you've set in its My Info preferences, but you'll often want to give songs different artist and composer credits or put them in different albums.

3. **If you want to compress the song to reduce the file size, select the Compress Using check box and choose the compression method:**

   ● Select AAC Encoder or MP3 Encoder in the Compress Using pop-up menu. AAC gives marginally higher quality than MP3 and is great for iPods, iPhones and iPads, and iTunes, but MP3 files are playable in more hardware and software players than AAC files, so it's a trade-off.

Note

If you deselect the Compress check box in the Send your song to your iTunes library sheet, GarageBand exports the song as an AIFF file.

   ● Choose the quality from the Audio Settings pop-up menu. Usually, it's best to choose Higher Quality to make your song sound good, but you can also experiment with the High Quality setting if you need to save some space. The AAC encoder also offers a Medium Quality setting (which is okay for music) and a Low Quality setting (which you should use for spoken audio only). The MP3 encoder also offers a Good Quality setting; this too is suitable only for spoken audio such as podcasts, not for any music you care about.

4. **Click Share.** GarageBand mixes down the song and adds it to your iTunes library. iTunes starts playing the new song automatically, even if you were listening to something else at the time.

Tagging a song

When you send a song to your iTunes library, GarageBand fills in the Name, Artist, Composer, Album, BPM, and Year tags.

This is a good start, but it's only a start. Before distributing a song, Control+click or right-click it in iTunes, choose Get Info, and then use the tabs of the Item Info dialog (see Figure 9.25) to edit these tags (if needed) and to add further tags and information to the song. Consider adding the following:

> Send your song to your iTunes library.
>
> | iTunes Playlist: | Acme Power Trio |
> | Artist Name: | Chris Thompson |
> | Composer Name: | Acme Power Trio |
> | Album Name: | APT Album |
>
> ☑ Compress
>
> | Compress Using: | AAC Encoder |
> | Audio Settings: | High Quality |
>
> Provides excellent sound quality but produces larger file sizes. Details: AAC, 192kbps, Stereo, optimized for music and complex audio. Estimated Size: 1.9MB.
>
> Cancel   Share

9.24 Exporting a song to iTunes. The Compress Using pop-up menu and Audio Settings pop-up menu appear only when you select the Compress check box.

- **Genre.** It's vital to set the genre so that people find the song when they browse by genre.

- **Track Number.** Fill this in so that the listener can sort your songs in the order you intended.

- **Artwork.** Drag one or more pictures to the box on the Artwork tab of the Item Info dialog, or click the Add button and use the Open dialog to pick the pictures. If you add multiple pictures, drag them into the order in which you want the audience to see them.

- **Album Artist.** Set this tag if the album artist is different from the artist.

- **Sorting tags.** If you want your song to be sorted by a different name, artist name, album artist, album, or composer, type the appropriate tags on the Sorting tab.

283

● **Lyrics.** If your song has words, add them on the Lyrics tab. Not only do most people like to know a song's lyrics, but you avoid the heartache of seeing your lyrics mangled by well-intentioned listeners on the Web's lyrics sites.

Unfunny Business

Summary	Info	Video	Sorting	Options	Lyrics	Artwork

Name
Unfunny Business

Artist | **Year**
Chris Thompson Power Quartet | 2011

Album Artist | **Track Number**
Chris Thompson | 2 of 14

Album | **Disc Number**
Turn On the Night Lights | 1 of 1

Grouping | **BPM**
| 120

Composer
Acme Power Trio

Comments

Genre
Stoner Rock ☐ Part of a compilation

(Previous) (Next)   (Cancel) (OK)

9.25 After exporting a song to iTunes, fill in as many tags as possible in the song's Info dialog. Most of the essential tags are on the Info tab, but adding lyrics and artwork is a great help.

Using a song in other iLife applications

Even without exporting a song from GarageBand, you can use it in your projects in the other iLife applications as long as you save an iLife preview of the song (as GarageBand prompts you to do when you close a project).

To use the song, simply open the Media Browser in the application and select the song in the GarageBand category.

If you haven't saved an iLife preview for the song, you won't be able to preview it in the Media Browser. Instead, when you select the song in the Media Browser, the application you use prompts you to open the song in GarageBand so that you can create a preview (see Figure 9.26). Click Yes if you want to use the song.

Creating an iPhone ring tone from a song

If you have an iPhone, you can quickly create a custom ring tone from a GarageBand project. You can use either the whole of a short GarageBand project (for example, one that you create specifically as a ringtone) or just part of a longer project. Either way, the maximum length for the ringtone is 40 seconds.

The project "Scorcher" cannot be used because it was not prepared with an iLife preview.

Would you like to open "Scorcher" in GarageBand so you can save it with an iLife preview?

No   Yes

9.26 The iLife application (here, iMovie) prompts you to open GarageBand and save an iLife preview for a song project that lacks one.

To create a ringtone, all you need do is select the part of the project and then choose Share ⇨ Send Ringtone to iTunes.

Provided that your selection is short enough to create a ringtone, GarageBand mixes down the audio and adds it to iTunes, placing it in the Ringtones category in the iTunes library. iTunes starts playing the ringtone (even if you were enjoying some other music at the time), so you can tell immediately if it has turned out the way you wanted.

If your selection is too long, GarageBand displays the Your iPhone ringtone length needs to be adjusted dialog (see Figure 9.27). Click Adjust to return to your song project, select a shorter section, and then choose Share ⇨ Send Ringtone to iTunes again.

Your iPhone ringtone length needs to be adjusted

A ringtone needs to be a repeating section of your song that is 40 seconds or less. To change the length manually, click Cancel and then click the Cycle button. Click Adjust to have GarageBand adjust it automatically. Once the ringtone length is set, choose Share > Send Ringtone to iTunes to have it appear as a Ringtone in your iTunes library.

Cancel   Adjust

9.27 GarageBand warns you if your selection is too long to create a ringtone.

How Do I Build a Web Site with iWeb?

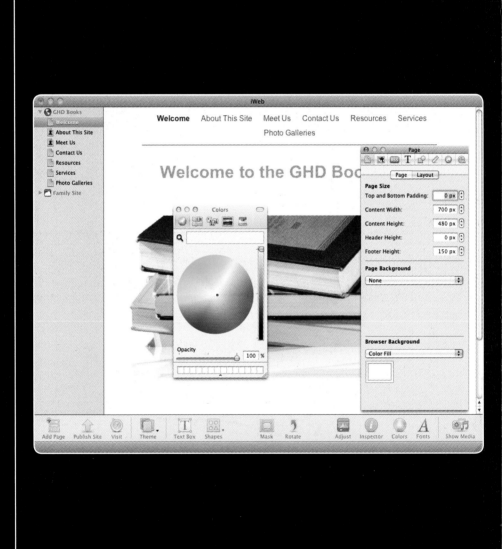

Have you ever wanted to create your own Web site without having to learn HTML? Apple's iWeb application lets you put together a sleek, well-designed Web site in minutes, publish it to the Web, quickly update it with new information whenever you need to, and even announce the updates automatically on Facebook. Whether you just want to display your own photos and writings or you want to include advanced features like online maps, videos from YouTube, and revenue-generating advertisements, this chapter shows you what you need to know.

Getting Started with the iWeb Interface

To get started with iWeb, launch the application by clicking the iWeb icon on the Dock (if there is one) or by opening the Applications folder and double-clicking the iWeb icon.

Note When you first launch iWeb, the application may display a MobileMe dialog prompting you to sign in to MobileMe if you're already a member or try MobileMe for free if you're not a member. Select the Don't show again check box if you don't want to see this dialog again. Click the Sign In button if you want to sign in to MobileMe, click the Learn More button if you want to find out about MobileMe, or click the No Thanks button if you just want to close the dialog.

Choosing a template for your Web site

iWeb expects you to start creating a Web site automatically if you don't already have one, so it displays the dialog shown in Figure 10.1. This is called the Template Chooser, and it lets you choose the theme and template for each Web page.

The theme is the overall design of the Web page. For example, the White theme has a white background, the Black theme has a black background, and the Goldenrod theme features golden tones and goldenrod daisies. Each theme contains several templates, each of which holds the layout for a particular type of page: the Welcome page, the About Me page, the Photos page, and so on.

If you click Cancel in the Template Chooser when your site doesn't contain a page, iWeb simply closes, so go ahead and start creating a page:

1. **Make sure All is selected in the pop-up list at the top of the Template Chooser.**

2. **In the list box on the left, click the theme you want to use for your Web site.** Each theme contains the same set of templates, so you can switch easily from one theme to another.

Genius The pop-up menu above the left list box lets you choose among showing all iWeb themes, the themes in iWeb 3.0, those in iWeb 2.0, those in iWeb 1.1, and those in iWeb 1.0. Choose All in the pop-up menu to give yourself the widest choice of templates. Choose one of the other selections if you want to see only the themes from an earlier version of iWeb.

3. **In the box on the right, click the Welcome page.** This is usually the best starting point for a Web site.

4. **Click Choose.** iWeb closes the Template Chooser and starts a Web page using the template you chose.

10.1 iWeb displays the Template Chooser the first time you launch the application so that you can create your first Web page immediately.

Meeting the iWeb interface

Now that iWeb is open, you can look at the user interface. Figure 10.2 shows the main areas of the iWeb window and the items you see at first.

- **Sidebar.** This area contains your Web sites, blogs, and Web pages. You can expand or collapse any item that has a gray disclosure triangle next to it. You can display any page on the Web page canvas by clicking it in the sidebar.

- **Web page canvas.** This the area on which you create the Web page.

- **Navigation area.** This area contains links to the different pages in your Web site, plus the text indicating the current page. Whichever page you're currently viewing doesn't have a link because you're already on it and don't need to navigate to it.

● **Toolbar.** This bar contains tools for quickly giving the most widely used commands in iWeb.

● **Add Page button.** Opens the Template Chooser so that you can create a new Web page.

● **Text placeholders.** These predefined areas contain sample text that you replace with your custom text.

● **Picture placeholders.** These predefined areas contain sample pictures that you replace with your own pictures.

● **Media pane.** This pane contains four tabs — Audio, Photos, Movies, and Widgets — that you use for inserting items in your Web pages. For example, the Widgets tab contains widgets (prebuilt sections of code) for adding a MobileMe Gallery or a YouTube video to a page. When you don't need the Media pane, click the Hide Media button on the toolbar to hide it.

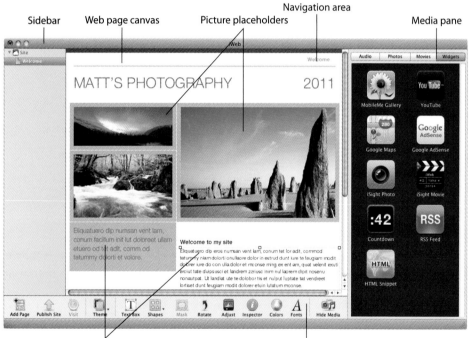

10.2 The main components of the iWeb user interface.

Understanding the four regions of the Web page canvas

In iWeb, each Web page is divided into four regions:

- **Header.** This area appears at the top of the page and contains the title of the page.

- **Navigation area.** This area appears near the top of the page — exactly where depends on the template used for the Web page — and contains links to the other main pages in the Web site.

- **Body.** This is the main part of the page. The body usually contains multiple placeholders for text and images.

- **Footer.** This area appears at the bottom of the page. Its contents depend on the Web page's template.

To see the divisions between the different areas of a page, choose View ➪ Show Layout or press ⌘+Shift+L. iWeb displays narrow lines marking out the different areas (see Figure 10.3). Press ⌘+Shift+L again or choose View ➪ Hide Layout when you want to hide the lines again.

Welcome

MATT'S PHOTOGRAPHY   2011

10.3 Displaying the layout lines by choosing View ➪ Show Layout lets you see the divisions between the header, footer, body, and navigation area.

Setting Preferences to Suit the Way You Work

Compared to most applications, iWeb has refreshingly few preferences, so you can set them in moments. The preferences make a big difference to the way iWeb behaves, so it's worth taking those moments.

Press ⌘+, (⌘ and the comma key) or choose iWeb ➪ Preferences to display the Preferences window (see Figure 10.4).

General Preferences

General

Automatic Correction:	☑ Use smart quotes (" ")
Hyperlinks:	☑ Automatically detect email and web addresses
Text:	☐ Show text imaging indicator
Alignment Guides:	▮▮▮
	☑ Show guides at object center
	☐ Show guides at object edges
Image Import:	☑ Optimize images on import
Warnings:	(Reset)
Auto Update:	☑ Check for iWeb updates automatically

10.4 Take a minute to set iWeb's preferences to suit your needs.

Here's what the iWeb preferences do, with suggestions of how you'll probably want to set them:

- **Use smart quotes (" ").** Select this check box to make iWeb automatically turn straight quote marks into "smart" quotes that curl the right way, just like in Pages or Microsoft Word. Smart quotes look better in Web pages, but some older browsers sometimes don't display them correctly.

- **Automatically detect email and web addresses.** Select this check box to have iWeb automatically create a link when you type an e-mail address or a Web URL. You can adjust the link afterward if you need to. This setting is usually helpful.

Genius

iWeb's trick of converting text in custom fonts to images makes sure anybody can see that text. But be aware that search engines normally don't read text in images. So if you want to make sure your Web site can be read by search engines, avoid using custom fonts for important text.

- **Show text imaging indicator.** This check box's name seems puzzling, but it's easy enough. When you use custom fonts in your Web pages rather than standard fonts, Web browsers on computers that don't have the fonts won't be able to display the text. To avoid this problem, iWeb converts text in custom fonts to images that any Web browser can download. When you select this check box, iWeb displays a yellow picture icon on any text box that it will convert to an image. This gives you a heads-up and lets you change the font if you want to keep the text as text.

- **Alignment Guides.** Choose the color you want to use for alignment guides, lines that help you align objects on your Web pages. You may need to change to a color that stands out against the template you're using.

- **Show guides at object center.** Select this check box to make iWeb show guidelines at the center of objects (see Figure 10.5). Whether you want the guides at the object center, edges, or both depends on which you find easiest.

10.5 Guides at the object center (as shown here) or object edges help you align objects quickly.

- **Show guides at object edges.** Select this check box to make iWeb show guidelines at the edges of objects.

- **Optimize images on import.** Select this check box if you want iWeb to alter images you include so that they're suitable for Web use. This feature is helpful because it helps you avoid lumbering your Web site with huge image files that take ages to download to a viewer's computer.

- **Reset.** Click this button to reset iWeb's various warnings to their default settings.

- **Check for iWeb updates automatically.** Select this check box if you want iWeb to automatically alert you to updates.

When you finish choosing preferences, click the Close button (the red button at the left end of the title bar) to close the iWeb Preferences window.

Planning Your Web Site

iWeb's flexibility and ease of use enable you to plunge straight into creating a Web site and feel your way along, but you'll probably make better progress if you take a minute to plan the pages you will create and the material you will use on them.

iWeb offers eight kinds of pages (see Table 10.1) for your Web sites. That may not seem like many, but they cover the full range of content you're most likely to use — and you can customize the pages if you need to create different looks.

Table 10.1 iWeb's Eight Kinds of Web Pages

Template name	Explanation
Welcome	The Web page on which the user arrives if he or she simply types the address of your site rather than the address of a specific Web page on it. Other applications call this the index page.
About Me	A page for describing yourself, showing a few pictures, and providing links to some of your favorite items (for example, songs or Web sites).
Photos	A page for showing a selection of your photos.
My Albums	A page that contains a summary of your photo pages and links to them.
Movie	A page on which you can present a video or movie.
Blog	A page for creating entries in your blog, your online journal. You look at how to create blog entries in Chapter 11.
Podcast	A page for creating audio or video podcasts. You look at how to create podcasts in Chapter 11.
Blank	A blank (or mostly blank, depending on the theme) page on which you can place whichever elements you need.

Choosing where to host your Web site

iWeb is built to make the most of MobileMe, so if you have a MobileMe account, this will normally be your first choice for hosting your Web site. You can sign up for a 60-day trial of a MobileMe account by choosing Apple menu ➪ System Preferences and clicking the MobileMe icon.

If you don't have a MobileMe account, you can use iWeb with other Web hosts easily enough, as you see later in this chapter.

Caution Several iWeb features work only with MobileMe, not with other Web hosts. These features are the hit counter, the blog search, blog comments, photo comments, enhanced slide shows, and password protection.

Creating Web Pages

After setting preferences, you can get right down to work and create your first few Web pages. iWeb makes the process as easy as possible, but this section gives you a few pointers.

Choosing a template

If you want to go ahead and create your first page using the Web page template you chose after you opened iWeb, stick with that. Otherwise, click that page in the sidebar and press Delete to delete it. That leaves you with no Web pages in your site, so iWeb opens the Template Chooser automatically to get you started creating a new page.

Click a theme that suits the character you're planning for your Web site, pick the template for the page, and then click Choose. For example, if your Web site's focus is showcasing your talents in the hope of landing you a job, choose a theme such as Elegant or Formal. For something more free-wheeling, try a theme such as Road Trip. Or for an events site, try Main Event.

Choose the template for the page, and then click Choose. iWeb adds the page to your site.

Genius

Don't worry too much about choosing the right template. You can change templates for a page at any time by clicking the Theme button on the toolbar and choosing another template from the panel that appears. You may have to rearrange your content to suit the new template, but that usually doesn't take long.

Adding text

Next, add text to the Web page. Simply click to select a text placeholder, click again to select the text in it, and then start typing your own text over the custom text.

If the text you type is too long for a placeholder, you have a couple of choices:

- **Resize the placeholder to make it big enough for the text.** To resize, click and drag one of the sizing handles on the corners or on the sides of the placeholder. To reposition, simply click and drag the placeholder wherever you want it to be.

- **Select the text and make it smaller.** Triple-click the placeholder to select the text. Press ⌘+− (⌘ and hyphen) to reduce the text to the next available size, or click the Fonts button on the toolbar to open the Fonts window, and then choose a different size.

Resizing and repositioning placeholders

You can resize and reposition any of the placeholders in the template you're using.

To resize a placeholder, click it, and then drag one of the sizing handles that appears. Drag a corner handle to resize the placeholder both horizontally and vertically at once, or drag a side handle to resize it only horizontally or only vertically.

To reposition a placeholder, click it and drag it to where you want it to appear. To help you position the placeholder accurately, iWeb displays alignment guides at the center of the placeholder, at the edges, or both, depending on the Alignment Guides choices you made in iWeb's Preferences.

Replacing the placeholder images

Your next move is to replace the placeholder images on the Web page with images of your own. To do so, follow these steps:

1. **If the Media Browser is hidden, click the Show Media button on the toolbar to display it.**

2. **Click the Photos tab at the top if it's not already selected (see Figure 10.6).**

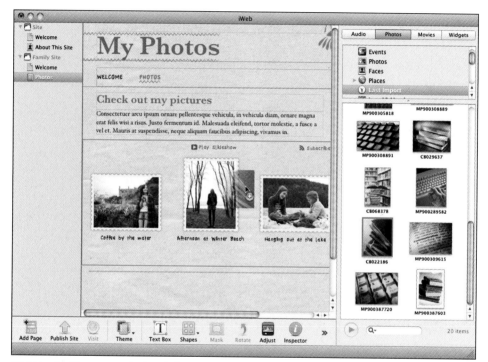

10.6 Use the Photos pane in the Media Browser to add photos to a Web page.

3. **Navigate to the iPhoto album or other item that contains the photo you want.**

4. **Drag a photo from the Media Browser to the placeholder in which you want to display it.**

Genius

If you prefer, you can drag a photo from iPhoto and drop it on a placeholder in iWeb. This move is handy when iPhoto already is open and showing a photo you want to use — you don't need to open the Media Browser and navigate to the photo again.

5. **If necessary, resize the placeholder to better accommodate the image.** Click the placeholder, and then drag one of its sizing handles.

6. **Zoom in on the image if necessary.** Drag the Zoom slider on the black pop-up window to zoom in or zoom back out.

7. **Change the part of the image displayed if necessary.** If the image is a different shape than the placeholder, part of it will be masked, so that it lies behind other elements on the Web page and isn't visible. If you zoom in on the image, much of it may be masked. To change the part of the image displayed:

   a. **Click the Edit Mask button on the black pop-up window to reveal the whole image behind other objects.**

   b. **Click within the image placeholder.**

   c. **Drag the image until the part of it you want appears in the placeholder.** Figure 10.7 illustrates dragging an image within a placeholder.

   d. **Click the Edit Mask button again to restore the mask.**

10.7 When an image is larger than its placeholder, click the Edit Mask button and drag the image to display a different part of it.

Placing Images in Text Boxes

iWeb doesn't limit you to placing images in image placeholders. You can place an image in a text box if you like. When you do this, iWeb treats the image as a floating object, which means it's not fixed in place and gets moved along as you edit the text.

Here's how to place an image in a text box:

1. **Click the text box to select it.**

2. **Click to place the insertion point between the characters where you want the image to appear.**

3. **Choose Insert ➪ Choose to open a dialog for choosing the image.**

4. **Select the image.** For example, scroll down in the sidebar, click Photos to display the contents of your iPhoto library, and then click the photo.

5. **Click Insert to insert the image.** You can then click the image within the text box and resize it as needed to suit the text box.

Adding your own text boxes and images

After replacing the placeholder text and images with your own content, you may need to add more text boxes and images to provide further content.

To add a text box, follow these steps:

1. **Make sure the insertion point isn't positioned in another text box (unless you want to place the new text box within that text box).**

2. **Click the Text Box button on the toolbar.** iWeb adds a new text box.

3. **Drag the new text box to where you want it to appear, and then resize it by dragging its corner handles or side handles.**

4. **Type the text you want in the text box.**

Genius

You can easily create a new text box or image by Option+dragging an existing one (to make a copy) and then changing its contents.

To add a new image, drag it from the Media Browser or from a folder and drop it where you want it to appear. You can then resize the image and adjust its mask as described earlier in this chapter.

Making text look the way you want

When you add text to a text box, iWeb automatically gives the text the formatting applied to the text box. If you want to change formatting or layout, you can do so easily by using the Text Inspector. Follow these steps:

1. **Select the text you want to affect.** To affect all the text in a text box, click the text box. To affect just some text within a text box, click the text box, and then drag to select the text you want to change.

2. **To change the font, click the Fonts button on the toolbar, and then work in the Fonts window (see Figure 10.8).**

   - **Font.** Choose a font collection in the Collection box (or simply choose All Fonts at the top), and then choose

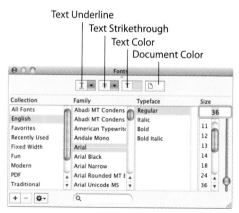

10.8 The Fonts window includes controls for applying and adjusting text shadows.

the font family in the Family box. In the Typeface box, choose the typeface — for example, Regular, Italic, Bold, or Bold Italic. Then choose the Size in the Size list, or drag the Size slider beside the Size list.

- **Underline and Strikethrough.** Use the Text Underline pop-up menu and the Text Strikethrough menu if you need to apply these effects.

- **Text Color and Document Color.** Click the appropriate button to open the Colors window, pick the color, and then click the Close button (the red button) to return to the Fonts window.

3. **To change alignment, spacing, wrapping, or bullets and numbering, click the Inspector button or press ⌘+Option+I to display the Inspector window.** The Inspector window provides eight Inspectors for different aspects of your Web site, including the pages, text, photos, and links. Figure 10.9 shows the button bar at the top of the Inspector window, which you use to choose the Inspector you need.

4. **Click the Text Inspector button to display the Text Inspector.**

5. **To change alignment and spacing, you use the Text tab of the Text Inspector (see Figure 10.10).** Click the Text button if it's not already selected.

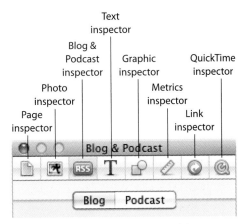

10.9 Use the button bar at the top of the Inspector window to select the Inspector you need. The title bar shows the current Inspector.

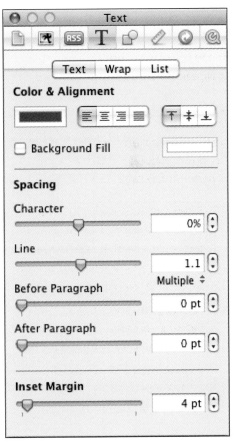

10.10 Use the Text tab of the Text Inspector to change color, alignment, spacing, and margins.

- **Alignment.** Choose the horizontal alignment — Align Left, Center, Align Right, or Justify — and the vertical alignment (Align Top, Align Middle, or Align Bottom).

- **Color.** Click the button to display the Colors window, and then choose the color and close the window. If you've already set the color using the Fonts window, you won't need to set it again.

- **Background Fill.** Select the Background Fill check box, and then use the Color button to choose the color. Again, if you've already set the background color using the Fonts window, you won't need to do this.

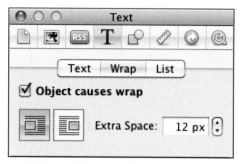

10.11 Use the Wrap tab of the Text Inspector to control how text wraps around an object you've placed in a text box.

- **Spacing.** Drag the Character slider, Line slider, Before Paragraph slider, After Paragraph slider, and Insert Margin slider to set the spacing you want. Alternatively, use the spin boxes and the Line Spacing pop-up menu. The Inset Margin measurement is the distance between the edge of the text box and the beginning of the text.

6. **If you've added an image or shape to a text box, click the Wrap button and set wrapping on the Wrap tab (see Figure 10.11).** Select the Object causes wrap check box, click the Alignment button, and then use the Extra Space box to change the amount of space if necessary.

7. **If you want to add bullets or numbering, click the List button, and use the controls on the List tab.** The controls that appear depend on which type of list you choose. Figure 10.12 shows the List tab for creating numbered lists.

10.12 You can choose from various formats for numbered lists.

8. **When you finish formatting the text, close the Inspector window by clicking its Close button (the red button) or by clicking the Inspector button on the toolbar in the main iWeb window.**

Adding shapes to your Web pages

To give a page visual interest, you can add a shape to it. iWeb provides 15 assorted shapes that range from a plain line and arrows to squares, circles, speech bubbles, stars, and pentagons.

To add a shape, click the Shapes button on the toolbar, and then choose the shape you want from the pop-up panel. iWeb places the shape in the middle of the page, leaving you to resize it and reposition it as needed.

You can add text to a shape by double-clicking the shape and then typing the text. If there's too much text to fit in the shape, iWeb displays a boxed plus (+) sign at the bottom of the shape. You can then either resize the shape to accommodate the text or reduce the text size to make it fit in the shape.

Adding hyperlinks to your Web pages

To enable visitors to navigate from one Web page to another. iWeb automatically creates a hyperlink in the navigation area for each main Web page you add to the site. iWeb doesn't create a navigation-area hyperlink in the navigation area to lower-level Web pages. For example, when you add a My Albums Web page, iWeb creates a hyperlink to that Web page, but not to the Web pages for the individual albums.

Adding hyperlinks manually from text or images

You can also add hyperlinks manually, either to your own Web site or to other sites. Here's what to do:

1. **Click the object (for example, an image) or select the text from which you want to create the hyperlink.**

2. **Click the Inspector button on the toolbar to open the Inspector window.**

3. **Click the Link Inspector button to display the Link Inspector.** Click the Hyperlink tab (see Figure 10.13) if it's not displayed at first.

4. **Select the Enable as a hyperlink check box to turn the object or text into a hyperlink.**

5. **In the Link To pop-up menu, choose the type of link you want to create.** The pop-up menu below the Link To pop-up menu changes its name depending on the choice you make:

   - **One of My Pages.** A page on your iWeb site. Choose the page by name from the Page pop-up menu.

   - **An External Page.** Any Web page outside your Web site. Type the URL in the URL box. Select the Open link in new window check box if you want the Web browser to open the page in a separate window rather than the same window.

Link

Hyperlink | Format

☑ **Enable as a hyperlink**

Link To: | An External Page ⬍

URL: | http://www.surrealmacs.com

☐ Open link in new window

☐ Make hyperlinks active

10.13 Use the Hyperlink tab of the Link Inspector to turn an object into a hyperlink.

Genius

Set a link to open in a new window when you want the visitor to be able to access the external Web site without leaving your site. Depending on the Web browser and the settings it's using, the link may open in a new tab in the same window rather than in a new window.

- **A File.** In the Open dialog that iWeb displays, click the file, and then click the Open button. iWeb enters the filename in the Name box.

- **An Email Message.** Type the e-mail address in the To box, and then type the default subject in the Subject box. (The visitor can change both the address and the subject if he or she wants, but entering a default subject helps avoid having the visitor send a message without a subject line.)

Formatting your hyperlinks

If you want to control the way a hyperlink appears on a Web page, follow these steps:

1. **Select the hyperlink you want to format.**

2. **Click the Inspector button on the toolbar to open the Inspector window.**

3. **Click the Link Inspector button to display the Link Inspector.** Click the Format tab to display its contents (see Figure 10.14).

4. **For each hyperlink state, choose the color you want to use, and decide whether to underline the hyperlink:**

   - **Normal.** This is the color in which hyperlinks the visitor hasn't yet hovered the mouse over or clicked appear.

   - **Rollover.** This is the color a hyperlink turns when the visitor moves the mouse pointer over it.

   - **Visited.** This is the color a hyperlink turns after the visitor clicks it.

   - **Disabled.** This is the color in which an unavailable hyperlink appears.

10.14 You can customize the colors iWeb uses for hyperlinks.

5. **If you want to use these same colors for other links you create on this Web page, click the Use for New Links on Page button.**

6. **Close the Inspector window.**

Making an image's colors match your Web page

To make an image fit in better with a Web page, you have two choices:

- **Adjust the image's colors to suit the Web page.** Click the image, click the Adjust button on the toolbar, and then use the controls in the Adjust Image window (see Figure 10.15) to change the image's colors. These controls work in a similar way to the controls on the Adjust tab of iPhoto's Edit pane (see Chapter 2). For example, the Enhance button attempts to improve the color balance and lighting automatically.

- **Adjust the Web page's colors to suit the image.** Click the Inspector button on the toolbar to open the Inspector window, click the Page Inspector button to display the Page Inspector, and then click the Layout button to display the Layout tab (see Figure 10.16). Use the Page Background controls to change the color of the page's background.

10.15 You can use the controls in the Adjust Image window to make an image fit its background better.

Creating an Email Me button on a Web page

One thing you'll want on many Web sites is a button that enables the visitor to start an e-mail to you. You can do this in moments by choosing Insert ⇨ Button ⇨ Email Me.

10.16 Alternatively, use the Page Background controls to change the page's background color to suit an image.

iWeb inserts the Email Me button in the footer (see Figure 10.17), where some visitors may miss it. You can drag it to a different area of the Web page to make it easier to see.

To tell iWeb which e-mail address to use for your Web site, click Site (or whatever name you've given to your Web site, as described a bit later) at the top of the iWeb sidebar to display the Site Publishing Settings, and then type the e-mail address in the Contact email box.

10.17 Add an Email Me button if you want to give visitors an easy way to contact you.

Adding a hit counter to a Web page

iWeb also makes it easy to add a hit counter to a Web page, allowing visitors to see how many visits that page has received. Simply choose Insert ➪ Button ➪ Hit Counter.

iWeb inserts the hit counter in the footer, but you can drag it to a different area of the Web page.

Genius

Having a very low score on a hit counter can make your Web site look unloved. You can increase the score of a hit counter by refreshing the display of the Web page in your Web browser. For example, in Safari, press ⌘+R to refresh the display.

Renaming your Web site and Web pages

iWeb names your first Web site simply Site (and subsequent sites, if you create them, Site 2, Site 3, and so on). To give your site a more descriptive name, double-click the name in the sidebar, type the new name in the edit box that appears, and then press Return.

Each Web page you add to the Web site receives its template name — for example, Welcome or About Me. You can rename a Web page by double-clicking its name in the sidebar, typing the new name, and then pressing Return.

Rearranging your Web pages

As you create new Web pages to your Web site, iWeb adds them to the list in the sidebar in the order you create them.

If you want to rearrange the Web pages in a site, drag them up and down in the sidebar. When you rearrange the Web pages, iWeb automatically changes the order of the links in the navigation area to reflect the new order.

Adding Photos and Albums from iPhoto

Because they consist of your own content and are (usually) personal, photos and albums from iPhoto make great content for your Web site. iWeb makes it simple to create Web pages that contain your photos or your albums.

Working with photo pages

You can create a Web page containing individual photos in a few moments. Follow these steps:

1. **Click the Add Page button to open the Template Chooser.**

2. **Click the theme you want, click the Photos template, and then click Choose.** iWeb adds a Photos Web page to the Web site.

3. **Click the Show Media button to open the Media Browser if it's hidden, and then click Photos to display your photos.**

4. **Drag a photo or an album over the placeholder (see Figure 10.18).** iWeb replaces all three sample photos with what you dragged and displays the Photo Grid window (see Figure 10.19).

5. **Choose settings in the Photo Grid window:**

   - **Album style.** Click the pop-up button and select the style you want — for example, with drop shadows or with rounded corners on the photos.

   - **Columns.** In this box, set the number of columns of photos to have on the page.

- **Spacing.** Drag this slider to increase or decrease the distance between photos.

- **Photos per page.** Choose how many photos to display on each page. The default setting is 99, but having more pages with fewer photos on each is usually easier to browse. If you add more photos to the page than the number set here, iWeb automatically creates multiple linked pages.

- **Caption lines.** Choose how many lines of text to display below each photo. (Choose 0 if you want no captions.)

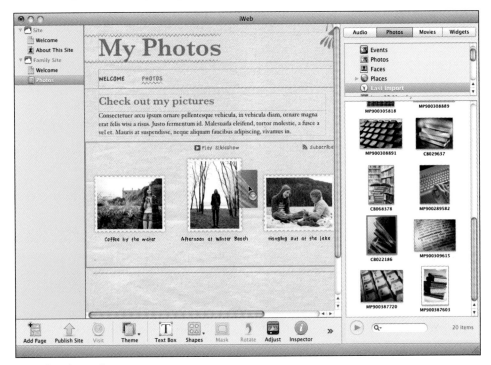

10.18 Creating a photo page.

6. **Drag the photos into the order you want, and edit the captions as needed.** You can leave the Photo Grid window open as you work, so that you can change the style as needed.

7. **Edit the text of the Web page as usual.**

10.19 From the Photo Grid window, you can quickly change how the photos are displayed and how many lines of text they include.

Creating an overview page of your photos

If you create several photo pages, you can create a single overview page to let visitors navigate among them easily. iWeb calls this page the My Albums page, but you can change the name in seconds.

Here's how to create an overview page:

1. **Click the Add Page button to open the Template Chooser.**

2. **Click the theme you want, click the My Albums template, and then click Choose.** iWeb adds a My Albums Web page to the Web site.

3. **Drag each of your photo pages from the sidebar to the Album placeholder on the My Albums page.** iWeb creates an album for each page you drag.

4. **To rearrange your overview page, click an album on it, and then choose settings in the Media Index window (see Figure 10.20).**

10.20 Use the controls in the Media Index window to change how your overview page looks.

- **Index style.** Click the pop-up button and select the design or colored background you want to use for the album pictures.

- **Columns.** In this box, set the number of columns of album photos to display on the page.

- **Spacing.** Drag this slider to increase or decrease the space between album photos.

- **Album animation.** In this pop-up menu, choose the animation to use for the album: None, Dissolve, Random, Reveal, Push, Fade Through Black, or Skim.

- **Show title.** Select this check box to display each album's title on the overview page.

- **Show number.** Select this check box to display the number of photos each album contains.

- **Allow subscribe.** Select this check box to include a Subscribe link that visitors can click to subscribe to your albums (so that they receive updates when you post new photos).

Genius

You can find other Web widgets at sites such as Widgetbox (www.widgetbox.com) and SpringWidgets (www.springwidgets.com/widgets/).

5. **To change the order in which the albums appear, drag the albums to where you want them.**

6. **If you want to rename the overview page, double-click its name in the sidebar, type the new name, and then press Return.**

Putting Web Widgets on Your Web Pages

Text, photos, and photo albums can make a great-looking Web site — but what if you want to take your Web site to the next level with active content? iWeb lets you easily add YouTube videos, Google Maps, AdSense ads, RSS feeds, and other items to your Web site.

To add the widgets, click the Widgets tab in the Media Browser (see Figure 10.21). If the Media Browser is hidden, click the Show Media button, and then click the Widgets tab.

Adding a MobileMe Gallery to a Web page

If you've published albums of your photos to your MobileMe Gallery, you may want to add the gallery to a Web page. To do so, follow these steps:

10.21 The Widgets tab in the Media Browser makes it easy to add Web widgets to your iWeb pages.

1. **Click the MobileMeGallery widget on the Widgets tab of the Media Browser, and then drag it to the Web page.** iWeb displays the MobileMe Gallery window (see Figure 10.22).

2. **Open the Display pop-up menu, and then click the gallery you want to add.**

10.22 In the MobileMe Gallery window, choose the gallery you want to add to the Web page.

3. **Resize and reposition the MobileMe Gallery widget on the Web page as needed.**

4. **Click the Close button (the X button).**

Adding a YouTube video to a Web page

Adding a video from YouTube to a Web page is a great way of illustrating a point or bringing a topic to life. Here's how to add a video:

1. **Steer your Web browser (for example, Safari) to YouTube and locate the video you want to add to your page.**

2. **Click the Embed button on the video's page to display the video's embed code, and then copy it.** For example, Control+click or right-click the embed code, and then click Copy on the context menu.

3. **In iWeb, click the YouTube widget on the Widgets tab of the Media Browser, and then drag it to the Web page.** iWeb displays the YouTube window.

4. **Control+click or right-click in the YouTube URL text box, click Paste on the context menu to paste the URL (see Figure 10.23), and then click Apply.**

10.23 It takes only moments to add a YouTube video to a Web page in iWeb.

5. **Deselect the Show Related Videos check box if you don't want to display related videos on your page.**

6. **Click the X button to close the YouTube window.**

7. **Resize and reposition the YouTube box on your Web page as needed.**

Now you can test the YouTube clip by clicking the Play button in its lower-right corner.

Inserting a Google map into a Web page

If you want to show someone where to find a particular place — your home, say, or the beach on which you're meeting for a party — you can add a map from Google Maps to a Web page. To do so, follow these steps:

1. **Create a new Web page if necessary, or make space on an existing page.**

2. **Click the Google Maps widget on the Widgets tab of the Media Browser, and then drag it to the Web page.** iWeb displays the Google Maps window.

3. **Type the address (see Figure 10.24) and choose options:**

   - **Zoom Controls.** Select this check box to display controls for zooming in and out on the map. These are usually helpful.

   - **Search Bar.** Select this check box to include a Google search bar in the bottom-left corner of the map.

   - **Address Bubble.** Select this check box to display a pop-up balloon showing the address. This too is usually helpful — and visitors can close it if it's in the way.

4. **Click Apply to insert the map, and click the X button to close the Google Maps window.**

5. **Resize the map as needed by dragging a sizing handle, or simply test the map to make sure it's working.**

10.24 Adding a Google map to a Web page is as simple as filling out the address and clicking the Apply button.

Inserting AdSense ads

If you need your Web site to pay its way, you can include AdSense ads on it. AdSense ads are relevant to a page's content (sometimes more relevant in theory than in practice) and earn you money from Google when visitors click them.

1. **Click the Google AdSense widget on the Widgets tab of the Media Browser, and then drag it to the Web page.** iWeb adds a Google AdSense placeholder and opens the Google AdSense Ad window (see Figure 10.25).

2. **In the Select ad format pop-up menu, choose the type, size, and shape of the ad:**

   - **Type.** You can choose among text ads, text and image ads, and text links.

   - **Size and shape.** The ads come in various sizes and shapes, from the 120-×-90-pixel text links to banner ads (wider than they are tall) and skyscraper ads (taller than they are wide).

10.25 Choosing the size and color scheme for a Google AdSense ad.

Note

To use AdSense ads, you need to have an AdSense account. If you don't have one already, iWeb displays the Set up a Google AdSense account dialog when you use the Google AdSense Ad command. Make sure the Email box shows the e-mail address you want to use, and then click Submit. You then receive an e-mail message that tells you how to complete the sign-up process. After you finish jumping through the hoops, it takes a couple of days for Google to finish setting up your account and start serving money-making ads. In the meantime, Google displays public-service ads in the placeholders.

3. **In the Select ad color pop-up menu, choose the ad color.** You may want the ad to match your Web page's background — or to stand out against it.

4. **Drag the ad placeholder to where you want it to appear on the Web page, and then click the X button to close the Google AdSense Ad window.**

In iWeb, you see only the AdSense placeholders, not the ads themselves. When you publish your Web site to MobileMe or another Web host, the ads themselves appear. The ads then change periodically without you needing to do anything.

Genius iWeb lets you use only a single Google AdSense account at a time. To change the account you're using, choose File ↪ Set Up Google AdSense to open the Google AdSense dialog. Click the Change Account button, and follow the procedure for either specifying a different existing account or setting up a new account.

Inserting an iSight photo

If your Mac has an iSight camera built in or attached, you can use it to capture a photo of yourself (for your About Me page, for example), or whatever you feel like sticking in front of the camera. Here's how it's done:

1. **Click the iSight Photo widget on the Widgets tab of the Media Browser, and then drag it to the Web page.** iWeb adds an iSight Photo placeholder and opens the iSight Photo window (see Figure 10.26).

2. **Position yourself (or whatever) in the line of the iSight camera.**

   10.26 Use the iSight Photo window to take a photo to insert into your Web page.

3. **Click the Capture a photo button.** iWeb counts down from 3, snaps the photo, and inserts the shot into the iSight Photo placeholder.

4. **Drag the placeholder to where you want it to appear on the Web page, and then click the X button to close the iSight Photo window.**

Inserting an iSight movie

Your Mac's iSight camera isn't just good for photos: You can use it to capture short movies as well. Here's how to use the iSight Movie widget to insert a short movie directly in a Web page:

1. **Click the iSight Movie widget on the Widgets tab of the Media Browser, and then drag it to the Web page.** iWeb adds an iSight Movie placeholder and opens the iSight Movie window (see Figure 10.27).

2. **Position yourself (or whatever) in the line of the iSight camera.**

   10.27 Use the iSight Movie window to record a movie to insert into your Web page.

3. **Click the Record a movie button.** iWeb counts down from 3 and then starts recording.

4. **Perform in front of the camera, and then click the Stop button.** iWeb inserts the video into the iSight Movie placeholder.

5. **Drag the placeholder to where you want it to appear on the Web page, and then click the X button to close the iSight Movie window.**

Inserting a Countdown widget

Do you have an upcoming event that you're discussing or promoting on your Web site? If so, you can add a Countdown widget to count down the number of days, hours, minutes, and seconds until the event happens. Here's how to add the Countdown widget:

1. **Click the Countdown widget on the Widgets tab of the Media Browser, and then drag it to the Web page.** iWeb adds a Countdown placeholder and opens the Countdown window (see Figure 10.28).

2. **Open the Style pop-up menu, and then click the style of timer you prefer.**

3. **Click and drag the ends of the Display control to specify the components you want to include in the timer: Years, Days, Hours, Mins, and Secs.** For example, drag the right handle to the left to remove Secs from the timer.

10.28 Use the Countdown window to set up a countdown timer on your Web page.

4. **If you want the timer to include labels for each component, leave the Labels check box selected.** Showing the labels is usually a good idea.

5. **Use the controls in the Countdown To section to specify the date and time to count down to.**

6. **Drag the placeholder to where you want it to appear on the Web page, and then click the X button to close the Countdown window.**

Inserting an RSS feed

A great way to add content to your site is to display posts from an RSS feed supplied by a blogger, news media organization, or other Web site that posts regular content. To display an RSS feed, you insert an RSS Feed widget like this:

1. **Steer your Web browser (for example, Safari) to the page that contains the site's RSS feed.**

2. **Copy the address of the RSS feed page.**

3. **In iWeb, click the RSS Feed widget on the Widgets tab of the Media Browser, and then drag it to the Web page.** iWeb adds an RSS Feed placeholder and opens the RSS Feed window (see Figure 10.29).

4. **Control+click or right-click in the Subscription URL text box, and then click Paste to paste in the feed address.**

5. **Use the Number of Entries spin box to set the number of posts you want to display.**

6. **Leave the Show Date check box selected if you want to display the post date at the top of each entry.**

7. **Click and drag the Article Length slider to set how much of each post you want to display.**

8. **If the feed includes photos, click and drag the Photo Size slider to set the display size, and use the Photo Orientation pop-up menu to select how you want the photos to appear.**

9. **Drag the placeholder to where you want it to appear on the Web page, and then click the X button to close the RSS Feed window.**

10.29 Use the RSS Feed window to display an RSS feed on your Web page.

Inserting an HTML snippet

When you want to add a Web-page feature that iWeb doesn't itself offer, such as creating a table or setting up a form, you can add the HTML code needed by inserting an HTML snippet. You can either create the code snippet yourself, if you have HTML coding skills, or you can find a prebuilt snippet online.

Here's how to insert an HTML snippet:

1. **Click the HTML Snippet widget on the Widgets tab of the Media Browser, and then drag it to the Web page.** iWeb displays the HTML Snippet window.

2. **Type or paste your HTML code in the large text box.**

3. **Click Apply.** iWeb renders the HTML code, as shown in Figure 10.30.

Services

HTML Snippet

```
<td align="center">Staffing</td>
<td>1 day</td>
<td align="right">$199.99</td>
</tr>
<tr>
<td align="right">AC104</td>
<td>Mailshot (one-off)</td>
<td align="center">Mailings</td>
<td>50 pieces</td>
<td align="right">$99.99</td>
</tr>
</table>|
```

Note: Be sure to visit your published page to verify that the widget behaves as expected.

Learn More

Apply

Services and Descriptions

Service	Description	Type	Service Details	Service Cost
AV101	Virtual Phone	Telecoms	1 day	$34.99
AV102	Virtual Assistant	Staffing	1 day	$49.99
AV103	Virtual Manager	Staffing	1 day	$199.99
AC104	Mailshot (one-off)	Mailings	50 pieces	$99.99

10.30 Use the HTML Snippet window to enter the HTML code that you want to add to your page.

4. **Drag the placeholder to where you want it to appear on the Web page, and then click the X button to close the HTML Snippet window.**

Caution

Even if your code snippet looks fine in iWeb, double-check that it works correctly after you post your Web site to your Web host.

Previewing Your Web Site

iWeb lets you see roughly how your Web site appears, but you'll probably want to preview your Web site before you publish it. You can do this in two ways: by making hyperlinks active in iWeb so that the links actually work, and by publishing the Web site to a folder.

Making your Web site's hyperlinks active

To make the hyperlinks in your Web site active, follow these steps:

1. **Click the Inspector button on the toolbar to open the Inspector window.**

2. **Click the Link Inspector button to display the Link Inspector.** Click the Hyperlink tab if it's not selected automatically.

3. **Select the Make hyperlinks active check box.** You can now position the mouse pointer over a hyperlink and click to jump to the linked page.

When you finish testing the hyperlinks, deselect the Make hyperlinks active check box, and then close the Link Inspector window.

Publishing your Web site to a folder

If you want to test your Web site in a browser, publish it to a folder on your Mac like this:

1. **Click Site (or the name of your Web site) at the top of the sidebar to display the Site Publishing Settings screen.**

2. **Click the Publish to pop-up menu and then click Local Folder.** iWeb displays the controls for publishing to a local folder (see Figure 10.31).

3. **Choose the folder in which to store the site — for example, in the Sites folder within your Home folder.** You can create a new folder by clicking the New Folder button, typing the name in the New Folder dialog, and clicking Create.

4. **If you haven't yet provided a snappy name for your site, type the name in the Site name text box.**

5. **Leave the URL for your site box blank.**

6. **Click the Publish Site button on the toolbar.** iWeb displays a dialog asking you to confirm that you have permission to publish your Web content.

10.31 To publish your Web site to a folder so that you can test it, choose Local Folder in the Publish to pop-up menu on the Site Publishing Settings screen.

7. **Click Continue.** iWeb publishes the site to the folder and then displays the dialog shown in Figure 10.32.

8. **Click Visit Site Now.** iWeb opens your default browser (for example, Safari) and displays the site. You can then see exactly how it looks and test the hyperlinks.

Your site has been published to the selected folder.

For Subscribe buttons to work, you must enter the website URL in Site Publishing Settings.

(Visit Site Now)   (OK)

10.32 Click Visit Site Now to preview your Web site in the folder to which you've published it.

Publishing Your Web Site to the Web

When you finish creating your Web site to your satisfaction, you can publish it quickly, either to your account on Apple's MobileMe service (formerly .Mac) or on a different online service.

Note

If you use MobileMe, your Web site appears at http://web.me.com/*Your-MobileMe-Name*/Site.

Publishing your Web site to MobileMe

Here's how to publish your Web site to MobileMe:

1. **Click Site (or the name of your Web site) at the top of the sidebar.** iWeb displays the Site Publishing Settings page.

2. **Click the Publish to pop-up menu and then click MobileMe.** iWeb displays the controls for publishing to MobileMe (see Figure 10.33).

10.33 To publish your Web site to your MobileMe account, choose MobileMe in the Publish to pop-up menu, and then fill in the information for the site.

3. **If you haven't yet provided a name for your site, type the name in the Site name text box.**

4. **In the Contact email text box, type the contact address for the site.**

> **Caution**
>
> For your site's contact address, use a secondary address rather than your main e-mail address. This way, you can avoid getting spam at your main e-mail address if spammers pick up the site's contact address.

5. **In the Privacy area, select the Make my published site private check box if you want to restrict access to your site.** You can then use the User Name text box and Password text box to set up a password for accessing the site. You'll then give the user name and password to the people who need access to the site.

6. **If you want to automatically update your Facebook profile with news of updates to the site, select the Update my Facebook profile when I publish this site check box in the Facebook area.**

7. **Click the Publish Site button in the toolbar.** iWeb displays the Content Rights dialog, asking you to confirm that you have permission to publish your Web content.

Note If you select the Update my Facebook profile when I publish this site check box, iWeb walks you through logging in to your Facebook account and giving iWeb access to your profile when you publish the site.

8. **Select the Don't show again check box if you want to avoid seeing the Content Rights dialog box in future.**

9. **Click Continue.** iWeb then displays the Publishing will now continue in the background dialog (see Figure 10.34) to warn you that publishing may take a few minutes, during which time you can't quit iWeb.

10. **Click OK.** iWeb publishes the site.

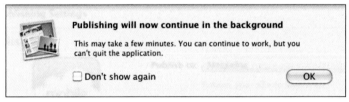

Publishing will now continue in the background

This may take a few minutes. You can continue to work, but you can't quit the application.

☐ Don't show again   (OK)

10.34 iWeb warns you that you can't quit while publishing is in progress.

Genius If you look at the File menu, you'll see there's a Publish Entire Site command as well as the Publish Site Changes command. You use the Publish Entire Site command if your Web site has become corrupted and you need to publish all the pages again. Normally, you use the Publish Site Changes command to publish only the pages that have changed since the last time you published.

Note

After you publish your site, you can view it at any time by clicking the Visit button on the toolbar or by choosing File ⇨ Visit Published Site.

Viewing your Web site

After uploading the files for your site, iWeb displays the Your site has been published dialog (see Figure 10.35). Click Visit Site Now to open the Web site in your default Web browser (for example, Safari) so that you can make sure it looks the way you want it to.

10.35 After publishing your site, you'll probably want to visit and check it out before announcing it to the world.

Announcing your Web site or your new pages

Alternatively, click Announce in the Your site has been published dialog to start a canned e-mail message using your default e-mail application (for example, Mail or Outlook). The message says that you've just updated your Web site, invites the recipients to check it out, and includes the URL for your site and URLs for new Web pages you've added.

Customize the message as needed, put your own address in the To box, add the recipients to the Bcc box (so each recipient sees only his or her own address), and then send it.

Publish on MobileMe with Your Own Domain Name

If you have your own domain name with another domain registrar, you can use it for your Web site on MobileMe. To make this work, you tell your domain registrar to redirect Web browser requests for your domain name to MobileMe.

That sounds awkward, but Apple has made the process as easy as possible. Here's what to do:

1. **In iWeb, choose File ⇨ Set Up Personal Domain on MobileMe.** iWeb launches your default Web browser, which connects to the MobileMe Web site.

continued

continued

2. **Log in with your MobileMe username and password (unless you've configured Mac OS X to log you in automatically).** Your Web browser displays your MobileMe account page.

3. **In the left column, click Personal Domain.** Your browser displays the Personal Domain page in Account Settings.

4. **Click the Add Domain button to display the Add Personal Domain page.**

5. **Type your domain name in the Domain Name box, confirm it in the Confirm Domain box, and then click Continue.** Your browser displays an information page with instructions.

6. **Open a browser tab or window manually and go to your domain registrar's Web site.** Log on to your account, and then set web.me.com to be the CNAME for your domain name. A CNAME (short for Canonical Name) is a sort of alias that you use to tell Internet clients where to look for a Web site.

7. **When your domain registrar has updated your domain with the CNAME change, return to your MobileMe account, and click Done on the Add Personal Domain page.**

Deleting a Web page from iWeb and from MobileMe

When you want to delete a Web page from your Web site, you first need to delete it from your site in iWeb and then publish the changes.

To delete the page, Control+click or right-click it in the sidebar, and then click Delete Page. Alternatively, click the page in the sidebar, and then press Delete. iWeb deletes the page and removes all links to it from other pages.

Note

If you delete a page in error, choose Edit ⇨ Undo Delete Page before you do anything else in iWeb.

After deleting the page in iWeb, publish the changes to MobileMe as described earlier in this chapter.

Publishing your Web site to a different Web hosting service

If you prefer to publish your Web site on a different Web hosting service than MobileMe, here's what to do:

1. **Click Site (or the name of your Web site) at the top of the sidebar.** iWeb displays the Site Publishing Settings screen.

2. **Open the Publish to pop-up menu and then click FTP Server.** iWeb displays the controls for publishing the site via FTP (see Figure 10.36).

3. **Use the Server address text box to type the address of your Web host's FTP server.**

4. **Use the User name and Password text boxes to type your FTP login credentials.**

5. **Use the Directory/Path text box to type the path to the server directory that you want to use to store your Web site files.**

6. **Use the Protocol pop-up menu and Port text box to specify your FTP connection settings.**

Caution

The path you type in the Directory/Path text box must point to an existing directory.

7. **In the Website URL section, use the URL text box to type the main (root) URL of your site.** iWeb uses this URL to set up your links correctly.

8. **Click the Publish Site button on the toolbar.** iWeb displays a notice asking you to confirm that you have permission to publish your Web content.

9. **Click Continue.** iWeb then displays the Publishing will now continue in the background dialog to warn you that publishing may take a few minutes, during which time you can't quit iWeb.

Note

At this point, it's a good idea to click the Test Connection button to make sure your FTP settings are configured properly. iWeb logs in to your FTP server and attempts to upload a file. If all goes well, click OK and continue publishing. Otherwise, double-check your settings and try again.

Site Publishing Settings

Publishing

Publish to: FTP Server
Publish to a web hosting service.

Site name: Surreal Macs
Contact email: info@surrealmacs.com

FTP Server Settings

Server address: ftp.pair.com
User name: ghd4280
Password: •••••••••••••••
Directory/Path: /users/ghd4280
Protocol: FTP   Port: 21

Test Connection

Website URL

URL: http://www.surrealmacs.com
Your site's root URL. Used for creating links and RSS feeds.

Add Page   Publish Site   Visit   Theme   Text Box   Shapes   Mask   Rotate   Adjust   Inspector   Colors   Fonts   Show Media

10.36 Choose FTP Server in the Publish to menu and then fill in your FTP settings.

10. **Click OK.** iWeb uploads your pages and then displays the Your site has been published dialog.

11. **Click Visit Site Now to load your site into your default Web browser.** Alternatively, click OK to return to iWeb.

Note

If you select the Update my Facebook profile when I publish this site check box, iWeb walks you through logging in to your Facebook account and giving iWeb access to your profile when you publish the site.

How Do I Publish Blogs and Podcasts with iWeb?

Do you have information to share with people frequently? If so, you can go beyond the limits of standard Web pages by publishing your own blog or podcasts on your Web site. A blog is a great way of distributing text-based information quickly, but you can also include photos, audio, or movies as needed. A podcast lets you quickly distribute either audio-based content or video-based content to listeners or viewers worldwide. Visitors can either browse or subscribe to your blog entries and podcasts on your Web site so that they automatically receive news of new entries and podcasts.

Publishing a Blog

A blog (short for Web log) is a journal that you keep on a Web site. A blog is a great way to communicate with your family and friends — or in a business setting with your colleagues and customers.

iWeb makes it easy to set up a blog, make it look good, and keep it updated with attractive content. When you add a new entry to a blog, it automatically appears at the top of the blog so that visitors see it first. Below it appear other recent entries, and older blog posts appear on archive pages.

Adding a blog to your iWeb site

Here's how to add a blog to your iWeb site:

1. **Click the Add Page button in the iWeb toolbar (or choose File ⇨ New Page) to open the Template Chooser.**

2. **In the list box on the left, choose the theme you're using for your Web site.**

3. **In the larger box, click the Blog item, and then click Choose.** iWeb closes the Template Chooser, adds a Blog item (containing an Entries item and an Archive item) to your Web site in the sidebar, and starts creating your first entry (see the chapter-opening illustration).

4. **Double-click the title placeholder to select it, and then type the name you want to give your blog.**

Understanding the Blog, Entries, and Archive items

When you start creating a blog, iWeb adds three items to the sidebar:

- **Blog.** This is a collapsible item that contains the Entries item and Archive item (discussed next). Click Entries to view the main page that visitors will see when they access your blog. This page contains the latest entries you've created.

- **Entries.** This is the page you use in iWeb to create new blog entries and manage older ones. This page appears only in iWeb, not on your Web site.

- **Archive.** This page contains all the entries in your blog — both those on your Blog page and older entries that don't appear there.

iWeb automatically creates a canned entry in the blog for you so that you can see how the blog works. This entry's title and content vary depending on the blog's template — for example, the "Day of longboarding" entry you see in the chapter-opening illustration. The easiest way to start is by customizing this entry.

Creating a blog entry

You can now create a blog entry as follows:

1. **Click Entries in the sidebar.** If you're working with the initial entry created by iWeb, skip Step 2.

2. **Click Add Entry.** iWeb creates a new blog entry and adds some default content.

3. **Double-click the default title in the entry to display an edit box.** (If the title's already selected and displaying an edit box, you're all set.) Type the title you want, and then press Return to apply it. iWeb automatically applies the change to the entry's title in the Title box at the top of the window.

4. **If you want to change the date from today's date, double-click the date to display a date picker (see Figure 11.1).** Choose the date you want the blog entry to show.

5. **Double-click the placeholder text for the entry, and then type your entry.**

6. **Replace the placeholder image with a photo of your own.** Click the Media button to open the Media Browser, display the Photos tab, and then drag the photo across. If necessary, zoom, recenter, or otherwise adjust the image, as you learned in Chapter 10.

If you need to delete a blog entry, click it in the list of blog entries, and then click the Delete Entry button. iWeb doesn't confirm the deletion, but if you delete the wrong entry, you can undo the deletion by immediately choosing Edit ⇨ Undo Delete Blog Entry.

11.1 Use the date picker to change the blog entry's date if necessary or to choose a different date format.

Setting up the main page for the blog

Next, set up the main page of the blog — the page that visitors see when they first go to your blog. Follow these steps:

1. **Click the Blog item in the sidebar to display the main page.** Figure 11.2 shows an example using the White theme. Some of the blog themes are much busier and have many more elements that you can customize.

11.2 The entry or entries you just created appear on your blog's main page, but you need to customize all the other elements.

2. **Change the title, main picture, description, and other elements on the main page.** As usual, double-click a text placeholder to select its contents, and then type the text you want. Replace the placeholder images by dragging photos from the Photos tab of the Media Browser.

3. **Click the Inspector button on the main iWeb toolbar to open the Inspector window.** Click the Blog & Podcast Inspector button on the toolbar across the top of the Inspector window, and then click the Blog tab to display its contents (see Figure 11.3).

4. **In the Blog Main Page area, set the Number of excerpts to show value and drag the Excerpt Length slider to choose how much of each entry to show.** You'll see the changes in the entry or entries you've created so far.

5. **In the Comments area, choose whether to allow comments and attachments:**

   - Select the Allow comments check box if you want to allow visitors to leave comments. iWeb displays the Allow Comments dialog to make sure you know how to manage comments. Click OK.

   - If you selected the Allow comments check box, you can select the Allow attachments check box if you want visitors to be able to leave attachments as well. iWeb displays the Allow Attachments dialog warning that you may get objectionable attachments or ones for which you don't have distribution rights. Click OK.

Blog & Podcast

Blog | Podcast

Blog Main Page

Number of excerpts to show: 5

Excerpt Length: = ⊙ ≡

Comments

☑ Allow comments

☐ Allow attachments

Search

☑ Display search field

11.3 Use the Blog tab of the Blog & Podcast Inspector to choose whether to allow comments and attachments on your blog.

6. **Select the Display search field check box if you want to allow visitors to search through your blog.** Usually, searching is helpful.

Caution

Each attachment can be up to 5MB in size. That's enough for a high-resolution photo or a four-minute song at reasonable quality (for example, 128 Kbps in AAC or MP3 format), but if your site gets a lot of 5MB attachments, it can chew through your MobileMe storage allowance and transfer allowance quickly.

Changing the layout of your blog template

From the main page of your blog, you can also change the layout of the entry pages. Here's how to do this:

1. **Click anywhere in the blog entries area on the main page to open the Blog Summary window (see Figure 11.4).**

2. **Deselect the Show photos check box if you want to hide the photo from the blog entry.** You can then skip the rest of this list because clearing this check box disables the other controls.

3. **To change the placement of a photo, open the Placement pop-up menu and click the placement you want to apply.**

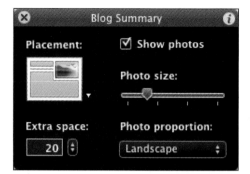

11.4 Use the Blog Summary window to rearrange the photos in your blog.

4. **To make the photo bigger or smaller, drag the Photo size slider.**

5. **To increase or decrease the amount of space around a photo, adjust the number in the Extra space box.** This measurement is in pixels.

6. **To change the shape of the photo box, open the Photo proportion pop-up menu and choose Original, Square, Landscape, or Portrait.**

7. **Click the X button in the upper-left corner to close the Blog Summary window.**

Adding multimedia to a blog entry

Blog entries are often text-only or text and pictures, but iWeb lets you easily add audio or video to your blog entries if you want.

To add an audio file, follow these steps:

1. **Click Entries and then click the blog entry to which you want to add the audio file.** If you want to create a new entry, click the Add Entry button, and then type the title and any text as usual.

2. **Click the Show Media button to open the Media Browser, and then click the Audio tab.**

3. **Drag the audio file to the blog entry and drop it there.** iWeb displays a Drag image here placeholder.

4. **If you want to add a photo to provide visual interest while the audio plays, click the Photos tab in the Media Browser, and then drag a photo to the placeholder.** Resize

the photo as needed. Figure 11.5 shows an example of a blog entry containing a photo with the audio controls under it.

Audio Excerpt: *Computing for Old and Young Alike*

Friday, May 27, 2011

Do you need a hand with your computer?

Listen to this audio excerpt from our great new resource for every computer user from toddler to grandparent.

11.5 When you include an audio file in a blog entry, you can add a picture to give visitors something to look at.

To add a video file from your Mac to a blog entry, follow these steps:

1. **Open the blog entry to which you want to add the audio file.**

2. **Click the Show Media button to open the Media Browser, and then click the Movies tab.**

3. **Drag the movie file to the blog entry and drop it there.** Resize the movie as needed.

Caution Avoid adding large video files to your blog because they will not only take a long time for visitors to download but they will take up your bandwidth allowance quickly. When you add a very large file, iWeb displays a warning dialog to make sure you're aware of the file's size. When this happens, click OK, but then delete the video from the blog page. Then either choose a different file or use iMovie to create a shorter edit of the video.

Publishing your blog

When you've created your blog entries, click the Publish Site button to publish your blog together with all the other changes you've made to your Web site. When iWeb tells you it has finished publishing the Web site, click the Announce button and send an e-mail to encourage friends and family to read your blog. If your blog is gripping, your visitors will subscribe for updates, so you may not need to send announcements via e-mail after your first few entries.

Managing visitor comments

One of the most compelling features of blogs is that visitors can contribute to them by adding comments. If you want, you can also let visitors attach files to their comments so that other people can download the files.

Visitor comments can greatly add to the appeal of your blog. But if you allow comments, you will need to review them frequently and delete any unsuitable comments.

Similarly, if you allow attachments, you must check the files frequently to make sure that none contains offensive material or copyrighted material that is being distributed without adequate permission. You will also need to make sure that attachments don't take your MobileMe account over its monthly storage limit or data-transfer limit.

Note   iWeb helps to protect you against "comment spam" by making anyone who tries to submit a comment type a displayed sequence of characters first. This "captcha," or Completely Automated Public Turing Test to Tell Computers and Humans Apart, aims to prevent automated programs from posting spam comments to your site. Some programs have been written that break captchas by deciphering and typing the word automatically, but at this writing these programs mostly target large sites such as Gmail and Hotmail.

Reviewing and removing comments and attachments

If you do permit comments (and maybe attachments) on your blog, you should review them regularly to make sure there's nothing you need to remove.

When visitors add comments to your blog, the iWeb icon on the Dock displays a telltale red icon showing the number of comments, just like Mail does for unread e-mail messages. You can force iWeb to check for comments by choosing File ⇨ Check for New Comments.

Figure 11.6 shows an example of comments in iWeb. One comment includes an attachment; the other does not.

To delete a comment, click the Delete button (the round button with an X on it). As long as your Mac is connected to the Internet, iWeb deletes the comment from the published version of your blog immediately as well as from the iWeb version. You don't need to publish your blog again to get rid of the comment from the published version.

11.6 Viewing the comments and attachments that visitors have left.

Deleting comments from your blog using a browser

Because the live version of your blog (on the Web) isn't kept strictly in sync with the version in iWeb, you can get into the situation where your blog has comments but you can't read them in iWeb because you've deleted the entries.

When this happens, you can use Safari or another Web browser to read the comments — and to delete them if necessary. Follow these steps:

1. **In iWeb, click the Visit button or choose File ⇨ Visit Published Site to open your blog in your default Web browser.**

2. **Click the Blog link, and then go to the blog entry that contains the comments.**

3. **Click the lock icon next to the number of comments.** The browser displays the Site Owner Login screen.

Understanding Your Blog's RSS Feed

RSS (short for Really Simple Syndication) is the group of standards used for blog subscriptions. By subscribing to your blog's RSS feed, a visitor can automatically receive news of your latest posts.

iWeb automatically provides an RSS link on your blog's main page and on the archive page, and most Web browsers display an RSS icon in the address box when you open one of these pages in them.

4. **Type your MobileMe ID and password, and then click the Login button.** The browser displays the Manage Comments page (see Figure 11.7).

11.7 You can also manage comments and attachments from Safari or another Web browser.

5. **Select the check box for the comment (or comment and attachment) you want to delete, or select the Select All check box, and then click Delete.** Click OK in the confirmation dialog that the browser displays.

6. **Click the Return to Entry link if you want to return to the blog entry.**

Creating Podcasts

Podcasts give you a way of broadcasting your own audio or video content easily on the Internet. You create a podcast episode and post it to your Web site, where anyone worldwide can download it. And if that person enjoys the podcast, he or she can subscribe and receive automatic notification of future episodes when you post them.

Putting a podcast up on the Web is a four-stage process:

1. **Add a podcast to iWeb.** Start by creating your Podcast item in iWeb. This Podcast item is the overall container for the podcast, in the same way as your Blog item is the container for your blog posts.

2. **Create the podcast episode.** To create a podcast, you use an audio or video application such as GarageBand.

3. **Create a Web page for the podcast.** In iWeb, you create a Web page using one of the Podcast templates. You then place the podcast episode on the page, together with any explanatory text it needs.

4. **Publish the podcast to the Web.** You publish the podcast from iWeb in exactly the same way as you publish other Web pages.

Genius If you want, you can also submit your podcasts to the iTunes Store. This can be a great way of putting your material in front of a larger audience than you can reach via your own Web site.

Add a podcast to iWeb

To add a podcast to your Web site in iWeb, follow these steps:

1. **Click the Add Page button in the iWeb toolbar (or choose File ⇨ New Page) to open the Template Chooser.**

2. **In the list box on the left, choose the theme you're using for your Web site.**

3. **Click the Podcast item, and then click Choose.** iWeb adds three items to the sidebar:

   - **Podcast.** This is a collapsible item that contains the Entries item and Archive item (discussed next). Click this item to view the main page that visitors see when they access your podcasts. This page contains an overview of your last few podcasts.

   - **Entries.** This is the page you use in iWeb to create new podcasts and manage older ones (for example, deleting them). This page appears only in iWeb, not on your Web site. iWeb creates a new entry for you by default.

   - **Archive.** This page contains all your podcasts — both those on your Podcast page and older podcasts that no longer appear on that page.

4. **Click the Podcast page in the sidebar, and then customize the text and image placeholders using the techniques you learned in this chapter and in Chapter 10.** This is the first page that visitors see when they click the Podcast link in your Web site.

5. **To change the layout of the podcast entry pages, click one of the entries, and then use the Blog Summary dialog as discussed earlier in this chapter.**

6. **When you finish customizing the Podcast page, click Entries in the sidebar to display the Entries page, and then delete the entry that iWeb created for you.** Click the entry in the list box at the top, and then click the Delete Entry button. You create a real podcast entry from GarageBand next.

Creating a podcast from GarageBand

GarageBand lets you create both audio podcasts and video podcasts. You can create a simple podcast that contains only audio or only video and audio, but GarageBand makes it easy to create enhanced podcasts that include artwork (in audio podcasts), navigation markers, and URLs the viewer can visit. This section shows you how to create enhanced podcasts.

Start creating a podcast

Here's how to start creating a podcast:

1. **Launch GarageBand from the Dock icon or the Applications folder.** If GarageBand is already open, choose File ⇨ Close to close the open project.

2. **On the GarageBand opening screen, click New Project in the left pane, click Podcast in the main pane, and then click Choose.** GarageBand displays the New Project from Template dialog (see Figure 11.8).

```
┌─────────────────────────────────────────────┐
│          New Project from Template          │
│                                             │
│   Save As: │GHD Books podcast 1      │  ▼   │
│                                             │
│   Where: │ 📁 GarageBand          │  ▲▼      │
│                                             │
│  ┌───────────────────────────────────────┐  │
│  │   Tempo: ──────────○───────────────   │  │
│  │  Signature: │ 4 / 4  ▲▼│ │ 120 │ bpm   │  │
│  │       Key: │ C     ▲▼│ │ major  ▲▼│    │  │
│  └───────────────────────────────────────┘  │
│                                             │
│                    ( Cancel )  ( Create )   │
└─────────────────────────────────────────────┘
```

11.8 In the New Project from Template dialog, name your podcast episode and pick the folder in which to store it.

3. **Type the name for the podcast episode in the Save As box, and pick the folder in the Where pop-up menu.**

4. **Click Create.** GarageBand creates the blank podcast project and displays it. Click the Podcast Track in the upper-left corner of the window to display the Podcast Markers pane, as shown in Figure 11.9.

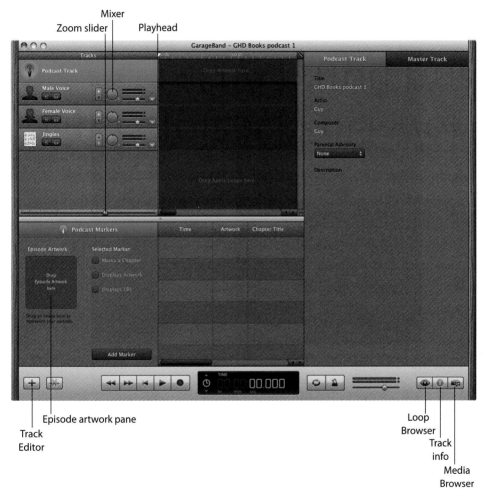

11.9 A blank podcast project includes a Podcast Track, a Male Voice track, a Female Voice track, and a Jingles track.

Here are the details of what you see in the figure:

⬤ **Podcast Track.** This is the track that contains the audio for the podcast. If you want to create a video podcast instead, you replace the Podcast Track with a Movie Track. A podcast can have only one of these at a time.

339

- **Male Voice track.** This is a Real Instrument track with settings optimized for making a male voice clearly audible in the podcast.

- **Female Voice track.** This is a Real Instrument track with settings optimized for making a female voice clearly audible in the podcast.

- **Jingles.** This track is for adding jingles, sound effects, and other short audio items to the podcast.

- **Podcast pane.** This pane contains the opening artwork for the podcast episode.

- **Markers pane.** This pane lets you create and work with markers in the podcast.

- **Media Browser.** As normal in the iLife applications, this browser lets you add audio, photos, and movies to your podcast.

- **Mixer.** As usual in GarageBand, the mixer controls let you adjust the volume, balance, and panning of different tracks in your podcast.

Adding audio to the podcast

You can add audio to the podcast either by recording narration or by adding musical tracks or loops.

Here's how to record narration:

1. **Double-click the Male Voice track header or the Female Voice track header (depending on the voice that will narrate) to display the Track Info pane (see Figure 11.10).**

2. **In the Input source pop-up menu, choose the microphone you will use — for example, your Mac's built-in microphone, recording in stereo.**

3. **If you want to hear what you're recording, choose On in the Monitor pop-up menu.** GarageBand automatically protects the input from feedback. You can also choose the On (no feedback protection) setting, but you may get feedback.

11.10 To record narration, choose the input source in the Track Info pane.

4. **Drag the Playhead to the time at which you want to start the recording.** If you add introductory music or jingles, leave enough space at the start. Otherwise, you can begin the recording right from the start.

5. **Click the Record button to start recording, and then start your narration.** Click the Stop button when you finish recording.

To add an audio file to the podcast, display the Media Browser, click the Audio tab, and then drag the file across to the podcast. GarageBand creates a new track for it, which you can adjust, as discussed in Chapter 8.

Similarly, you can add Software Instrument or Real Instrument tracks to the podcast. Just click the Loop Browser button to display the Loop Browser, select the loop, and drag it to the podcast.

Replacing the Podcast Track with a Movie Track

If you want to create a video podcast, you replace the Podcast Track with a Movie Track. To do so, choose Track ⇨ Show Movie Track, and then click Replace in the dialog (see Figure 11.11) that GarageBand displays.

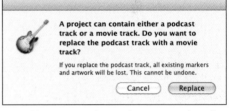

A project can contain either a podcast track or a movie track. Do you want to replace the podcast track with a movie track?

If you replace the podcast track, all existing markers and artwork will be lost. This cannot be undone.

Cancel   Replace

GarageBand displays the Movie Track at the top of the track list. You can then drag a movie from the Movies tab in the Media Browser and drop it on the Movie Track. GarageBand adds

11.11 To create a video podcast, you replace the Podcast Track with the Movie Track.

the movie to the Movie Track and adds a Real Instrument track named Movie Sound containing the audio from the movie. You can edit this track just like any Real Instrument track — you can even mute it if you want to suppress it altogether and accompany the movie with narration or other audio content instead.

Adding episode artwork

Each podcast can have one piece of episode artwork — the image that represents the episode and that appears on the podcast's Web page in iWeb and your Web site.

To add the episode artwork, follow these steps:

1. **If the Track Editor isn't already displayed, click the Track Editor button to display it.** If you don't see the Podcast Markers pane, click the Podcast Track.

2. **If the Media Browser isn't already displayed, click the Media Browser button to display it.** Click the Photos tab to display its contents.

3. **Find the photo you want, and then drag it to the Episode Artwork pane in the lower-left corner of the GarageBand window.**

4. **If you need to edit the photo, double-click it in the Episode Artwork area to open the Artwork Editor window (see Figure 11.12).** Drag the slider to resize the photo, and then drag the photo so that the border frames the part you want to display. Click Set when you finish.

Adding markers to a podcast episode

If you're creating an enhanced podcast episode, you can add markers to it. The markers break up the podcast track into marker regions that show you how long each section lasts. You can move marker regions or resize them using the same techniques you use for audio clips.

11.12 Use the Artwork Editor window to resize a photo and to select the part you want to display.

Here's the easiest way to add a marker:

1. **Position the Playhead where you want the marker region to start.** Either drag the Playhead or play through the podcast to reach the right point, and then stop playback.

2. **Click the Add Marker button or choose Edit ⇨ Add Marker (or simply press P).** GarageBand adds a marker to the Track Editor (see Figure 11.13).

11.13 Markers make your podcast episode easier to navigate and let you add URLs the viewer can reach.

3. **Add artwork for the marker by dragging it from the Photos tab of the Media Browser to the marker's placeholder in the Artwork column in the editing area.** If you need to edit the photo, double-click it in the Artwork column to open it in the Artwork Editor, and then resize it and select the part you want, as described earlier in this chapter.

Genius

You can also create a new marker and add artwork to it by dragging a photo from the Photos tab of the Media Browser to the appropriate point on the Podcast Track.

4. **Click in the marker's row in the Chapter Title column in the editing area, type the title, and then press Return to apply it.**

5. **If you want to add a URL to the marker, click in the URL Title column in the marker's row, and then type the text you want to display for the URL.** Then click in the URL column and type or paste the URL itself. The URL title can be the same as the URL itself if you want, but often it's helpful to display a URL title that's shorter than the URL, more descriptive, or both.

Genius

Adding a chapter title to a marker is optional, but it enables someone playing back the podcast in iTunes, iDVD, or QuickTime to move quickly from one marker to another.

Adding sounds or jingles

To help you jazz up your podcasts, GarageBand also provides jingles, sound effects, and stingers (attention-grabbing sounds). Here's how to add these sounds to a podcast episode:

1. **If the loop browser isn't open, click the Loop Browser button.**

2. **Click the Podcast Sounds View button.** GarageBand displays the sounds in Podcast Sounds View (see Figure 11.14).

3. **Navigate to the sound you want.** For example, click Sound Effects in the Loops column, click the category in the second column, and then click the sound. Or type a search term in the Search box and press Return to find sounds that match that term.

4. **Drag the sound to the Jingles track, and position its beginning at the time you want it to start.**

Ducking backing tracks to keep narration audible

If your podcast episode includes audio tracks as well as one or more narration tracks, you can duck the audio tracks to make sure that the narration is always audible. To do this, you tell GarageBand which tracks are lead tracks and which tracks are backing tracks. When playing or mixing your podcast episode, GarageBand ducks (lowers) the backing tracks when any of the lead tracks have a sound. You can adjust the amount of ducking to get the effect you need.

Here's how to duck the backing tracks:

1. **If GarageBand isn't displaying the ducking controls (see Figure 11.15), choose Control ⇨ Ducking or press ⌘+Shift+R to display them.**

2. **To make a track a lead track, click the upper arrow button so that it turns yellow.** If the button is already yellow, the track is already a lead track.

3. **To make a track a backing track, click the lower arrow button so that it turns blue.** If the button is already blue, the track is already a backing track.

11.14 The loop browser's Podcast Sounds View lets you quickly browse through the jingles, stingers, and sound effects.

Play back the episode to see whether the ducking is how you want it to be. If not, adjust the ducking like this:

1. **Click the Track Info button to open the Track Info pane.**

2. **Click the Master Track tab.**

3. **Click the Edit tab.**

4. **In the Ducker pop-up menu, choose the preset you want — for example, Fast - Maximum Music Reduction:**

   - **Speed.** There are three speeds: Fast, Slow, and Slowest. These control how fast the ducking happens.

   - **Degree of reduction.** There are three degrees of reduction: Maximum Music Reduction, Moderate Music Reduction, and Slight Music Reduction.

5. **If none of the Ducker presets suits you, create your own setting like this:**

   - Choose Manual in the Ducker pop-up menu.

   - Click the picture button to the left of the Ducker pop-up menu to display the Ducker window, as shown in Figure 11.16.

   - Drag the sliders to set the amount of ducking you need, and then click the Close button (the red button in the upper-left corner of the Ducker window).

Adding episode information to the podcast episode

After creating the content for your podcast episode, add the episode information like this:

1. **Double-click the Podcast Track to open the Track Info pane.**

2. **Click the Podcast Track tab to display the Episode Info pane, as shown in Figure 11.17.**

11.15 In the ducking controls, the yellow arrow pointing up indicates a lead track, and the blue arrow pointing down indicates a backing track.

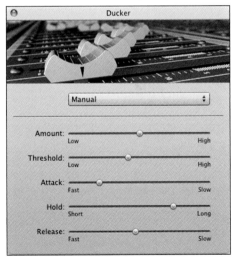

11.16 You can use the Ducker window to create custom ducking for your podcast episode.

Genius In the Ducker window, the Threshold slider controls the threshold level at which GarageBand starts to apply the ducking. The Attack slider controls the speed at which the ducking takes effect, and the Release slider the speed at which the ducking ceases. The Hold slider controls how long the ducking remains on.

3. **Type the title and adjust the artist and composer information as needed.**

4. **If you want to apply a parental advisory to the episode, open the Parental Advisory pop-up menu and choose Clean or Explicit, as appropriate.** If you don't want to apply a parental advisory, choose None.

5. **Click in the Description box and type a description of the episode's contents.**

When you finish creating your podcast episode, save it by pressing ⌘+S.

Sending the podcast to iWeb

When you complete the podcast, send it to iWeb like this:

1. **Choose Share ⇨ Send Podcast to iWeb. GarageBand displays the Send your podcast to iWeb dialog (see Figure 11.18).**

2. **In the Compress Using pop-up menu, choose AAC Encoder if you want to use AAC format, or MP3 Encoder if you want to use MP3 format.** AAC gives marginally better quality, but MP3 is usually a better choice because many more players can play MP3 than AAC. MP3 is also a better choice for playing from within a Web page.

3. **In the Audio Settings pop-up menu, choose the quality:**

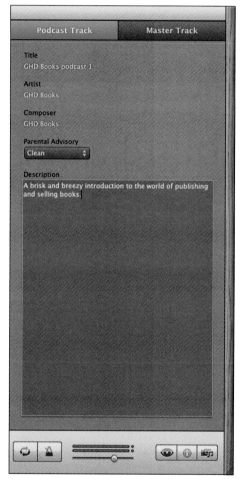

11.17 Use the Episode Info pane to set the title, artist, and composer information, apply a parental advisory if needed, and add a description.

- **Mono Podcast.** Uses the 32 Kbps bit rate and mono (one channel) rather than stereo. The files download quickly and help conserve Internet bandwidth, but the audio results are disappointing — as if you were podcasting on AM radio.

- **Spoken Podcast.** Uses the 64 Kbps bit rate and stereo. This sounds fine for voice, but music and other complex audio suffers.

- **Musical Podcast.** Uses the 128 Kbps bit rate and stereo. Music sounds fine to anyone except audiophiles.

Send your podcast to iWeb

Compress Using: AAC Encoder

Audio Settings: Musical Podcast

Ideal for enhanced podcasts with voice and music. Download times are moderate. Details: AAC, 128kbps, Stereo, optimized for music and complex audio. Estimated size: 3.6MB.

Publish Podcast: ☑ Set artwork to recommended size for podcasts (300 x 300 pixels) when exporting

Cancel   Share

11.18 Before you can add your podcast to your Web site, you need to export it using this dialog.

- **Higher Quality.** Uses the 192 Kbps bit rate and stereo. Music sounds great to most people, but the file sizes are that much larger.

- **iTunes Plus.** (AAC Encoder only.) Uses the 256 Kbps bit rate and stereo. This produces high-quality sound at the expense of larger file sizes.

- **Custom.** Opens the AAC Encoder dialog or MP3 Encoder dialog (depending on the encoder you chose in the Compress Using pop-up menu) so that you can choose exactly the settings you want. Figure 11.19 shows the MP3 Encoder dialog. Click OK when you make your choices.

MP3 Encoder

Bit Rate: 320 kbps

☑ Use Variable Bit Rate Encoding (VBR)

VBR Quality: Highest

Channels: ⦿ Stereo ◯ Mono

☑ Use Joint Stereo

☑ Filter Frequencies Below 10Hz

Default Settings   Cancel   OK

11.19 Use the MP3 Encoder dialog or the AAC Encoder dialog when you need to create super-high-quality podcasts.

4. **If you're using the AAC Encoder, select the Set artwork to recommended size for podcasts when exporting check box if you want GarageBand to resize the art automatically.** This is usually a good idea. This setting doesn't apply to MP3 podcasts.

5. **Click Share.** GarageBand exports the podcast and passes it to iWeb, which prompts you to decide which blog you want to send it to.

6. **Choose the blog or podcast, and then click OK.** iWeb adds the podcast to the Entries list for the blog or podcast.

Genius

Use custom audio settings when you need to crank the quality as high as possible. In the AAC Encoder dialog or MP3 Encoder dialog, choose a high bit rate — up to 320 Kbps if you can afford large file sizes. Turn on Variable Bit Rate Encoding to squeeze the highest quality into your files. Select the Stereo option button unless you need mono. For MP3, turn off joint stereo for bit rates more than 160 Kbps — joint stereo is a space-saving measure that reduces audio quality, so you shouldn't use it at higher bit rates.

Publishing the podcast from iWeb

After you add the podcast episode to iWeb from GarageBand, you need to finalize its Web page, set series, and episode information, and then publish it to your Web site.

Finalizing the podcast's Web page

When GarageBand creates an entry in iWeb's Podcast category for the podcast episode, it copies across the title and artist information you supplied. Often, you need to edit this information to make the entry's Web page look compelling. For example, you may want to improve the description, give the podcast a snappier title, or change the date.

Setting series and episode information

Next, set the series and episode information for the podcast like this:

1. **Click the Inspector button on the tool-bar to display the Inspector window.**

2. **Click the Blog & Podcast Inspector button to display the Blog & Podcast Inspector.** Click the Podcast tab to display it, as shown in Figure 11.20.

3. **Choose serieswide options in the Podcast Series area:**

Blog & Podcast

Blog | Podcast

Podcast Series

Series Artist

GHD Books

Contact Email

admin@ghdbooks.com

Parental Advisory

Clean

☑ Allow Podcast in iTunes Store

Podcast Episode

Duration: 3:39 Minutes

Episode Artist

GHD Books

Parental Advisory

Clean

☑ Allow Podcast in iTunes Store

11.20 Enter the series and episode information for your podcast on the Podcast tab in the Blog & Podcast Inspector.

- **Series Artist.** Type the name you want to use for the artist for the podcast series. (This may be different from the artist for individual episodes.)

- **Contact Email.** Type the address you want to use for the podcast series.

- **Parental Advisory.** Choose Clean or Explicit if you want to apply a parental advisory to the series. Choose None if you don't.

- **Allow Podcast in iTunes Store.** Select this check box if you want the podcast series to appear in the iTunes Store for free download. This is a great way of getting distribution for your podcast.

4. Choose options for this episode only in the Podcast Episode area:

   - **Episode Artist.** Type a different artist's name here if necessary.

   - **Parental Advisory.** Choose Clean or Explicit if you want to apply a parental advisory to this podcast episode. (This rating can be different from that which you applied to the podcast series.) Choose None if you don't.

   - **Allow Podcast in iTunes Store.** Select this check box if you want the podcast episode to appear in the iTunes Store for free download.

5. **Click the Close button (the red button in the upper-left corner) to close the Inspector.**

Publishing the podcast

Your podcast is now ready for publishing. To publish it, click the Publish Site button in the lower-left corner of the iWeb window.

How Do I Design, Build, and Burn DVDs in iDVD?

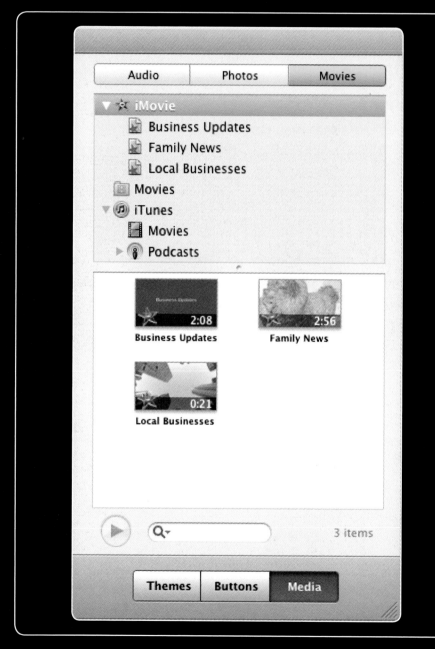

DVD lets you create professional-looking DVDs from your movies, photos, and compositions, complete with customized menu screens including pictures, video, and audio. You can either take full control of the process of creating the DVD, or use the Magic iDVD feature to jump-start the process for you and then finish it yourself. You can even use the OneStep DVD feature to burn a DVD directly from your DV camcorder without your intervention. The first essential is to understand the process of creating a DVD in iDVD. Let's look at that quickly, and then get to work.

Understanding the Process of Creating a DVD

Before getting into creating a DVD, let's go quickly through the steps you need to take. The process is straightforward once you know what you're doing.

1. **Get your content ready in the other iLife applications:**

   - **Movies.** Create movies in iMovie and export them directly to iDVD or to the Media Browser. If you have movies already prepared in other folders, you can use them directly from there.

   - **Photos.** If you want to create slide shows in iDVD, prepare the photos in iPhoto. For example, put your edited photos in a photo album so that you can grab them all at once.

   - **Music.** Compose songs in GarageBand and save previews of them in the Media Browser so that iDVD can access them. You can also export the finished songs to iTunes and use them from there. And you can use any song or playlist from your iTunes library — so you may want to assemble a suitable playlist for a DVD.

2. **Start creating a DVD project in iDVD.** You can create either a regular DVD project, which gives you total control right from the start, or use the Magic iDVD feature to jump-start creating the DVD. If you use Magic iDVD, you avoid Step 3 altogether, and Magic iDVD takes care of Step 4 for you.

Note The majority of this chapter shows you how to create a DVD manually. If you want to use the Magic iDVD feature to start your DVD project quickly, see the end of the chapter.

3. **Add content to the DVD.** At this point, you add your movies, photos, and music to the DVD. You may need to add chapter markers to a movie or create a scene selection menu for a movie; the latter involves a bit of work outside iDVD but is well worth the effort.

4. **Customize the menu screen for the DVD.** The menu screen is the background on which the various buttons for controlling the DVD appear. You can add movies and slide shows to the menu screen to give it more impact.

5. **Check the DVD's status and inspect the items it contains.**

6. **When the DVD project is ready, burn it to DVD.**

After skimming over the previous six steps, you may have already taken care of Step 1, preparing the contents. (If not, go and do so.) The following sections take you through the remaining five steps in turn.

Starting a DVD Project

Now that you understand the process of creating a DVD, it's time to launch iDVD and start a project.

Launch iDVD by either of these ways:

- **Click the iDVD icon in the Dock.**
- **Click the desktop, choose Go⇨Applications, and then double-click the iDVD icon in the Finder window.**

The first time you launch it, iDVD displays the iDVD opening screen shown in Figure 12.1.

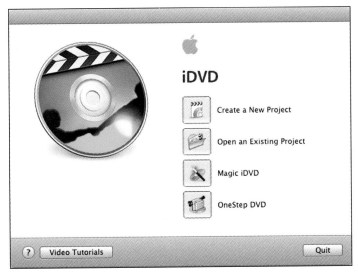

12.1 On the iDVD opening screen, choose the type of DVD project you want to create.

Note Once you create a DVD project (or several), each time you launch iDVD, it opens the last project you were working with. If you close that project (by choosing File⇨Close Window), iDVD displays the iDVD opening screen again.

Choosing which kind of DVD to create

Before you can get started with iDVD, you need to pick a task from the iDVD opening screen. This screen lets you create three kinds of DVD projects or open an existing project:

- **Create a New Project.** Click this button to start a new DVD that you create manually, as described in the bulk of this chapter. This is what you'll probably want to do most of the time.

- **Open an Existing Project.** Once you start a DVD project or two, you can click this button to open one of them to work on it further. Choose the DVD project in the Open dialog, and then click the Open button to open it.

- **Magic iDVD.** Click this button to create a DVD the quick-and-easy way. Like the Magic GarageBand feature in GarageBand for starting custom songs in a snap, Magic iDVD lets you create a customized DVD with minimal effort while providing you with control over the DVD's contents, menus, and appearance.

- **OneStep DVD.** Click this button to grab movie content from the tape on your DV camcorder and drop it directly onto a DVD. When you do, you don't get to use iMovie to edit the movie content and pretty it up, so OneStep DVD is best for content that's either final (for example, a movie project someone has exported to the DV camcorder) or that you're simply not planning to edit. You find details of OneStep DVD later in this chapter.

Creating a new project

Here's how to create a new project:

1. **Click the Create a New Project button from the iDVD opening screen.** iMovie displays the Create Project dialog (see Figure 12.2).

2. **Type the name for the project in the Save As box in place of iDVD's suggestion (My Great DVD).**

12.2 Start by naming your DVD project, choosing its aspect ratio, and deciding where to save it.

3. **In the Where pop-up menu, choose the folder in which to save the DVD project.** iDVD suggests the Documents folder, but it's better to use a different folder so that your Documents folder doesn't get cluttered. If necessary, expand the Create Project dialog so that you can see the sidebar and create a new folder.

4. **In the Aspect Ratio area, select the Standard (4:3) option button if you're creating a DVD for standard-format screens.** Select the Widescreen (16:9) option button if your audience will use wide screens; anyone viewing a widescreen DVD on a standard-format screen will see it letterboxed with black bands above and below.

5. **Click Create.** iDVD creates the project and displays it in the main iDVD window.

Setting preferences to meet your needs

Now that you have iDVD open, you can set preferences to tell iDVD how you want it to work and how to encode your video. Choose iDVD ⇨ Preferences to open the iDVD preferences window, and then click the General button on the toolbar if it's not already selected.

Setting General preferences

The General preferences (see Figure 12.3) contain the following settings:

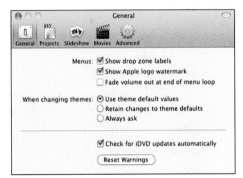

- **Show drop zone labels.** Select this check box to have iDVD label the areas on the menu screens where you can drop background music, photos, or movies. These labels are usually helpful.

- **Show Apple logo watermark.** Select this check box if you want to make an Apple logo appear as a watermark on the menu backgrounds of your DVD.

12.3 The General preferences include settings for fading out audio on menu loops and choosing how to handle theme changes.

- **Fade volume out at end of menu loop.** Select this check box if you want iDVD to gradually fade out the volume at the end of each loop.

- **When changing themes.** Tell iDVD what to do about changes you've made to a theme when you switch a DVD project from one theme to another. Select the Use theme default values option button if you want to use the values in the new theme. Select the Retain changes to theme defaults option button if you want to keep your changes. Select the Always ask option button if you want iDVD to prompt you to decide at the time.

● **Check for iDVD updates automatically.** Select this check box if you want iDVD to automatically look for its own updates. Deselect the check box if you prefer to check manually by choosing iDVD ➪ Check for Updates or by using Software Update.

● **Reset Warnings.** You can turn off many of iDVD's warnings by selecting a Don't ask me again check box in them. Click this button if you need to reset all iDVD's warnings.

Setting Projects preferences

The Projects preferences (see Figure 12.4) let you choose the following settings:

● **Video Mode.** NTSC is the format generally used in North America, whereas Europe is PAL territory. The two formats use different numbers of frames per second of video and different numbers of horizontal lines, so a DVD in one format won't play properly on a TV that uses the other format.

12.4 Choose the video mode and encoding type in the Projects preferences.

● **Encoding.** This is a vital setting. Choose Best Performance if you want iDVD to encode movies for DVD as you work so that they're ready to burn when you finish the project. Choose High Quality to encode at higher quality when you start to burn your project. Choose Professional Quality to encode at the highest quality available, again when you start to burn your project.

● **DVD Type.** Choose whether to create Single-Layer or Dual-Layer discs. If your Mac's SuperDrive can burn only Single-Layer discs, this pop-up menu is unavailable.

Genius

The High Quality and Professional Quality settings in the Encoding pop-up menu in the Projects preferences give visibly better results than the Best Performance setting. The disadvantage is that, because neither of them starts encoding until you start burning the DVD project, the burning process takes that much longer. Professional Quality takes about twice as long as High Quality to encode the video, so plan ahead if you intend to use it.

Setting Slideshow preferences

The Slideshow preferences (see Figure 12.5) let you choose the following settings:

- **Always add original photos to DVD-ROM contents.** Select this check box if you want to include original, full-size photos on the DVD as well as the smaller versions used for the slide shows. This setting is helpful if you distribute the photos.

12.5 The Slideshow preferences let you add original photos to the DVD, stay in the TV Safe Area, fade the volume out, and include titles and comments.

- **Always scale slides to TV Safe Area.** The TV Safe Area is that part of a wide-screen project that will appear on a standard-format TV screen (whose aspect ratio is 4:3 rather than 16:9). Select this check box if you want to make sure the full photo always appears on the TV screen. This is a good idea unless you're certain the DVD will be viewed only on widescreen monitors.

- **Fade volume out at end of slideshow.** Select this check box if you want iDVD to fade the volume out at the end of a slide show. This effect can be useful with music, but you won't usually want to use it with voiceovers.

- **Show titles and comments.** Select this check box if you want to include the titles and comments with the photos. Having the titles and comments can be useful when you make DVDs for yourself, but you'll probably want to omit them when you make DVDs for other people.

Setting Movies preferences

The Movies preferences (see Figure 12.6) let you choose the following settings:

- **When importing movies.** Select the Create chapter submenus option button if you want iDVD to automatically create a submenu screen to let the viewer access the chapters (the scenes) in the movie.

- **Look for my movies in these folders.** If you want iDVD to look for movies in other folders than your ~/Movies folder, your iTunes Movies, and the Media Browser, add the folders to this list.

12.6 In the Movies preferences, choose whether to create chapter submenus. You can also add folders iDVD should scan automatically for movies.

Setting Advanced preferences

The Advanced preferences (see Figure 12.7) let you choose the following settings:

- **Look for my themes in these folders.** iDVD automatically searches your Mac's /Library/Application Support/iDVD/ Themes folder for themes. If you have themes in another folder, add that folder by clicking Add.

- **OneStep DVD capture folder.** The readout shows the folder iDVD is using to store the data it captures from your camcorder for creating OneStep DVDs. If

12.7 The Advanced preferences let you add themes, change your OneStep DVD capture folder, and set your preferred DVD burning speed.

you're running out of space on your Mac's hard drive, you may need to switch to a folder on an external drive. Click Change, select the folder in the Open dialog, and then click the Open button.

- **Preferred DVD Burning Speed.** In this pop-up menu, choose the DVD burning speed you want to use. Usually, it's best to choose Maximum Possible and let iDVD handle the speed. But if you find that full-speed burning produces DVDs containing errors, choose a lower speed here.

Closing the Preferences window automatically saves your new preferences settings.

Genius

If you changed any of the Projects preferences, you have a chicken-and-egg situation here: The new settings you chose apply only to new projects you create from now on, not to the new project you just created in order to be able to set the preferences. To implement the changes, close your project (choose File ⇨ Close Window) and create a new one.

Navigating the iDVD interface

Now that you've got a project open in iDVD, it's time to come to grips with the application's interface. Figure 12.8 shows the main iDVD window.

Genius

If you find you've chosen Standard format for your DVD project instead of Widescreen, or vice versa, you can change by choosing Project ⇨ Switch to Widescreen or Project ⇨ Switch to Standard. You can also flip between the formats by pressing ⌘+Option+A.

Applying a theme

A theme is a complete set of formatting for the DVD, including the layouts, background, fonts, and background music.

Here's how to apply a theme:

1. **In the Themes pop-up menu at the top of the Themes pane, choose the category of themes you want to see:**

    - **All.** All the themes you've installed

    - **7.0 Themes.** Themes from iDVD '08, '09, and '11

    - **6.0 Themes.** Themes from iDVD '06

    - **Old Themes.** Themes from earlier versions of iDVD

    - **Favorites.** Themes you've marked as your favorites

2. **To see the other screens a theme includes, click the disclosure triangle next to it.**

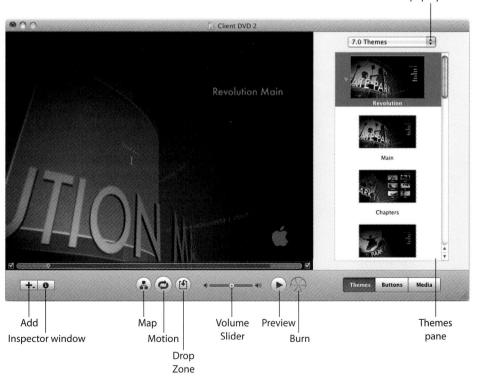

12.8 The main iDVD window.

3. **Click the theme you want.** iDVD applies the theme to the project. If the theme doesn't appear in the main iDVD window, try running Software Update from the Apple menu.

If you're creating a standard-format project and choose a widescreen-format theme, iDVD displays the Change Project Aspect Ratio dialog, as shown in Figure 12.9, asking if you want to change aspect ratio and giving you three choices:

12.9 You may need to decide whether to change the project's aspect ratio to match the ratio of the theme you applied.

- **Keep.** Click this button to maintain the aspect ratio. This is usually the best choice because changing the aspect ratio gives the DVD the wrong aspect ratio for your movie.

- **Change.** Click this button to change the project to the theme's aspect ratio.

- **Cancel.** Click this button to cancel applying the theme. You can then pick another theme that uses the right aspect ratio.

Adding Content to the DVD Project

Next, add content to your DVD project. You'll probably want to add one or more movies to the DVD project, but you can also create a powerful DVD by using slide shows either with movies or instead of them.

Adding a movie

To add a movie to your DVD, follow these steps:

1. **Click the Media button in the lower-right corner of the iDVD window to display the Media pane.**

2. **Click the Movies button at the top of the Media pane to display the Movies tab.**

3. **In the box at the top of the Movies tab, choose the source of the movies:**

   - **iMovie.** These are the movies you've added to the Media Browser from iMovie.

   - **Movies.** These are the movies stored in your Movies folder.

   - **iPhoto.** These are movies you've imported to iPhoto from your digital camera.

   - **iTunes.** These are movies you've exported to iTunes from iMovie or otherwise added to iTunes. Click the disclosure triangle to display the Movies category within iTunes.

   - **Folders.** These are movies in the folders you've told iDVD to search for movies. You can add other folders as described in the nearby sidebar.

Note The box at the top of the Movies tab in the Media pane shows only the movie sources that contain movies.

4. **Click the thumbnail for the movie you want to add, and then drag it to the menu in the main part of the iDVD window.** You can drop it anywhere that the mouse pointer includes a green circle containing a + sign, as shown in Figure 12.10. iDVD adds a menu button with the movie's name on it.

12.10 Drag a movie thumbnail from the Movies tab of the Media pane to the main part of the iDVD window.

Caution

Make sure you don't drop the movie in one of the drop zones — if you do, iDVD makes it part of the menu screen rather than a separate movie.

5. **If you want to change the button's text, click the button once, and then click it again to display the text-editing controls (see Figure 12.11).** Edit the text as needed; choose the font, style, and size; and then click elsewhere to apply the changes.

12.11 You can easily change the text or formatting of a menu button.

Adding chapter markers to a movie

To break a movie up into scenes among which the viewer can easily navigate on a DVD you add chapter markers to the movie. Unfortunately, iDVD's feature for adding chapter markers is severely limited: It lets you place chapter markers only at regular intervals — for example, every three minutes. This is better than nothing, but unless you've shot and edited your movie with unnatural precision, the chapter markers won't coincide with the beginning of scenes.

Genius

If you find working on the main DVD screen confusing, try using the DVD map instead, as discussed later in this chapter. This shows you a layout of the DVD's contents that is much less graphical and (for many people) much easier to interpret.

Here's how to add chapter markers in iDVD:

1. **Choose Advanced ➪ Create Chapter Markers for Movie.** iDVD displays the dialog shown in Figure 12.12.

2. **Set the number of minutes in the Create marker every box.**

3. **Click OK.** iDVD adds the markers to the movie.

12.12 iDVD lets you add chapter markers to a movie, but they can only be at regular intervals.

These chapter markers give viewers a rudimentary way of navigating quickly through the movie on your DVD. But if you want to create a proper scene-selection menu tied to chapter markers that appear where you want them to, you need to do a bit more work, as described next.

Adding Other Folders to the Movies Tab

If you keep your movies in various folders, you may want to make them appear on the Movies tab in the Media pane. You can add the folders like this:

1. **Choose iDVD⇨Preferences to open the Preferences window.**

2. **Click the Movies button in the toolbar to display the Movies preferences.**

3. **Click the Add button to display the Open dialog.**

4. **Select the folder that contains the movies, and then click Open. iDVD adds the folder to the Look for my Movies in these folders box.**

5. **Add more folders as needed, and then click the Close button (the red button) to close the Preferences window.**

Creating a scene selection menu

Here's the workaround for creating a scene selection menu tied to chapter markers that you position yourself instead of having iDVD position automatically. It takes more effort, but the results make it worthwhile.

Before you start this procedure, open iDVD preferences (choose iDVD⇨Preferences), click the Movies button, and make sure you've selected the Create chapter submenus option button in the When importing movies area of Movies preferences. This setting causes iDVD to create the scene selection menu when you import a movie that contains chapter markers.

Follow these steps:

1. **In iMovie, export the movie to the Media Browser.** You may have done this already.

2. **Launch GarageBand.** If GarageBand opens your last project, choose File⇨Close to close it so that the GarageBand opening screen appears.

3. **Click New Project, click Movie, and then click Choose.** GarageBand displays the New Project from Template dialog.

4. **Type the name for the project and choose the folder in which to save it.** The best place to save the project is in your ~/Movies folder because then iDVD shows this folder's movies automatically in the Movies pane.

5. **Click the Create button.** GarageBand creates the project.

6. **If the Media Browser isn't already displayed, click the Media Browser button (the button at the right end of the toolbar) to open it.**

7. **Click the Movies button at the top of the Media Browser.**

8. **Click the movie and drag it to the Movie track at the top of the project.** GarageBand adds the movie to the project and creates thumbnails to represent it.

9. **Choose Edit ⇨ Add Marker (or press P) to display the chapter-editing pane (see Figure 12.13).** GarageBand automatically adds a marker for the beginning of the movie. If you want to keep it, click in the Chapter Title box and type the name to give it. If you don't want the marker, click it, and then press Delete.

12.13 Creating chapter markers for a movie in GarageBand.

10. **Play the movie (click the Play button or press the spacebar) or drag the playhead to where you want to create the next marker.** Drag the Zoom slider to zoom in on the thumbnails if you need to get a better view.

11. **Click Add Marker in the Markers pane to add a marker.** Click in the Chapter Title box and type the name for the marker.

12. **Continue until you've added all the markers you want.**

13. **Choose File ⇨ Save to save the project.**

14. **Choose Share ⇨ Export Movie to Disk to display the Export your movie to disk dialog.**

15. **In the Video Settings pop-up menu, choose Full Quality.**

16. **Click Export.** GarageBand displays the Export to Disk dialog.

17. **Choose the folder in which to save the new movie.** For example, use your Movies folder.

18. **Click Save.** GarageBand exports the movie file.

Now go back to iDVD and add the movie to your project either by using the Media Browser (if you saved the movie in a folder that iDVD is monitoring) or by dragging it from a Finder window. iDVD automatically creates a scene selection menu, which you can customize as needed.

Adding a slide show

Here's how to add a slide show to your DVD project:

1. **Make sure you're on the main menu for your DVD project.**

2. **In the lower-left corner of the iDVD window, click the Add button, and then choose Add Slideshow.** iDVD adds a button named My Slideshow to the menu.

3. **With the My Slideshow button still selected, click the button to select the text, and then type the name you want to give the slide show.** You can also change the font, style, and size if you want. Click outside the button when you finish.

4. **Double-click the slide show button.** iDVD opens the slide show editor and selects the Photos tab in the Media pane.

5. **In the Photos pane, select the category or album that contains the photos you want.** For example, select the Flagged category if you want to use photos you flagged.

6. **Click and drag one or more photos — or an album — to the slide show editor to add them to the slide show (see Figure 12.14).** To select multiple photos at once, click the first, and then ⌘+click each of the others.

   - If you add a photo you don't want, click it and press Delete to delete it.

   - To view more photos at once, click the Grid View button in the upper-right corner of the slide show editor.

7. **When you've added all the photos you want, click and drag them into the order you want.** You can play back your slide show at any point by clicking the Play button. Click the Stop button to exit the preview window and return to the slide show editor.

8. **If you want to add a song as the soundtrack for the slide show, click the Audio tab at the top of the Media pane.** Locate the song in either GarageBand or your iTunes library, click it, and then drag it to the slide show. Drop it anywhere, and iDVD applies it to the whole slide show.

9. **Set the duration for each slide in the Slide Duration pop-up menu.** iDVD applies this duration to each slide; you can't set different numbers of seconds for different slides.

10. **In the Transition pop-up menu, choose the transition to use for the slides, or choose None if you want no transition effect.** If the direction button to the right of the Transition pop-up menu is available, select the direction in which you want the transition to move — for example, a Push transition from the top or bottom.

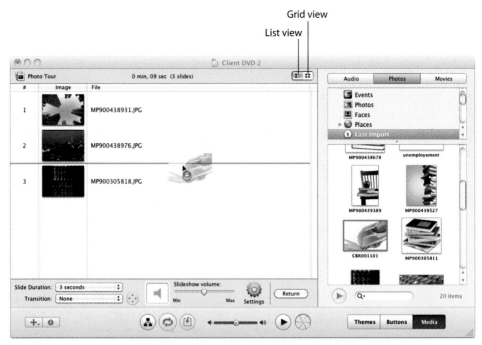

Grid view

List view

12.14 Adding a photo to a slide show in the slide show editor in iDVD.

11. **Set the volume for the slide show by dragging the Slideshow volume slider.**

12. **To choose other settings for the slide show, click the Settings button, select the appropriate check boxes in the settings dialog (see Figure 12.15), and then click OK:**

12.15 Slide show options include looping the slide show, displaying navigation arrows, and including titles and comments.

- **Loop slideshow.** Select this check box to make the slide show repeat itself until the viewer stops it.

- **Display navigation arrows.** Select this check box to display forward and back arrow buttons on the slides.

- **Add image files to DVD-ROM.** Select this check box if you want to include original, full-size photos on the DVD as well as the smaller versions used for the slide shows.

- **Show titles and comments.** Select this check box if you want to include the titles and comments with the photos. This can be useful for your personal DVDs — for example, if you're reviewing the photos to pick the best.

- **Duck audio while playing movies.** Select this check box if you want iDVD to lower (duck) the volume on the slide show when the viewer is playing a movie. This is almost always a good idea.

13. **When you finish setting up your slide show, click the Return button to go back to the main menu screen.**

Customizing the Menu Screen for the DVD

Your next move is to customize the menu screen for the DVD by adding photos, slide shows, or movies to it. To add these items, you use the drop zones, the marked areas on the menu screen.

Finding out how many drop zones a menu screen has

iDVD's various themes have different numbers of drop zones in their menu screens, but all menu screens have at least one drop zone, and many have several. What's tricky is that in some menu screens, drop zones appear all at the same time, but in other screens, they play in sequence, so you see only one at a time.

To find out how many drop zones are in the menu screen you're using, click the Drop Zone button on the toolbar at the bottom of the iDVD window. iDVD displays the drop zone editor (see Figure 12.16).

Adding a movie to a drop zone

A great way to add life to a menu screen is to place a movie in one of the drop zones. The movie then plays when the viewer opens the menu screen.

Genius

Normally, it's best to use short movies for your drop zones because most viewers won't want to linger on the menu screens. You can also make iDVD play only part of the movie in the drop zone, as you see in a moment.

Drop zones for menu screen

Drop zone button

12.16 Use the drop zone editor to check how many drop zones a menu screen contains.

Here's how to add a movie to a drop zone and choose which part to play:

1. **If the drop zone editor isn't open, open it as explained in the previous section.**

2. **Click the Media button to display the Media pane, and then click the Movies tab.**

3. **Click the movie you want to add, and then drag it to the drop zone in which you want to place it.** iDVD displays a thumbnail of the movie in the drop zone.

4. **Add movies to any other drop zones in which you want to use movies rather than photos.**

5. **Click the Drop Zone button to return to the main menu, which now shows the movies you added in the drop zones.** Figure 12.17 shows an example in which only the first movie appears.

6. **Set the start point and endpoint of each movie you added:**

   - If your menu screen plays movies in a single drop zone, drag the Motion playhead along the playback bar across the bottom of the menu screen to make the drop zone display the right movie.

Drop zones

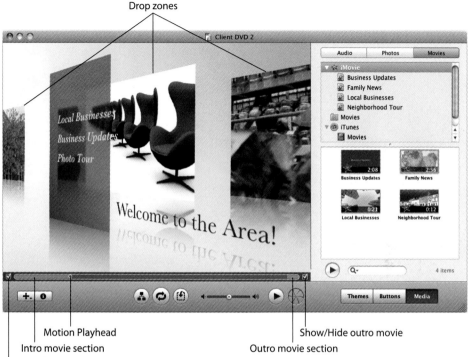

Motion Playhead

Intro movie section

Show/Hide intro movie

Show/Hide outro movie

Outro movie section

12.17 The movies you added appear in the drop zones. This menu screen has only one drop zone (on the left), in which the movies play in succession.

- Click the drop zone. iDVD displays a yellow-and-black border around it and opens the Movie Start/End panel, as shown in Figure 12.18.

- Drag the start marker to select the starting frame. The movie scrubs through the frames as you drag.

- Drag the end marker to select the ending frame.

- Click elsewhere to close the Movie Start/End panel and apply your changes.

- Repeat the procedure for each of the other movies.

7. **If you want to turn off the movie intro, deselect the Show/Hide intro movie check box.** Likewise, if you want to turn off the outro, clear the Show/Hide outro movie check box.

8. **Click the Motion button to loop through the movies in your drop zones and see how they look.** Click this button again to stop the playback.

12.18 Use the Movie Start/End panel to choose the frames at which to start and end the movie in the drop zone.

Adding photos to a drop zone

Instead of a movie, you can add a still photo or a photo slide show to a drop zone. Follow these steps:

1. **If the drop zone editor isn't open, click the Drop Zone button to open it.**

2. **Click the Media button to display the Media pane, and then click the Photos tab.**

3. **Click the photo you want to add, and then drag it to the drop zone in which you want to place it.** iDVD displays a thumbnail of the first photo in the drop zone.

4. **Click the Drop Zone button to return to the main menu, which now shows the drop zone to which you added the photos.**

5. **Set up the slide show to meet your needs:**

   - Click the drop zone once. iDVD displays a yellow-and-black border around it and opens the Photos panel.

- Click and drag the slider in the Photos panel to view the photos.

- If you need to rearrange the photos, click the Edit Order button in the Photos panel to open the photos in the slide show editor. This is the same slide show editor discussed earlier, but when you create a slide show for a drop zone, you can't add music or transitions or set slide durations.

- Rearrange the photos as needed by clicking and dragging them. You can also drag in other photos from the Photos pane if you want.

- Click the Return button. iDVD displays the drop zone editor.

- Click the Drop Zone button to return to the menu screen.

6. **Click the Motion button to loop through the movies and slide shows in your drop zones and see how they look.** Click this button again to stop the playback.

Change a menu's background and audio

To change the background and audio of a menu screen, follow these steps:

1. **Click the Inspector Window button on the toolbar or choose View ⇨ Show Inspector to open the Menu Info window (see Figure 12.19).**

2. **To change the background image for the menu screen, click a photo in the Photos pane and drag it into the center well in the Background area.**

3. **To change the duration of the loop, drag the Loop Duration slider.**

4. **To add audio to the menu, click a song in the Music pane and drag it into the Audio well.** Drag the Menu Volume slider to set the volume.

5. **If necessary, change the menu's button settings:**

   - If you want to reposition the menu's buttons freely, select the Free positioning option button instead of the Snap to grid option button. You can then drag the menu buttons to where you want them.

12.19 Use the Menu Info window to change the background of a menu and add audio.

- To change the highlight color, click the Highlight button, and use the Colors window to pick the color you want. For example, choose a color that works better with the new menu background you've applied.

6. **Deselect the Show drop zones and related graphics check box if you want to hide these items.**

7. **When you finish making changes, click the Inspector Window button on the toolbar again to close the Menu Info window.**

Checking Your Project's Status and DVD Space

To see how much of your DVD project iDVD has encoded, or to see how much space you have left on the DVD, choose Project ➪ Project Info (or press Shift+⌘+I). iDVD displays the Project info window (see Figure 12.20).

12.20 The Project info window shows you how much space your material will occupy on the DVD and whether the components have been encoded.

If necessary, you can also change the following settings:

- **Disc Name.** Just type the new name.

- **Video Mode.** Choose NTSC or PAL.

- **Aspect Ratio.** Choose Standard or Widescreen.

- **Encoding.** Choose Best Performance, High Quality, or Professional Quality, as needed.

- **DVD Type.** Choose Single-Layer or Dual-Layer.

If you change the setting in the Encoding pop-up menu from Best Performance to High Quality or Professional Quality, iDVD displays the Changing Encoding Mode dialog, as shown in Figure 12.21, to make sure you understand that iDVD must reencode all the material it has already encoded. Click Yes if you're okay with this change; otherwise, click Cancel to restore the project's previous encoding.

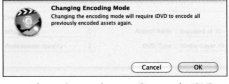

12.21 If you change the encoding mode, iDVD warns you that it must reencode all the material it has already encoded. This can take several hours.

When you finish using the Project Info window, close it by clicking the Close button on its title bar or choosing File ⇨ Close Window.

Using Map View to Inspect Your DVD

iDVD's menu screens are neat, but they can make it hard to see exactly what your DVD contains and where all the content is. When you need to get a clear picture of what's on the DVD, click the Map button to display the DVD map, as shown in Figure 12.22.

If you can't see enough of your project, you can change the view in these ways:

- **Drag the Zoom slider to zoom out (revealing more of your project) or zoom in.**

- **Click an upward or left disclosure triangle to collapse the content underneath it.** Click a downward or right disclosure triangle to expand its contents.

- **Click the Vertical View button to switch the map to vertical view, or click the Horizontal View button to switch to horizontal view.**

These are the main actions you can take in the DVD map:

- **Delete an item.** Click the item and drag it outside the iDVD window, where it vanishes in a puff of smoke. Alternatively, click the item and then press Delete.

Project icon   Disclosure triangles

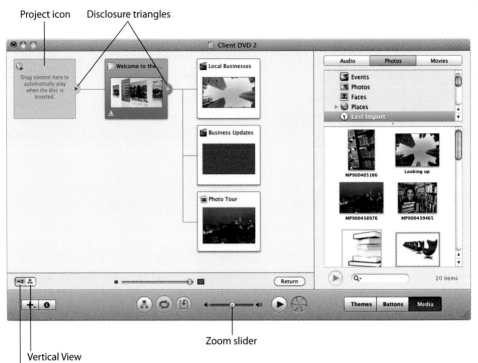

Zoom slider

Vertical View

Horizontal View

12.22 Use the DVD map to get a clear view of where all the files are in your DVD project and to add an autoplay movie.

- **Add an item.** Click and drag a movie, photo, or album to a menu button. iDVD adds a new item to the menu.

- **Change a movie or slide show.** Click and drag another movie, photo, or album to the button to replace its contents.

- **Add an autoplay movie or slide show.** Click and drag a movie or album to the project icon. If you drag an album, double-click the project icon button to open the Autoplay Slideshow editor and arrange the photos into your preferred order.

When you finish working in the DVD map, click the Map button to return to the menu screen.

Genius

You can double-click a slide show button in the DVD map to display the photos in the slide show editor so that you can rearrange the photos, delete some, or add others.

Burning the DVD

When you finish adding content and have previewed the DVD project, you can burn it to disc. Follow these steps:

1. **If your DVD project contains unsaved changes, press ⌘+S or choose File ⇨ Save to save them.**

2. **Click the Burn button on the toolbar.** iDVD prompts you to insert a recordable DVD.

3. **Insert a disc in your Mac's DVD drive.** If it's a drawer-style drive, close the drawer.

4. **Wait while iDVD burns the disc.** When it has finished, test the disc, remove it, and label it.

To create a disc image, choose File ⇨ Save As Disc Image. In the Save Disc Image As dialog (see Figure 12.23), type the filename, choose the folder in which to save it, and then click Save.

12.23 Save a DVD project to a disc image so that you can burn it to DVD multiple times using Disc Utility.

Creating a Disc Image or a VIDEO_TS File

Instead of burning your DVD project to a DVD, you can save it as a disc image or as a VIDEO_TS file.

- **Disc image.** If you create a disc image, you then have a file containing the completed DVD that you can burn to multiple DVDs using Disc Utility without having to encode it each time. This can save you a considerable amount of time over encoding the same DVD multiple times. Creating a disc image is also handy if you're working on a Mac that has no DVD burner. You can then transfer the completed disc image to a Mac that does have a burner.

- **VIDEO_TS folder.** A VIDEO_TS folder contains the video files for the DVD but not the DVD menus. You can play the contents of the VIDEO_TS folder using either DVD Player or third-party software such as the free VLC Media Player (www.videolan.org).

To create a VIDEO_TS folder, follow these steps:

1. **Choose File ⇨ Save as VIDEO_TS Folder.**
2. **In the Save VIDEO_TS folder As dialog, type the filename.**
3. **Select the folder in which to save the folder.**
4. **Click Save.**

Creating a OneStep DVD

Do you ever find you have finished content on your DV camcorder that you need to burn to DVD? If so, you can use iDVD's OneStep DVD feature to quickly import the footage and burn it directly to DVD without putting it into iMovie first.

Here's how to use OneStep DVD:

1. **Open iDVD if it's not already running.** Leave it at the iDVD opening screen for the time being.
2. **Load the tape containing the movie footage.**
3. **Choose the starting point if necessary:**

- If you want to capture only part of the footage on the tape, wind or play the tape until that point is ready to play.

- If you want to capture all the footage on the tape, either rewind the tape or just let iDVD rewind it for you.

4. **Connect the DV camcorder to your Mac via a FireWire cable, just as you would for importing into iMovie.** Usually, you'll need a four-pin (small) plug at the camcorder end and a regular six-pin plug (for FireWire 400) or a regular nine-pin plug (for FireWire 800) at the Mac's end.

5. **Move the camcorder's switch to VCR mode or Playback mode (whichever the camera calls it).**

6. **In iDVD, click the OneStep DVD button on the opening screen.** iDVD notices the camcorder and prompts you to insert a recordable DVD.

7. **Insert a disc in your Mac's DVD drive.**

8. **iDVD displays the Creating your OneStep DVD screen.**

9. **iDVD winds the camcorder's tape back to the beginning.** If you want to start playback from the point you chose, press the Play button on the camcorder immediately to prevent iDVD from winding the tape back.

Genius

You can also stop iDVD's capture at any point by clicking Stop in the Creating your OneStep DVD dialog. If you let the capture run, it continues until it finds a ten-second blank section of tape or until the end of the tape.

10. **Wait while iDVD captures the video from the camcorder's tape, prepares the DVD, processes the movie, and then burns the DVD.** iDVD shows you its progress (see Figure 12.24).

11. **When iDVD finishes the burn, it ejects the DVD and displays the Disc Insertion dialog, prompting you to insert another DVD if you want to burn another copy.**

12.24 OneStep DVD automatically captures the footage from your DV camcorder and burns it to DVD.

12. **Insert a blank DVD and repeat the recording process, or click Done to close the OneStep DVD window.**

Genius

If you like burning DVDs this easily, try choosing File ⇨ OneStep DVD from Movie to burn a DVD directly from a movie.

Jump-Starting a DVD with Magic iDVD

If you've played with the Magic GarageBand feature in GarageBand for creating custom songs in a snap, you'll grasp Magic iDVD at once: It gives you a way of creating a customized DVD with as little effort as possible, while providing you with control over the DVD's contents, menus, and appearance.

Here's how to create a DVD using Magic iDVD:

1. **Open iDVD if it's not already running.**

2. **Open the Magic iDVD window (see Figure 12.25):**

   - If you're looking at the iDVD opening screen, click the Magic DVD button.

   - If you have a project open in iDVD, choose File ⇨ Magic iDVD.

3. **Select the default title (My Great DVD) in the DVD Title box and type the title you want.**

4. **In the Choose a Theme box, click the theme for the overall look of the DVD.** To see a different selection of themes, open the pop-up menu above the right end of the Choose a Theme box and choose the theme category you want. See the discussion earlier in this chapter for an explanation of the various categories of themes.

5. **Click and drag one or more movies from the Movies pane on the right to the wells in the Drop Movies Here box.**

   - You can click and drag movies from either of the Movies folders shown in the Movies pane.

   - You can also click and drag movies from the Movies folder in iTunes.

   - If your movies are in another folder, open a Finder window to that folder, and then click the movie and drag it to the well in iMovie.

Genius

If you need to delete a movie or slide show from a well, simply click the well and then press Delete. You can also drag an item out of a well and drop it outside the iDVD window, where it vanishes in a puff of smoke.

12.25 The Magic iDVD window looks like this when you open it.

6. **If you want to add one or more slide shows to the DVD, follow these steps:**

   ○ Click the Photos button in the upper-right corner of the Magic iDVD window to dis-play the Photos pane.

Genius

Adding a slide show to a DVD with Magic iDVD is a bit weird because what you may want to do is add the slide shows you created in iPhoto. Frustratingly, you can't actu-ally do this. What you do instead is create a new slide show in iDVD by adding the photos and then (if you want) selecting music for them.

   ○ Select the photos you want. You can select an album, a group of photos you've selected, or a single photo.

   ○ Drag your selection to a photo well in the Drop Photos Here box. If you drag a single photo, you'll probably want to add others to its photo well; otherwise, it won't make much of a slide show.

   ○ To add audio, click the Audio tab in the upper-right corner of the Magic iDVD window to display the Audio pane. Click the song or playlist you want, and then drag it to the photo well for the slide show.

7. **Click the Preview button.** iDVD assembles a preview of the project and displays it in the iDVD preview window, together with an on-screen remote control. Use the controls on the remote to navigate the DVD. Click the Exit button to return to the Magic iDVD window, where you can add or delete content as needed.

8. **When your project has the contents you want, click Create Project.** Magic iDVD creates the project and then displays it in a window. You can now tweak the project as discussed earlier in this chapter, burn it to DVD, or simply leave it until later.

Genius

If you're satisfied with the project when you preview it, you can burn it directly from Magic iDVD. Simply click the Burn button, insert a blank DVD, and wait for the burn to take place.

Appendix

How Do I Upgrade to iLife '11 and Keep It Updated?

If you buy a new Mac with iLife '11 installed, you're all set to get started with iPhoto, iMovie, GarageBand, iWeb, and iDVD. But if you buy a copy of iLife '11 to install on a Mac that already has an earlier version of iLife, you need to upgrade to iLife '11; before you do, you should back up your iPhoto library. And whether you upgrade or not, it's a good idea to keep the iLife applications updated with the latest fixes and improvements Apple releases.

Buying iLife '11

You can buy iLife '11 from the online Apple Store (http://store.apple.com) or various other online retailers (such as Amazon.com) or from a physical Apple Store or another bricks-and-mortar retailer.

If you have more than one Mac to use iLife on, you can save money by buying the iLife Family Pack instead of two or more single iLife boxes. You're allowed to install the Family Pack on up to five Macs, which is plenty for most households (and many small businesses).

Backing Up Your iPhoto Library

The iLife '11 upgrade routine is straightforward, as you see in a moment, but upgrading to the initial release of iLife '11 caused problems with some existing photo libraries in iPhoto. These problems occurred on only some Macs — but those who suffered the problems had to recover their photo libraries from backups.

So before you upgrade to iLife '11, make sure that you have a current backup of your photo library. For example

- **Run Time Machine.** If you use Mac OS X's Time Machine feature to back up your Mac, run Time Machine to create an extra backup or make sure that your previous backup ran properly. From iPhoto, you can choose File ⇨ Browse Backups to browse your Time Machine backups of your photo library and make sure the most recent backup is present and correct.

- **Copy the folder that contains your photo library.** If you don't use Time Machine or another automated backup system, open a Finder window to the folder that contains your Photo Library. Copy the folder and paste it to a safe location, such as an external hard drive or an SD card.

Upgrading to iLife '11

After you back up your photo library, you're ready to upgrade to iLife '11. Insert the iLife DVD in your Mac's optical drive, and then click the Install iLife icon in the Finder window that Mac OS X displays.

The iLife installation is straightforward, and you can simply accept all the default settings if you want to install all the applications in their default location, which is to the Applications folder on your Mac's main hard drive.

If your Mac has multiple hard drives or hard drive volumes, you can choose on which of them to install iLife by clicking the appropriate icon on the Select a Destination screen.

If you don't want to install all the applications, click Customize on the Installation Type screen (see Figure A.1).

A.1 If you want to choose which applications to install, click Customize on the Installation Type screen.

The Installer then displays the Custom Install screen (see Figure A.2). Deselect the check box for each item you don't want to install, and then click Install to proceed with the installation.

A.2 On the Custom Install screen, deselect the check box for any application or item you don't want to install.

Updating iPhoto

Before you run iPhoto '11 for the first time, use Software Update to download the latest updates for iPhoto. These updates include a fix for the problem that corrupted some photo libraries created with earlier versions of iPhoto.

Note

Just to be clear — this problem applies only if you're upgrading to iPhoto '11 from an earlier version, not if you're going straight to iPhoto '11

To run Software Update, choose Apple ➪ Software Update, and then wait while Software Update checks for updates. (Software Update checks for updates to Mac OS X and all your Apple software, so it may take a while.)

When Software Update returns the results, click Show Details to show the details of the updates you're getting (see Figure A.3).

Make sure the updates include the iPhoto Update, and deselect the check boxes for any updates you don't want to install at this point. Then click Install to download the updates and install them. If Mac OS X prompts you to restart your Mac to allow some updates to take place, save your documents, close your applications, and then click Restart.

After installing the updates, launch iPhoto by clicking its icon on the Dock or double-click its icon in the Applications folder. When iPhoto displays the dialog shown in Figure A.4 telling you that it must upgrade your photo library, click Upgrade.

⚪⚪⚪   **Software Update**

New software is available for your computer.

If you don't want to install now, choose Apple menu > Software Update when you're ready to install.

Install	Name	Version	Size
☑	iPhoto Update	9.1	186.5 MB
☑	Safari	5.0.3	39.2 MB
☑	Mac OS X Update	10.6.5	741.6 MB

This update adds several new print product options to iPhoto '11. It also improves overall stability and addresses a number of other minor issues.

- Provides the ability to create and order calendars in iPhoto.
- Additional letterpress holiday greeting card themes are now available.
- Fixes an issue that prevented videos downloaded from MobileMe or Flickr from importing correctly into iPhoto events.

The update is recommended for all users of iPhoto '11.

Note: Use of this software is subject to the original Software License Agreement(s) that accompanied the software being updated. A list of Apple SLAs may be found here: http://www.apple.com/legal/sla/.

○ You must restart your computer after the updates are installed.

(Hide Details)   (Not Now)   (Install 3 Items)

A.3 Verify that the software updates include the iPhoto Update.

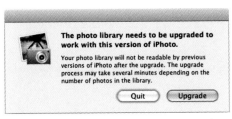

The photo library needs to be upgraded to work with this version of iPhoto.

Your photo library will not be readable by previous versions of iPhoto after the upgrade. The upgrade process may take several minutes depending on the number of photos in the library.

(Quit)   (Upgrade)

A.4 Click Upgrade to upgrade your existing photo library to work with iPhoto '11.

Keeping the iLife Applications Updated

To get the best performance out of the iLife applications, it's a good idea to install the latest updates that Apple releases.

You can check for updates from within any of the iLife applications by opening the application's menu and choosing the Check for Updates command (for example, choose iMovie ⇨ Check for Updates from within iMovie). But because using the command this way causes the Software Update utility to run, it's usually easier to run the utility directly or have it run automatically.

To run Software Update directly, choose Apple ⇨ Software Update.

To make sure that Software Update runs automatically, and to control how frequently it runs, follow these steps:

1. **Choose Apple ⇨ System Preferences to open the System Preferences window.**

2. **Click the Software Update icon in the System category to display the Software Update pane.**

3. **On the Scheduled Check tab, select the Check for updates check box and then choose the frequency in the pop-up menu.** Daily is the best choice, but you may prefer to check Weekly. Don't use Monthly — it's not frequent enough to keep your system protected against bugs and Internet attacks.

Index